Comparative Higher Education

COMPARATIVE HIGHER EDUCATION

Research trends and bibliography

PHILIP G. ALTBACH

Mansell, London, 1979

Mansell Publishing,
3 Bloomsbury Place, London WC1A 2QA

First published 1979

British Library Cataloguing in Publication Data

Altbach, Philip Geoffrey
    Comparative higher education.
    1. Education, Higher—Study and teaching
    2. Comparative education
    I. Title
    378   LA174

    ISBN 0 7201 0825 X

Printed photolitho in Great Britain by
Ebenezer Baylis and Son Limited,
Worcester, and London

Contents

THE BIBLIOGRAPHY

Acknowledgements

This volume stems from my earlier work, *Comparative Higher Education*, published in 1973 and now out of print. The essay substantially expands on the earlier volume, and the bibliography is much more extensive. I am indebted to the E.R.I.C. Clearing House on Higher Education for sponsoring the first edition and to the American Association for Higher Education for publishing it. Segments of this volume are reprinted with their permission.[1] This volume is also related to two bibliographical publications I edited for the International Council for Educational Development.[2] The I.C.E.D. and its chairman, Dr James Perkins, provided support for these bibliographical ventures. The comments of Lionel Lewis, Sheila McVey and Thomas O. Eisemon were very helpful. This volume is part of the continuing research program of the Comparative Education Center, Faculty of Educational Studies, State University of New York at Buffalo.

PHILIP G. ALTBACH

Buffalo, New York
February, 1978

Introduction

This volume has several main purposes, and is divided into two sections: an essay and a bibliography. The essay provides a discussion of the origins and development of comparative higher education as a field of study; it also includes a trend report of key issues and developments in this field, stressing topics which are of current importance to higher education. The highly selected bibliography contains some 1,100 items which have been deemed to be of significance to the field and to important contemporary issues. The project is necessarily exploratory since the field itself is new and there have been few other efforts to synthesize and define it. Further, there are no established methodological foci, few established authorities, and only a limited, widely-used literature. Nevertheless, comparative higher education is a field of study which has attracted increasing attention in recent years and which is in the process of establishing itself as a topic of inquiry and relevance not only to scholars concerned with education, but to policy-makers, government officials, and administrators who must deal with the immediate and long-term problems of post-secondary education. The essay is aimed at both audiences as it seeks to provide scholars with an orientation to a new field of study and policy-makers with a guide to the literature on relevant topics relating to post-secondary education.

The organization of the essay requires some explanation. It is basically straightforward. The first section deals with the emergence of the field of comparative higher education itself and with some of the key resources, such as journals and centers for research, which exist. In addition, some of the orientations of the research are discussed. The rest of the essay is concerned with substantive aspects of comparative higher education. The anatomy of the international academic crisis is discussed. This is followed by a consideration of the international linkages of universities, and particularly the historical transfer of institutional models from nation to nation. The largest segment is concerned with an analysis of six key areas of comparative higher education. It concludes with a section concerning university reform, a topic which in a sense includes elements of many of the previous topics. Thus, while the bulk of the essay is concerned with presenting some of

For notes see pp. 93–113.

the basic literature of the field, it is also peripherally interested in discussing the origins and directions of an emerging area of scholarly inquiry.

This volume has many limitations. Because it is among the first efforts to provide a synthesis of this field, it necessarily covers a large amount of material briefly. No claim is made for completeness of coverage. Further, materials in the English language are much better represented than those in other languages, although an effort is made to provide some coverage of relevant publications in French, German and Spanish. The lack of adequate bibliographical materials for a number of countries – particularly those in the Third World – also biases the coverage in this volume. Limitations of space have meant that only a small proportion of what is available to this researcher has been included in the essay and bibliography. Other bibliographies provide specific coverage and some of these are listed in the bibliography section. Despite these limitations, it is hoped that this volume will provide a first step toward defining an emerging dynamic field of research and analysis.

We are concerned with 'comparative' higher education, and by that we mean studies which deal with more than one country. But in fact most of the materials in this essay and in the bibliography that follows concern single nations. Only a small proportion of the literature is truly comparative in nature. Thus the title 'comparative' is somewhat misleading. The field of comparative higher education, in the strict sense of the term, is slowly emerging. The reasons for the lack of specifically comparative materials are complex. Research emphases and funding have been largely national in orientation, and there has not been much interest in insights from abroad. In many cases, scholars have followed the orientations of their sponsors. Overseas data has not generally been considered 'relevant' to specific national problems. The methodologies of comparative research are difficult and often quite expensive. Scholars have often avoided comparative empirical work because of its expense and methodological problems. Much of the limited comparative literature is based on analysis of secondary materials. For these, and other reasons, comparative higher education has been slow in emerging, and largescale research projects have been few in number.[3]

In addition to the methodological problems of doing comparative research, there are also problems of definition. The literature refers, almost interchangeably, to higher education, post-secondary education, universities, colleges, academies, and recently to post-compulsory education. In some countries, one or more of these terms have quite specific meanings and the imprecise use of terminology can be confusing. In the United States, for example, a college usually means a post-secondary educational institution offering a maximum of four years of instruction. A university generally offers graduate training in one or more fields. In Britain, these terms have somewhat different meanings. In the United States, graduate education means post-baccalaureate training of some sort. The same type of education in Britain is called post-graduate, while in France the baccalaureate is a certificate given on the completion of secondary education. The chief administrative officer of the American university is usually called the president or chancellor, while in Britain and most Commonwealth countries the equivalent title is vice-chancellor and in Germany and much of Eastern Europe rector. Nomenclature for the academic profession also differs from country to country, as do the powers associated with these titles. The traditional European professor had wide powers and much authority; he was generally head of his department or institute. In the United States, the term professor is applied more widely as the senior ranks of the academic system are proportionately larger than in Europe. Academic titles such as privat-docent, reader, associate professor, lecturer, and others exist in various countries, and have quite specific meanings. Thus, it is important to carefully define terms with reference to specific countries and universities. The essay refers rather broadly to universities and includes most post-secondary institutions, but there is an effort here to be specific about other terms.

Select List of Abbreviations

AAUP	American Association of University Professors (Washington, D.C.)
A.U.P.E.L.F.	Association des Universités Partiellement ou Entièrement de Langue Française (Montreal, Canada)
E.R.I.C.	Educational Resources Information Center (U.S.A.)
H.M.S.O.	Her Majesty's Stationery Office (London, Britain)
I.A.U.	International Association of Universities (Paris, France)
I.C.E.D.	International Council for Educational Development (New York, U.S.A.)
I.I.E.P.	International Institute for Educational Planning (Paris, France—United Nations Agency)
M.I.T.	Massachusetts Institute of Technology (Cambridge, Mass., U.S.A.)
O.E.C.D.	Organization for Economic Cooperation and Development (Paris, France)
O.U.	Open University (Milton Keynes, Britain)
P.P.B.S.	Program Planning Budgeting System
R.I.H.E.D.	Regional Institute for Higher Education and Development (Singapore)
S.D.S.	Students for Demoncratic Society (U.S.A.)
U.G.C.	University Grants Committee (London, Britain)
UNESCO, Unesco	United Nations Educational, Scientific and Cultural Organization (Paris, France—U.N. Agency)

THE ESSAY

The Emergence of a Field of Study: Historical, Political and Disciplinary Perspectives

Comparative higher education is emerging as a field of scholarly and policy inquiry, and is developing the 'infrastructures' customary to a research speciality. There is some debate as to whether the field will emerge as a formal academic discipline. While this is unlikely, it is clear that comparative higher education is developing as a speciality. Several journals[4] focusing on the field have been established in recent years, and a number of publishing firms in different countries have given higher education an emphasis in their programs.[5]

The relevance of comparative perspectives on higher education has also been recognized by national agencies charged with studying higher education in their own countries. The Carnegie Commission on Higher Education in the United States, for example, published two volumes[6] dealing with non-American issues and commissioned several foreign scholars to write on American universities from their own perspectives.[7] The Robbins Committee in Britain, which issued its influential report in 1963, included a volume focusing on higher education outside of the United Kingdom.[8] Japanese educational planners have taken an active interest in developments in other countries, and a sizeable number of volumes concerning higher education outside Japan have been translated and published.[9] Official commissions concerning higher education in the Third World have typically included at least one expert from another country, and often several foreigners. The evaluations of educational systems done by the Organization for Economic Cooperation and Development (O.E.C.D.) have been done by international teams of experts. This outside participation has broadened the scope of many inquiries, but in the case of the Third World might emphasize European educational models and policies too strongly. Among the countries that have used outside members on official educational commissions have been India, Nigeria, Ghana, and others.[10] And, as will be indicated in this essay, there has been a great deal of cross-fertilization of ideas about universities. Academic models have been transferred, with varying results, from one nation to another, and specific reforms emanating from one country have often been applied in others.[11]

Despite the modestly increased attention given to comparative higher

For notes see pp. 93–113.

education, the main cause for the growth of interest in the study of universities has been the particular problems facing individual countries, and this research has not been cross-national in nature. The expansion of the post-war era and the strains put on the academic system by this expansion have generated unprecedented interest in understanding post-secondary education and in dealing with the challenges which have arisen. Universities have moved to the center of their societies. They provide training—and credentials—for increasing proportions of the population. They are key research institutions. And in almost all countries their cost has increased dramatically. Thus, the growth in research concerning higher education is due largely to specific interest in answering quite pragmatic policy-related questions rather than to the initiative of the academic community. The research which has been conducted is for the most part limited to the particular country in which it is undertaken, and researchers have generally been quite parochial in their orientations. Comparative studies are considered esoteric and of little direct value by most researchers and policy-makers. Indeed, it is part of the focus of this essay to indicate that comparative studies have relevance to pragmatic national issues as well as providing a broader—and in the long run useful—overview concerning higher education.

Because higher education research remains largely a 'national' matter, the literature is very uneven. It is likely that more than half of the writings on higher education have been done by Americans and deal largely with the United States. There are many reasons for this imbalance. The American academic system is the largest in the world, and it is a system which has stressed research and scholarly publication. The American administrative apparatus in higher education is the largest in the world, and administrators have actively promoted research on problems relating to universities. Higher education as an academic speciality was first developed in the United States and there are at present graduate programs focusing on the study of higher education and the preparation of administrative personnel at more than thirty American universities.[12] A network of journals, professional organizations and meetings has emerged to service this growing professional community.[13] There is no question but that the existence of departments and centers in established universities which focus their attention on higher education has been a major factor in stimulating research, analysis, and publication. These academic programs have been stimulated by the pragmatic need for highly-trained administrators and for focused research. Combined with the emergence of an academic speciality concerned with higher education, a number of American social scientists have taken a strong interest in studies of post-secondary education. The reasons for this sudden interest are complex, but certainly relate to the emergence of the university as a major public institution in the United States, to the increasingly visible problems of the universities, and to research funds made available by government agencies and foundations for the study of higher education.

Other countries present a mixed picture concerning publications on higher education. A few, such as West Germany and Britain, have established research programs and publications. In West Germany, the Westdeutsche Rektorenkonferenz and several other agencies have taken an interest in research for a long period and several journals dealing with higher education exist. The Max Planck Institut für Bildungsforschung in Berlin has focused on higher education as well. Several journals exist in Britain which concentrate on higher education. These include the comprehensive *Times Higher Education Supplement*, which is unequaled anywhere in the world in its coverage and quality and the *Universities Quarterly*, which has recently transformed itself into a general intellectual journal. Scholarly work appears in the *Higher Education Review*, published only occasionally, and in two new journals, *Studies in Higher Education* and the *Higher Education Bulletin*. The former is sponsored by the Society for Research into Higher Education and the latter by the Research Institute on Post-Compulsory Education at the University of Lancaster. *Higher Education*, an international journal, features a substantial number of articles concerning Britain.

Most industrialized countries have at least one research center or journal which takes a major interest in higher education. It is beyond the scope of this volume to indicate each one, and most tend not to pay much attention to developments in other countries. With the exception of India, the countries of the Third World have not paid much attention to research on higher education and have few organized research activities and a relatively modest stock of published material concerning higher education.[14] Much of the research that does exist has been conducted by scholars from industrialized nations or by international agencies. Thus, while the overall amount of material on higher education has expanded dramatically, large gaps still exist in the literature. For a number of nations, even basic statistical data is unavailable.

It is probably true that the major stimulus which has accounted for the expansion of research on higher education has been the various 'crises' which have involved post-secondary education. Academic attention has focused on problems of higher education and funds have become available for research. In addition, the emergence of higher education as a field of expertise and professional training has also stimulated research and writing. For the first time there is a group of academics and researchers who have a 'vested interest' in research on higher education. There is also a growing cadre of administrators and others concerned with the operation of universities who are consumers of research. Many of these individuals are employees of government

ministries and are not scholars in the traditional sense; they are concerned with understanding how universities work. Since it is likely that
the academic speciality of higher education will continue to develop in
direct consequence of the continued need for adminstrative staff and
research knowledge, the community of individuals who will produce
research will continue to develop. It will also spread to countries in
which such a community does not now exist as post-secondary education seems to be changing from an 'elite' to a 'mass' system throughout the world. The larger university systems almost inevitably require
increased administrative staff. The establishment of a journal in mid-
1977 by the O.E.C.D. entitled *International Journal of Institutional
Management in Higher Education* is a dramatic indication of this current.
In addition, the demand by government officials and university administrators for research work and their willingness to fund relevant
research will continue to exist, although the rate of funding may fluctu-
ate with the perceptions of crisis and the availability of funds.

A Early writings on comparative higher education

While much of the literature concerning comparative higher education
is recent, and the field is only beginning to establish its own identity,
studies concerning higher education have a long tradition in more than
one country. Many of the early writings were descriptive in nature,
reporting on visits to various universities or intended to instil an interest
in foreign educational models in one's own nation. C. F. Thwing,
writing in 1911, described European universities in a volume based on
his travels.[15] An academic administrator, Thwing also wrote extensively on American higher education. Many of the early writings were
concerned with publicizing reforms made in other countries or con-
vincing skeptics that alternative educational policies can work. One
early such work is V. A. Huber's *The English Universities*, published in
Germany in 1843.[16] Several Americans wrote persuasively of innovations in Europe, especially in Germany, during the nineteenth
century, a period of dramatic change in American higher education. In
part as a result of these persuasive writings, elements of the German
university system were adopted in the United States, including graduate training, increased emphasis on research, and the importance of the
doctoral degree.[17]

Historians were among the most prolific and best analysts of higher
education prior to World War II. Hastings Rashdall's classic, *The
Universities of Europe in the Middle Ages* remains the classic discussion of
the medieval university.[18] Robert Rait also wrote about the medieval
university.[19] John Tate Lanning wrote of the history of higher education in Spanish America.[20]

Academic crisis also stimulated writing about higher education in earlier periods as it does at the present time. Abraham Flexner's influential volume was stimulated in part by problems perceived in the American university of the twenties.[21] His was one of the earliest efforts at specific comparative analysis, and it has become a classic in the field although its enthusiastic description of the German universities was quickly changed by the realities of Nazi power only a few years after Flexner's volume was published. Max Weber's writings on higher education, collected recently by Edward Shils, constitute another commentary on academic crisis by a well known social scientist.[22] Two volumes by Walter Kotschnig concern the economic crisis of the 1930s and how the Depression and related dislocations affected the academic community.[23] These two volumes also considered higher education in a comparative perspective. Frederick Lilge, in an effort to analyze the role of the universities in Nazi Germany wrote an influential volume on this topic.[24]

B Research currents

The field of comparative higher education did not emerge without stimulation as a 'natural' academic development. Unlike certain subfields in the physical sciences, the study of higher education is not a natural outgrowth of intellectual inquiry. Although universities have existed for a long time, it is only recently that analytic attention has been devoted to them. While it is not possible to provide a sociological analysis of the emergence of higher education as a field of study in this essay, it is worthwhile looking at some of the roots of the field.

As indicated in the previous section, early writings were in part 'travellers' tales', in part exhortation to adopt particular reforms or innovations, and in part the result of scholarly research in history. The total amount of writing was quite small and for many nations virtually non-existent. Further, as historians, and in the twentieth century political scientists, sociologists and others in the emerging social sciences dealt peripherally with higher education they generally did not maintain their research interest in higher education. Universities, it is fair to say, were a passing interest of a few scholars whose concerns were not the development of a field of academic speciality in higher education.

Post-secondary education was similarly ignored by professional educators as university-level schools of education which grew, in the United States at least, in the late nineteenth century and more dramatically in the twentieth. As the training of teachers gained professional status and school teachers were required to have some higher education and then some instruction in the methods of teaching, professional schools of education were established. In the United States, these institutions gradually gained university status. In some European countries, colleges of education remained separate entities, usually with lower status than the established universities. As teaching training became more specialized and professional, research took on an increasingly important role. Journals were established and education became a specialized field of study. The schools and colleges of education, however, remained closely tied to primary and secondary education, and virtually no attention was paid to higher education.

It is worth noting that in the United States education emerged as a professional field as it assumed a key position in society and became a 'mass' phenomenon. Once the common school took on key training and socialization functions, expertise was required of teachers and there was interest in understanding the nature of education. Similarly, as universities became more important to modern technological societies and as academic institutions affected more people, there has been an interest in understanding more about higher education and in professionalizing the operation of post-secondary educational institutions.

In addition to the lack of an academic home for higher education studies scholars were reluctant to undertake studies of their own institutions. Universities, until recently, were seen as relatively unimportant institutions in society, and they did not attract widespread interest from social scientists. In addition, there was probably some feeling that universities were somehow 'above' analysis in that they were devoted to intellectual pursuits. Finally, academics may have felt some reluctance to 'demystify' higher education by subjecting it to social science analysis. For these, and probably other reasons analytic research on higher education developed slowly.

The growth of research on higher education has been stimulated in large part by the increasingly important role that universities have in modern societies. A recent report, for example, indicates that more than half of the basic scientific research done in the United States is conducted in universities.[25] Enrollments have expanded dramatically in most countries, doubling or tripling in a few decades. And crises such as student revolts, demands for curriculum reform and accountability, and other factors have all focused public and governmental attention on higher education. The fact that public expenditures for higher education rose dramatically also contributed to interest in how universities spent these funds. It is clear that the growth of research on higher education in the post-World War II period is based not on pure academic interest but rather on the fact that universities have become centers of public attention. As has been pointed out earlier, funds for research on higher education have become available and social scientists and others have endeavored to obtain these research funds.

While statistics are unavailable, it is fairly clear that most funded research on higher education has a policy orientation or is somehow 'practical' in the sense that the funding agencies have specific uses in mind for the research. Despite the orientation of specific research projects, useful data is often generated which can be applicable for more disinterested analysis of educational issues.[26] Government commissions and research projects have been aimed at dealing with enrollment growth, understanding specific problems affecting higher education, student activism, planning entirely new systems of higher education, and for other purposes have provided not only plans and information concerning the specific aims of their inquiry, but have often generated useful data on a range of issues. The largest was probably the American Carnegie Commission on Higher Education, a privately funded effort which sponsored a series of policy recommendations concerning American higher education, but also generated more than sixty volumes of research on a wide range of topics. The Commission's research findings constitute one of the richest sources of data on American higher education.[27] The Commission's activities did not include much comparative emphasis, and in this way reflects the dominant trend toward discussion of only domestic educational questions.

Policy research has some important characteristics which have affected the nature of the field of studies in higher education. Research questions are usually framed by the funding agency rather than by the researcher, and it is sometimes the case as well that the methodologies are also dictated by those granting funds. The questions asked are relatively narrow and focused on specific and often immediate needs rather than broad issues that will increase understanding of systems as a whole. Those engaged in research usually function under constraints and do not feel free to go beyond the specific questions. The ideological framework of the research questions and methodologies—and therefore the results that emerge—are usually in keeping with the assumptions and policy parameters of the funding agencies.[28] Research personnel, especially at the senior levels, usually represent the mainstream orientations in social science in their countries, and critics are seldom recipients of large research grants or at the head of official commissions.

In the United States, and increasingly in other countries, individual universities have established research offices to collect data concerning their own institutions so as to help with management, planning, and often student services. These offices of institutional research, as they are often called in America, have a narrow focus as well and seldom engage in what might be called 'basic' research concerning higher education. Typically, they collect data on specific issues such as student attrition rates or financial aspects of university administration. They are usually most efficient in collecting statistics. Research done by university research departments is seldom published in established journals, and is often difficult to obtain. While the kinds of case-study materials generated by institutional research offices may be useful in comparative research, it is especially difficult to obtain in other countries.

Private foundations in the United States and those few other countries in which such agencies are active have taken some interest in higher education research and have funded a modest amount of comparative work as well. Perhaps the most notable effort in this area has been that of the International Council for Educational Development (I.C.E.D.) in New York, which has not only undertaken some research studies on behalf of private and international agencies, but has attempted to spread a consciousness of comparative higher education and has published a number of bibliographies and occasional papers. The I.C.E.D.'s basic funding came from the Ford Foundation, which permitted it to engage in some non-project oriented activities,[29] but it was also dependent on specific grants from agencies to work on directed research tasks such as an evaluation of aid to higher education in developing countries.[30] The I.C.E.D. also sponsored several international meetings focusing on problems of comparative higher education. However, the general funding for I.C.E.D.'s work ended, and the agency has become almost completely limited to focused research studies. More recently, Yale's Institution for Social and Policy Studies has begun a program of research on comparative higher education.

Other American philanthropic foundations have taken an active interest in higher education, largely as a result of their efforts to assist universities overseas. The Ford and Rockefeller Foundations have been most active in sponsoring research and assistance to universities, notably in the Third World, and a small part of their aid has been invested in research studies relevant to understanding higher education.[31] Some of the most interesting research consists of evaluations of their own programs, and this material is unpublished and often unavailable to scholars. While private philanthropic agencies have greater autonomy than government agencies, the purposes of their research and assistance programs do not seem to differ basically from governmental efforts.

International agencies have also been increasingly concerned with higher education, and have sponsored research programs and projects. Among the international agencies which have engaged in research and publication on higher education are the United Nations and its specialized agencies (particularly UNESCO), the Organization for Economic Cooperation and Development (O.E.C.D.), the Council of Europe, the World Bank, the International Association of Universities,[32] the Commonwealth Secretariat, and others. The research programs of these organizations differ substantially. Some, like the UNESCO-sponsored International Institute for Educational Planning, have a clear mission and focus their research and other activities. Others, like the O.E.C.D., have defined their research activities more broadly from time to time. Many of the international groups have extensive publications programs and some of them sponsor journals. UNESCO's *Prospects* and the *International Social Science Journal* are widely disseminated and often feature general articles on higher education. The international organizations are among the richest sources of comparative statistics on higher education. The two international organizations which have been most active in publishing on higher education are the O.E.C.D. and UNESCO, both with headquarters in Paris. O.E.C.D., which has a membership limited to the industrialized nations of Western Europe, North America and Japan, has had an impressive program of research and publication on higher education. It has sponsored wideranging inquiries into the educational systems of its member countries and these reports feature some analysis of post-secondary education.[33] In addition, the O.E.C.D. has sponsored research studies on such topics as higher education reform, which resulted in several excellent publications, on short-cycle higher education, on educational planning, and on the economic problems of higher education. O.E.C.D. publications are sometimes single-country case studies but they often include comparative materials.[34] Several statistical volumes concerning higher education trends in member nations have also been published.

UNESCO's higher education programs are varied and geographically dispersed. The International Institute for Educational Planning has published a number of studies relating to post-secondary education.[35] The UNESCO Institute for Education in Hamburg publishes the *International Review of Education* and has sponsored some research as well. These agencies, and others such as the Council of Europe, provide the particularly valuable function of maintaining communications among specialists on higher education, reinforcing the concerns of individual governments in research on higher education.[36] Their seminars, planning groups, and conferences provide needed stimulation for comparative thinking and sometimes result in research and publication.

Like the national government agencies, however, most of the research sponsored by international agencies, is focused on specific topics related to the research concerns of the particular agency or program within the agency. Thus, researchers have only limited leeway in the topics for research or even in the nature of the results. In addition, political criteria in the selection of research topics and occasionally of personnel are sometimes evident, particularly in UNESCO. Some of the international organizations have bureaucratic structures which may hinder research.

This discussion has several major generalizations. It is clear that research on higher education, for the most part, does not emanate from the scholarly interests of individual researchers but is part of national, regional, and international networks of agencies which sponsor and fund research. The freedom of inquiry of individual scholars, the kinds of topics which are funded, at times the methodologies employed in research, and the financial resources available, are all part of this institutional sponsorship. International agencies generally sponsor research which is aimed at specific problems perceived by the funding agencies. Research sponsors are not interested in an overall analysis of higher education, and usually not in the relationship of their 'problem areas' with other topics. They are concerned with the collection of specific information, the solutions to specific problems, or the training of specific individuals. Many research sponsors have assumptions about the nature of the university, about the nature of society, about appropriate economic relationships, and other matters. They are unlikely to sponsor research which does not conform to these assumptions or which does not promise to find solutions to perceived problems. An understanding of the 'political economy' of research networks can help to make sense of the kinds of research work undertaken, the general parameters of the available data, and even of the methodologies employed in research and analysis.

The International Academic Crisis: Causes and Controversies

One of the most dramatic, widely publicized and serious crises for higher education in modern times came during the 1960s and its repercussions continue to be felt even at the present time. Most academic systems throughout the world were affected to some extent by this crisis and much was written about it. It is the purpose of this section to discuss some of the immediate and long-term causes for this crisis, and to indicate some of the literature relating to it. In later parts of this essay, some of the major ingredients of the academic situation of the present period will be considered in more detail. In this section, we are concerned with general analysis.

Academic crisis is manifested in many ways. In France, Thailand, Japan, and South Korea student dissent brought governments to the brink of disaster. In Italy, the academic system has become unworkable as the result of expansion. In Britain, the academic system suffers from a major fiscal problem. In Sweden and West Germany, efforts to implement change in the system have caused disruption and dissent. In short, while the manifestations differ, elements of strain exist in most nations at the present time.[37] And while academic systems remain basically unchanged in most nations, few have escaped recurring difficulties and pressure.

Many of the problems outlined here have no easy solutions. They are a part of the broader structural dilemma of higher education. It is my basic contention that the so-called crisis of recent years is the culmination of a range of demands which have been placed on higher education which universities have tried to meet without basic alteration in academic style, organization or governance, or for the most part in curriculum. In a sense, the logical consequence of these demands are now being felt, often with dramatic consequences for institutions and systems.

While it is very difficult to discuss the crisis in an international framework because national academic systems do differ and the particular forms of crisis are determined to a substantial extent by national conditions, it is nevertheless possible to make some generalizations. At the risk of over-simplification, the following factors have contributed to the

For notes see pp. 93–113.

difficulties in which many academic systems find themselves:

*Expansion. Universities in most countries have expanded dramatically since World War II, and particularly in the last two decades. Student numbers have in many countries more than doubled in a short time. This expansion is unprecedented, and has had major implications for the universites.

*Changing roles for universities. As technology has expanded and research has become increasingly important to modern societies, the importance of universities has increased and roles have expanded. Many new functions have been added to the traditional university responsibilities of teaching and preservation of the established culture.[38]

*Increased expenditures. As universities have expanded their roles and numbers of students, their budgets have naturally risen as well. Most of the additional funds have come from governmental sources, and one consequence has been increased government and public interest in how academic institutions spend their money. In addition, increased budgets inevitably require a more complex bureaucratic structure to administer the funds.

*Student diversity. As enrollments have expanded and the social class-base of the student population diversified, there were fewer links among the students and more disagreement about the goals of education, academic styles, and other factors.

*Curriculum. The traditional liberal arts and professional curriculum have been under attack and in some countries virtually destroyed. But there is no common agreement on a coherent curriculum to replace them. This lack of agreement—and often strife—concerning the curriculum has been a disruptive force in the academy.[39]

*Accountability. Demands by government and other external authorities to know exactly how academic institutions spend their funds and to provide documentation for academic programs have been perceived as a threat to academic autonomy and to traditional patterns of university governance.

*Elite versus mass higher education. Universities have traditionally been elite institutions serving small populations for specific purposes. In a sense they maintain elements of this elitism, but in the context of societies which claim democratic forms and ideologies. Tension is an inevitable result.

*Politicization. As universities have assumed central roles in their society, they have necessarily increasingly reflected the political concerns and problems of that society. Student and faculty activism in some countries are part of this current.[40]

The 'university crisis' has generated a considerable literature in recent years. Indeed, for most countries, at least one anthology has appeared which attempts to deal with the broader issues. Wallerstein

Approximate enrollment rates for Higher Education

Country	Age groups	1950–1	1955–6	1960–1	1965–6	1968–9
Austria [1]	19·24	...	3·0	4·5	6·4	8·3
Belgium	18·23	4·0*	5·4	8·0	11·0	13·7*
Denmark	19·25	5·0	5·4	7·7	9·6	10·9
Finland	19·24	4·2	5·5	7·1	10·2	14·0*
France	18·23	4·8*	6·0	8·7	12·5	13·9
Germany	20·25	3·8	4·4	5·8	8·3	9·0†
Greece	18·24	...	1·9	2·8	6·5	7·65*
Ireland	18·22	3·9*	4·6*	7·3	8·0*	10·0*
Iceland	......	...	...	...	...	...
Italy [2]	19·25	4·2	44·1	5·5	8·7	10·0
Japan	18·22	4·9	7·1	8·1	12·0	14·1
Luxembourg [3]	20·25	...	...	3·8	6·1	...
Netherlands	18·24	4·4	5·2	7·4	8·6	9·0
Norway	19·24	3·4*	3·1*	5·0*	8·7	9·4*
Portugal	18·24	1·4	1·7*	2·5	3·6	5·7†
Spain	18·24	...	2·6*	3·8	6·0	7·1*
Sweden	20·24	4·8	6·3	8·6	12·6	16·9†
Switzerland	20·25	4·5	4·5	5·5	6·6	7·1†
Turkey	18·23	1·0*	1·3*	2·3	3·2	4·4†
United Kingdom	18·22	5·2*	6·3*	8·7	10·7	13·5*
Yugoslavia	19·25	2·7	2·9	6·1	9·2	11·5†
Canada [4]	18·23	6·5*	8·1	13·6	18·9	28·0†
United States	18·23	16·8	21·1	25·9	31·4	35·0

[1] Austrian students only.
[2] 1951, 1956, 1961 and 1966.
[3] 1960 and 1966.
[4] 1951, 1956, 1961 and 1965.
*Estimate of enrollments.
†Estimate of age group.
Source: *Towards New Structures of Post-Secondary Education* (Paris: O.E.C.D. 1971).

and Starr's two-volume collection deals with the American scene in the 1960s.[41] David Martin's volume considers the British situation.[42] Other volumes deal with France and Germany. Useful books concerning India[43] and Africa have also been published recently.[44] Many other countries have also been analyzed in terms of their academic problems in volumes which differ substantially in quality, methodological and intellectual approaches and along other variables. Many of these volumes have only limited lasting interest as they were written in the heat of a contemporary crisis and often without careful analysis. But it is fair to say that the 1960s generated a large volume of material on higher education, some of it quite useful. And without the air of crisis, it is unlikely that much of this research and writing would have been done.

A number of useful cross-national volumes were also published during the 1960s. Most of these volumes are edited collections, often featuring essays on individual countries. A key source for factual data on university systems in nine countries is a volume written by Barbara Burn and collaborators.[45] Christopher Driver's excellent volume concentrates mainly on the United States, Britain, France and Japan and provides a historical and contemporary overview of recent changes in higher education.[46] Paul Seabury's edited volume focuses on Western Europe, and reflects the concerns of traditionally-minded academics.[47] Two volumes edited by W. R. Niblett include essays on a number of countries and provide a very useful background to university problems in those countries.[48] Similarly, Brian Holmes and David Scanlon's edited volume provides wide geographical coverage and deals with some of the key issues relating to the 'crisis'.[49] Michael Stephens and Gordon Roderick have also edited a volume dealing with problems of the contemporary university.[50] In addition to these volumes, articles in such journals as *Minerva* and *Higher Education* regularly feature descriptions and analyses of the specific problems of universities. Margaret S. Archer's collection of papers links student activism in various countries to the broader problems of academic institutions in an effective volume.[51] Finally, Eric Ashby's collection of papers on contemporary higher education provides characteristically useful insights.[52]

While these volumes provide an overview of some of the problems faced by universities both in cross-cultural perspective and in some specific countries, there has been a good deal of analysis of the various components of the academic crisis. The theme of expansion has been considered by many writers. Ladislav Cerych's I.C.E.D. occasional paper provides a context for European higher education expansion.[53] Several reports issued by the O.E.C.D. discuss the nature of European higher education expansion and discuss its implications.[54] George Bereday's volume discussed policy alternatives for mass systems of higher education.[55] The Council of Europe has also been concerned

with the implications of the expansion of higher education.[56] These
analyses provide detailed statistical data for much of Western Europe,
and indicate some of the policy alternatives as well.

Very few of these analyses provide guidelines as to how to deal with
the implications of the expansion which has been so accurately pre-
dicted. As Bowman and Anderson have pointed out, the United States
was the first country to deal with major expansion of higher education,
and it encountered various challenges.[57] And while there has been
considerable interest in Europe in understanding the American experience, European nations have been slow to develop comprehensive
plans to adapt their universities to the realities of increased numbers of
students, and it has been only recently that plans have been approved in
such nations as Sweden and the Netherlands. Britain, with the publication of the Robbins Report in 1963, was one of the first European
nations to deal comprehensively with expansion and its implications.[58]

The stresses of the 1960s reflected the consequences of rapid expansion and new roles, and a period of substantial political unrest in many
societies. The nature of that crisis has changed in the seventies, and it is
difficult to predict what the next set of challenges for higher education
will be in the coming decades.[59] In a sense, the present decade is a
quieter period, and the substantial societal interest in higher education
and massive social pressures of the 1960s are, at least for the present,
ended. But the problems facing the universities are nevertheless serious.
It is the purpose of the following discussion simply to raise some of the
key issues and not to include a comprehensive discussion of them.
Clearly, some of the issues indicated previously, such as accountability,
remain critical in the 1970s, and the implications of the massive expansion of the past twenty years remain in most countries. Yet, some new
issues have arisen, and have attracted the attention of the academic
community as well as planners and government officials.

*Stable enrollments. After several decades of unprecedented growth,
enrollments in many countries, particularly in Western Europe and
North America, have levelled off or have even declined somewhat.

*Stable resources. After years of increasing budgets for higher educa-
tion, funds from public sources are no longer growing. The implications
for academic institutions are substantial.[60]

*The academic profession. Great expansion in recent years followed by
little growth has distorted the age structure of the profession, in many
countries damaged the sense of community, and in general created
strains.

*Public distrust of universities. Due in part to the strains of the 1960s,
both the public and government authorities have come to distrust
universities. This has had implications for enrollments, budgets, and
other matters.

American commentators have called this combination of circumstances a 'steady state' and have contrasted it with the growth of previous years.[61] Demographic factors, most notably a decline in the numbers of college age individuals, have contributed. In most industrialized nations, the proportion of the age group attending post-secondary education is not continuing to grow, and this has added to current difficulties.[62] At the same time that enrollments have stabilized, governments have been increasingly reluctant to provide additional funds to higher education. The shift from rapid growth to no growth has been especially difficult for the universities. In some countries, funding is closely tied to enrollments, while in others expenditures for universities grew so rapidly that many feel that the saturation point was reached. All this has combined with public disenchantment with higher education for failing to solve key social problems. Even the great stress on science and technology of the post-World War II period has been blunted by a realization that pollution and other problems accompany scientific advancement.

Academic Models and Institutional Transfer: Philosophical, Historical and Contemporary Perspectives

The contemporary problems of universities cannot be fully understood without knowledge of the history of higher education. Universities have long historical traditions, and also have a consciousness of these traditions and their impact on the evolution of higher education. Ideas about the nature of universities have helped to create the modern academic institution. Academic models have been influential across national borders. This section is intended to provide some perspectives on the relevance of these factors on the modern university. The modern university is basically a Western institution, even in the Third World, where indigenous institutions of higher learning have virtually died out only to be replaced by Western transplants.[63] In the Arab World, for example, the traditional Al-Azhar University still exists, and it retains considerable authority over Islamic scholarship, but the newer Western-style Cairo University has more impact on modern Egyptian life.[64] The process of adaptation and transplantation of higher education from one culture to another and over long periods of time within a nation is an extremely important one. Eric Ashby has written most perceptively on the process of institutional transfer from West to East.[65] Ashby pioneered the idea of an 'ecology' of higher education which takes into account the various elements of academic development.

It is often difficult to analyze the sometimes competing influences of philosophical and historical tradition, the specific national historical circumstances and current demands on higher education in discerning the causes for particular academic developments. It is often the case that planners and others seeking change in higher education ignore important academic traditions in seeking to make higher education responsive to immediate needs.[66] It is the purpose of this section to point to some of the key literature which has tried to analyze the various elements in the developments of modern higher education.

A Philosophical aspects

Philosophers, from Aristotle to Confucius to the present time have

For notes see pp. 93–113.

speculated about the role and techniques of education. But relatively few have dealt specifically with higher education. Medieval religious and secular thought was very much a part of the development of the University of Paris in 1200. In more recent times, the writings of John Henry Newman,[67] José Ortega y Gasset,[68] Karl Jaspers[69] and others have influenced thinking on higher education.

In the contemporary period, several philosophers have written persuasively on higher education, including the Americans, Robert Hutchins,[70] Robert Paul Wolff,[71] Sidney Hook[72] and others. There is an established tradition of speculative essays on higher education in Latin America. Others have also written on philosophical questions relating to higher education.

While not formally a philosophical statement on higher education, Clark Kerr's *The Uses of the University*, the volume which put the term 'multiversity' in common usage, is an accurate contemporary statement about the direction of American higher education which has relevance to the rest of the world.[73] Opposing Kerr's vision, Robert Nisbet argues that American higher education should return to its traditional values.[74]

While many of the major policy questions which affect higher education, the reform proposals, and discussions of curriculum, relate directly to major philosophical questions, the number of philosophical works on higher education is relatively small. Relatively few academic philosophers have turned their attention to higher education, and the discipline of philosophy of education as it is practised in schools of education generally concerns itself with issues of relevance mainly to primary and secondary education.

B Historical studies

There is a considerable body of literature on the history of higher education in the West. It is, without question, crucial to understand the historical roots of the university if one is to fully comprehend its modern characteristics. The permutations of historical tradition are complex, and it is difficult to generalize on the basis of individual countries. The experience of the German universities was very different from that of the British. Eastern European universities were affected directly by Germany, while much of the Third World was influenced by British models. These and other academic systems stem basically from the two major university models which emerged in the Middle Ages. The dominant model—the professor-oriented University of Paris —has been most influential internationally. It has basically shaped the world's academic systems. The other model, the Italian student-oriented Bologna University, has been virtually shunted aside as a working academic model, although it has had some impact in Latin America. The literature on the medieval university is substantial and can provide a fairly thorough understanding of both of these models[75]

The differences between the two medieval models are important and have implications for modern higher education. The University of Paris was founded by a faculty seeking to protect their employment, provide a coherent curriculum, and in general to codify what had been a loose system of providing advanced study in theology and law. The power rested in the hands of the professors, who controlled virtually all internal aspects of the university, subject in some matters to clerical or state authority. The tradition of faculty control was established early and remained a powerful element of the ideology of higher education. From the beginning the University of Paris was involved in disputes with external authorities. The University faculty were involved in clerical disputes and played an important role in mediating disagreements between the Church and the rising authority of the French state. Indeed, university professors often had to play a careful diplomatic role in maintaining a degree of university autonomy from the competing influences of Church and state. Due to its location at the heart of the emerging French state which was in periodic conflict with the power of the Roman Catholic Church, the University of Paris was more embroiled in political affairs than was the student-run University of Bologna.

The medieval universities were quite different from their modern successors in a number of respects. Research was not part of the function of the university, and the curriculum was highly structured and very restricted. Although what has come to be known as the liberal arts was evident in some respects in early universities through the trivium and quadrivium, the core of the curriculum was studies in the traditional professions of the clergy, law, and medicine. In addition, the medieval universities were small and did not have elaborate campuses. Indeed, the University of Bologna periodically moved from city to city in Italy as it became embroiled in town-gown disputes of various kinds.[76]

Academic governance, however, was not dramatically different from that which is familiar in the modern period, particularly at the University of Paris.[77] Virtually all decisions relating to the internal governance of the institution were made by the faculty. Degree requirements, the curriculum, the appointment of staff, and the other key academic decisions were all made by the professors. The administration of the institution was uncomplicated. A chief administrative officer, usually called the rector, was chosen from among the senior faculty and served for a short period. The powers of the rector were limited, and seem to have been largely limited to dealing with the outside world. Because institutions were small and their roles fairly limited, elaborate administrative structures were for the most part unnecessary.[78] The reasons why the Paris model proved to be the dominant one are complex. The fact that students are, by definition, associated with their universities for only a short time and administrative and curricular continuity is therefore easily broken is part of the reason. In addition, higher education expanded rapidly in Northern Europe and the students at Paris who returned to their home countries took with them the Paris model. It is also possible that the government and clerical authorities who sponsored universities in general preferred to deal with professors rather than students. For whatever reasons, it is clear that European universities adopted the Paris model of professorial control rather than the student-run Bologna model.

Universities in Europe gradually took on national rather than international characteristics, and this was a key turning-point in the history of higher education. The early universities used Latin as the medium of instruction, and thus had an international clientele and flavor. With the rise of nationalism and the growth of institutions in most parts of Europe, the language of instruction gradually shifted to the national language of the region in which the university was located and the international flavor of the student body gradually diminished.

Universities in Europe slowly expanded during the period after 1500, and were established in most parts of the continent. Many common elements existed—the curriculum remained fairly uniform throughout the continent, the purposes of the universities were similar, and the ethos of higher education was fairly common as well. Yet, differences did exist and institutions of higher learning began to take on more national characteristics. During the Protestant Reformation, universities were in many cases forced to take sides, and most followed the persuasion of the dominant religion in their regions.

In England, universities were established at Oxford and Cambridge and these became important centers of learning in Britain.[79] They eventually played a crucial role in providing models for the emergence of higher education in the United States and later in the former British colonies. Universities also developed in Scotland at an early date and differed considerably from the English model.[80]

Universities also grew in Eastern Europe, in the German states, and in other parts of Northern Europe.[81] Many of these institutions were impelled by the Reformation, or the later Counter-reformation or by the ambitions of the German princes to bring learning to their domains.

Italian universities continued to grow, but as Italy's intellectual and cultural influence in Europe declined, the Italian universities lost some of their importance. To some extent Spain's universities were tied to the Italian model, but were also influenced by Northern European institutions.[82] The Latin American universities, established by the

Spanish in the eighteenth century and reflecting the Spanish model and ethos, were among the earliest 'transplanted' universities, and their history has been relatively neglected.[83]

The seventeenth and eighteenth centuries might, with some exceptions, be called the dark ages of European higher education. Universities continued to exist during this period, but for the most part they did not play a very important role in the creative intellectual life of their respective countries. Their roles were relatively circumscribed— training sections of the élite and upholding the traditional and established culture. In most parts of Europe, universities did not expand dramatically in size. Research was not part of the academic system, and few professors were creative intellectuals. Of course, individual academics in some countries played an active intellectual role, and institutions from time to time took on societal functions. All this is especially dramatic because this period was one of tremendous intellectual and scientific creativity in Europe. The Enlightenment, the roots of the Romantic movement, the beginnings of nationalism in the German states, and perhaps most important, the scientific and technological discoveries and inventions that led to the industrial revolution, were all occurring at this time. Such key intellectuals as Voltaire, Marx, Watt, the French Encyclopediasts, and many others had no ties with the universities. The modern notion that universities are absolutely crucial to scientific and intellectual life is clearly false, since during this creative historical period, the unviersities were not directly involved in important intellectual advances.

The history of higher education in Europe was not one of uninterrupted growth, development and high intellectual achievement. As Ben-David and Zloczower point out, universities were relatively dormant during the eighteenth and early nineteenth centuries.[84] The lack of a real intellectual function, stress on transmission of established culture and a sharp circumscribed societal role all contributed to the lack of dynamism. Perhaps the lesson of this period is that universities are not necessary ingredients of scientific and intellectual achievement. It is possible for academic institutions to flounder at a time when considerable intellectual growth takes place.

C The emergence of the modern university

This historical discussion indicates that universities have common roots and that the idea of institutional transfer and adaptation can be seen in the history of higher education. Academic institutions reflect their own national surroundings in curricular, structural, and philosophical terms, but their common roots are evident in many respects. In addition, it is clear that international academic models have played an important role in the development of higher education throughout the world, and they continue to do so. The exact history of higher education in any particular country is a combination of many factors. For example, the particular foreign influence used is often an accident of history. Indian universities reflect a British model because of colonialism. Japanese universities are patterned on German models in part because the Japanese were shopping for institutional models at a time when the German universities had much influence. While the development of universities is a complex process, it is clear that their international roots have played an important role in shaping the destiny of higher education in many countries.

The nineteenth century brought major change in higher education throughout the world, and indeed in a sense recreated the university in its modern form.[85] Curricula changed, universities took on research as one of their activities, they became involved in societal concerns, and their organizational structures were dramatically altered. There was a good deal of cross-cultural borrowing as well. While it would be hard to argue that historical circumstances forced this transformation, for various reasons in most European countries and in the United States, it did occur. Some countries felt the forces of change more than others. Germany, the United States and Japan were probably the most active nations in reforming their universities. Britain and France changed much more slowly, and some of the smaller European nations altered very little. Latin American universities were reformed in the early twentieth century,[86] and universities were established for the first time in India, Thailand, and some other Asian nations. Africa was still virtually without higher education.

Germany was the first European nation to substantially alter its higher educational system, and it provided a model for Eastern Europe, the United States, Japan, and to a lesser extent, Britain and France. A number of forces came together in Germany in the nineteenth century which helped to stimulate a basic transformation of higher education. German nationalism was on the ascent, and it needed intellectual underpinnings. The gradual unification of much of German-speaking central Europe under the leadership of Prussia created an increasingly powerful state concerned with education and willing to foster universities. The emerging German state was concerned with catching up with the industrial advances of Britain and France, and used the universities in part to harness technological innovations. Thus, research became a key part of the responsibility of the universities. The structure of the university was also changed and institutes and professorial chairs were created which coincided with the emerging disciplines and scientific fields. All of this was highly innovative and set the German universities apart from other institutions.[87]

The architect of the 'new' German university, Wilhelm von Humboldt, founded the University of Berlin in 1810. In the new university, professors were state civil servants and had the prestige and income of senior officials. Their academic freedom, at least in their scientific work and in their teaching, was also protected. Professors were expected to organize scientific research and they were often provided with resources to carry on research, to establish institutes, and appoint assistants. The concepts of *lehrfreiheit* and *lernfreiheit* characterized academic life. These concepts provided freedom to the professor to choose his subjects for research and teaching and the student had the liberty to choose his subjects of concentration and the ability to matriculate at universities of his choice. When compared to the rigidity of the traditional academic curriculum, the new German system allowed unprecedented freedom, and the faculty took advantage of this situation by reorganizing the very bases of knowledge, especially in the sciences.[88]

Within several decades, the German universities were radically altered. The impetus for change came mainly from the outside—from the state—but the professoriate generally supported the transformation and greatly benefited from it through greater prestige, more autonomy, and funds to engage in research. Universities lost some of their sense of community as chair-holding professors became semi-autonomous barons.[89] Political freedom was not part of the German concept of academic freedom, so socialists and other dissenters were generally barred from teaching positions.[90] But as the German academic profession was generally conservative, these political limitations did not create much stress.[91]

The German university fulfilled its expectations. It made major contributions to the growth of the German state both by assisting in scientific and industrial development and by providing the cultural, intellectual and historical underpinnings for German nationalism. At the same time, the German universities became a model for scholars and others abroad who wanted universities to participate in research and become a part of a rapidly changing scientific and technological scene. Americans and others travelled to Germany to study and returned convinced that the German university was the wave of the future. In much of Eastern Europe, at the time under German political and cultural influence, higher education was profoundly influenced by the German pattern.[92] German influence was also strong in Russia, and it proved the major model for the Japanese when they established Western-style universities at the end of the nineteenth century.

To summarize, the German university broke from traditional academic models in the following ways:

*It emphasized the research function as an integral element of the academic role;

*It reorganized the structure of the university around the chair (full professor) and institute and invested in the chair-holder unprecedented power and prestige. These chairs generally reflected the newly emerging disciplines;

*It provided funding from the state, and also involved the state more directly in influencing the direction of higher education. Academic staff became civil servants;

*Universities were expected to participate in national development through basic and applied research.

The American university, which until the 1860s had been a relative backwater of American society, slowly emerged as a key institution in the modernization of the United States. Two basic influences contributed to the transformation of American higher education in the years after the Civil War. The first of these was the Morrill Act of 1863, which provided grants of land to the states to build up universities provided that these universities offered certain kinds of applied subjects such as agriculture. The 'Land Grant' Act provided the funds which permitted the establishment of expansion of many of America's major state universities. The University of Wisconsin is perhaps the best example of the growth of an institution which, by the turn of the twentieth century, provided major service to agriculture and commerce as well as producing research.[93]

The other major influence on the American university during the later nineteenth century was the new German model.[94] While the adaptations made in the United States were suited to local conditions, and the German system was not used entirely, the following elements were part of the transformation of the American university:

*The departmental system was based on the German idea of the chair system and the division of the academic work of the university according to the discipline;

*Research was increasingly emphasized as an integral part of the university, and doctoral degrees were established as the pinnacle of academic training;

*The university and the state grew closer, and government funding of research became widespread;

*The prestige of the professor grew, as did autonomy and access to research funds.

The American adaptation of the German model was suited to local conditions. Curricular offerings which would have been considered unsuitable for academic study in Germany were readily admitted to the American university curriculum. Engineering, applied agriculture, and later education were included in the university. While the German university emphasized basic research, its American counterpart often included applied research as well.[95] The power of the chair-holder was diffused in the American system to a kind of oligarchy of the full professors, with substantially more participation from the lower ranks of the teaching staff than was the case in the German system. The fact that American universities are governed by lay boards of trustees and even the state universities have some insulation from the direct participation of the state in governance has been a key feature of the American system.

Germany was not the only nation to provide an influential academic export model in the nineteenth century. Britain, as a major world power and with widespread colonial holdings, provided an important export model as well. The British universities themselves were slowly adapting to the German system, and the newer civic universities at Manchester and Birmingham as well as the University of London made use of some German academic ideas. The British model has had a profound impact on Britain's colonies and continues to provide the basic academic framework to many Third World nations. In addition, Canada, Australia, South Africa and other nations are still influenced by the British pattern.[96]

Higher education expanded in the British colonies as much due to indigenous pressure as to the desire of the colonial authorities to spread education. Further, the British perception that the expansion of Western-style higher education in India had led to political disaffection caused them actively to limit expansion, at least at the university level, in Africa.

The British export model was not that of Oxbridge but rather of the University of London or one of the civic universities. Thus, the British were not transferring their 'first class' institutions, but rather a type of higher education which colonial administrators felt more 'practical' for the colonies. This early export model has shaped the structure, mission, and ethos of higher education to the present time. Further, the curriculum, with few exceptions, was based on liberal arts—legal studies and science developed only much later.

British colonial higher education expanded slowly and provided education for a tiny proportion of the indigenous population and was limited, in general, to urban areas. While colleges were established in India as early as 1800 and universities were established in 1857, the resources devoted to higher education were very limited.[97] Much of the initiative came from Indians who wanted to use advanced degrees for remunerative employment in the growing civil service and in the private sector. The model used for the first Indian universities was that of the University of London, and many colleges were linked to institutions which became largely affiliating and examining bodies rather than creative intellectual institutions.[98] African higher education moved even more slowly, and its models reflected the civic universities in Britain rather than London University. Indeed, African higher education was so limited than when Independence came to Anglophone Africa, there was a dramatic shortage of trained personnel, and higher education expanded quickly to meet the new demands.[99]

The Japanese case is an interesting example of the adaptation of foreign academic models. After experimenting with several European models, the Japanese, after the Meiji Restoration in 1868, used the German model and patterned their universities after the reformed German institutions.[100] The German pattern fit most efficiently the needs of a highly centralized state seeking to quickly modernize its industrial and scientific base. In addition, the German university was the dominant academic institution in the world at the time. The Japanese universities were structured according to a rigid 'chair' system, although institutions were less concerned with basic research than were their German counterparts.

D The United States as a paradigm for higher education

The previous section has noted that institutional transfer has occurred throughout history and has been a key element in the development of universities. This discussion will focus in more detail on the role of American higher education as a paradigm for other countries in the post-World War II period. There is no question but that higher education planners and others often look to the United States as the most relevant model for academic development in their countries. On the surface at least, it would seem that the American experience has much to offer other countries. According to a paradigm set up by Martin Trow, the United States is the only country to have moved from an 'elite' to a 'mass' and now to a 'universal' academic system in terms of numbers of students enrolled, access to the system, and its role in society.[101] Enrollment increases, for example, are common throughout the world, and in fact are often proportionately larger than in the United States. But since the United States was the first nation to achieve a mass system of higher education and is now poised on the threshold of a universal system, with about 40 per cent of the age group going on for some kind of post-secondary education, nations in which the proportion entering post-secondary education is now increasing from 5 or 8 to 15 or more per cent, look to the United States as a model. As Ladislav Cerych indicates, most countries will move toward the United States in terms of proportions of individuals in post-secondary education.[102] The pattern of expansion has significantly slowed in the United States and in most Western European nations, but the worldwide trend toward mass higher education continues unabated. Further, most countries continue to cope with the growth that took place in the 1960s in terms of institutional arrangements and financing for higher education. The United States is also a powerful nation which has provided considerable educational assistance to the Third World, and through this aid its educational models have been publicized and stressed.[103]

The American university seems relevant in other countries not only because of its adaptation to large numbers of students, but for other reasons as well. New disciplines and innovations in curriculum have been more readily incorporated into American universities than has been the case in most other countries. In a period when the basis of knowledge is changing rapidly and demands in many countries for increased 'relevance' in the universities have been heard, the American model has been seriously considered. The American pattern of university governance has maintained a degree of academic autonomy at the same time that increasing amounts of public funds are spent on higher education, although there is a continuing debate about autonomy and many see it threatened. And the research productivity of American higher education, combined with its catering to undergraduate teaching, has attracted the interest of foreign observers. American campuses are, in many cases, quite large, and this too has been seen by others as a possible solution to expansion in countries where individual institutions are traditionally small. While many observers have pointed to the difficulty of change in the American university, there is no question but that the United States has adapted more easily to most of the challenges of the post-war period than have universities in other parts of the world. A common European response to the desire to innovate has been to copy elements of the American departmental system, which at least democratizes the faculty and permits younger professors more latitude for innovation and research. It is surprising that Europeans have taken to this aspect of American higher education at the same time that many American reformers have begun to question the department as the best means of academic organization and several universities, such as the University of Wisconsin at Green Bay, have moved away from the department idea.[104]

Other, perhaps less important aspects of American higher education have also been emulated by other countries. Student personnel services, for example, are an innovation in nations where academic institutions have traditionally paid no attention to the extra-curricular lives of their students. The concept of the semester, the course-credit system, and continuing assessment and grading are all increasingly popular overseas. The American practice of including such 'new' fields

Annual Growth of Enrollments in Post-secondary Education (in%)

	1960-5	1965-70	1965-6	1966-7	1967-8	1968-9	1969-70	1970-1	1971-2	1972-3	1973-4
GERMANY											
university type	(4·7)	8·4	7·0	3·2	6·6	6·5	9·1	13·7	15·1	10·6	5·5
non-university type	(5·2)	6·8	1·4	1·7	3·8	7·2	3·3	31·1	-5·2	11·8	16·2
total post-secondary	(4·8)	7·9	5·8	2·9	6·0	6·8	7·9	17·1	10·6	10·8	7·6
BELGIUM											
university type	9·4	8·9	10·2	10·0	9·5	7·5	7·9	7·9	3·9	2·1	1·9
non-university type	10·6	13·0	7·3	8·0	16·3	4·7				12·7	
total post-secondary	10·1	10·8	9·0	9·2	12·3	6·3				6·4	
DENMARK											
university type	15·7	9·1	11·4	12·5	5·5	7·4	8·7	9·1	8·9	5·0	4·9
non-university type	5·2	5·9	5·5	3·8	18·0	2·0	0·8	5·0	16·6	(2·7)	5·9
total post-secondary	10·4	7·7	8·8	8·8	10·6	5·0	5·4	7·5	11·9	(4·1)	5·3
FRANCE											
university type	13·1	9·4	10·0	13·5	15·6	4·6	3·8	6·5	5·1	0·8	(2·1)
non-university type	13·5	6·8	1·0	8·6	10·3	10·4	3·8	8·9	8·2	6·0	(1·6)
total post-secondary	13·2	8·9	8·4	12·7	14·7	5·5	3·8	6·9	5·6	1·7	(2·0)
ITALY											
university type	8·5	11·0	12·1	9·7	10·4	12·0	10·8	11·3	(5·8)	(4·5)	
non-university type	5·8	4·8	18·2	0·7	2·4	-0·1	3·5	3·8	(2·1)	8·9	
total post-secondary	8·4	10·8	12·3	9·4	10·1	11·7	10·7	11·2	(5·7)	4·6	
NETHERLANDS											
university type	9·7	9·9	10·6	9·3	8·8	10·4	10·4	9·2	3·3	4·2	4·3
non-university type	5·2	7·4	5·0	9·7	8·5	7·0	6·9	5·7			
total post-secondary	6·9	8·5	7·4	9·5	8·6	8·5	8·5	7·3			

UNITED KINGDOM											
university type	(7·6)	8·4	14·1	9·8	8·0	5·9	4·3	4·2	2·9	2·6	
non-university type	(9·4)	5·1	8·3	10·7	4·9	-0·3	2·2	0·9	-0·1	0·4	
total post-secondary	(8·5)	6·7	11·1	10·3	6·4	2·8	3·3	2·6	1·5	1·6	
SWEDEN											
university type	13·0	12·8	16·9	22·1	18·4	-0·5	8·5	-1·3	-5·0		
non-university type	9·4			7·8	10·0	21·4	11·2	(-19·4)	-1·3		
total post-secondary	14·2			19·2	15·0	3·0	8·9	-4·7	-4·4		
YUGOSLAVIA											
university type	1·3	9·2	3·3	6·8	15·0	9·7	11·3	7·7	8·3	11·6	7·2
non-university type	16·7	3·4	9·7	9·6	1·7	-7·2	4·0	9·2	3·4	2·6	15·1
total post-secondary	5·7	7·1	5·7	7·8	9·8	3·6	8·9	8·2	6·8	8·9	9·5
UNITED STATES											
university type	8·4	6·1	(6·4)	(6·8)	(5·9)	5·6	5·6	1·6	1·3	1·9	
non-university type	13·3	14·1	(12·3)	(14·4)	(19·3)	18·5	6·6	5·8	3·8	7·2	
total post-secondary	9·1	7·5	(7·4)	(8·1)	(8·1)	8·0	5·8	2·5	1·8	3·0	(4·5)
JAPAN											
university type	8·4	8·5	11·7	10·8	9·4	6·7	3·9	4·4	4·1	4·4	
non-university type	12·1	12·3	32·1	20·4	8·7	3·2	-0·05	4·6	4·6	7·6	
total post-secondary	8·9	9·0	14·2	12·6	9·3	6·1	3·2	4·4	4·2	4·9	

Source: I. Hecquet, *et al., Recent Student Flows in Higher Education* (New York: I.C.E.D., 1976), pp. 25–6.

as education, management, computer science and the like in the university curriculum is increasingly followed overseas as well. Study teams from other countries are often investigating American academic practices, and there is considerable interest in American higher education overseas.

The Third World has been particularly influenced by American academic models. Through foreign aid programs, advisors, and the fact that thousands of students from the Third World have studied in the States and return with ideas about academic organization based on their own student careers, there has been much interest in American patterns and often funds available for utilizing American academic programs. For example, the 'land grant' model has been widely copied and adapted in the Third World, American curricular innovations, textbooks, and many other elements have also been adopted by Third World countries.[105] While many of these aspects of the American system are probably useful in the Third World context, they often have consequences which are not always anticipated. It is probably fair to say that of all the major metropolitan university systems, the American has the most impact on the Third World at the present time.

Because of America's political and economic power, and because it has faced some of the challenges now being faced by other countries, it will probably remain one of the key sources of ideas about higher educational innovations. In a sense, the American university functions in somewhat the same role as the German university did at the end of the last century. It is carefully studied by scholars from other countries.[106] It welcomes a large number of foreign students, many of whom return home with their ideas about higher education shaped by their American experiences.[107] The American university is a productive source of research, scholarship, and technological innovations which are used abroad.[108] Thus American notions of science and scientific development have a disproportionate influence around the world. Just as academic systems in the nineteenth century did not become fully 'Germanized', it is unlikely that other university systems will completely adopt the American system. But without question, the American 'model' of higher education, and particularly its prestigious graduate-oriented universities, exercise wide influence around the world.

Key Fields of Inquiry in Comparative Higher Education

Most of the rest of this essay is devoted to a discussion of six key issues which are important to higher education in almost every nation. These are topics which have generated a significant literature in recent years, and on which some analysis of a comparative nature has been done. These issues: planning, the professoriate, governance, university-society relations, student activism, and higher education in the Third World, are by no means the only topics which might be discussed. Others, such as the curriculum, psychological aspects of academic life or the economics of higher education, have all received some attention and are of importance. These brief analyses of key elements in the literature on higher education are not complete, but are intended as surveys of some of the more important literature available, mainly in English. The final segment of this essay deals with university reform, a topic which includes elements of the six areas of research discussed in this section and which is also a key issue.

A Planning in higher education

The art—some would say science—of planning in higher education has become widespread in recent years as one means of coping with the challenges of expansion. Self-conscious planning in higher education is a new phenomenon, since the traditional stability of universities and their relatively slow change made technical planning unnecessary. All that has changed. The size of institutions and their increasing use of management techniques, the necessity to expend efficiently substantial sums of money, and the need to coordinate highly complicated and diverse academic and research programs has contributed to efforts to plan academic programs and institutions efficiently.

Academic planning takes on many forms. Probably the largest amount of planning takes place in individual institutions. This planning concerns the coordination of individual programs, budget allocations, or the creation of a 'master plan' for an entire institution. Increasingly, large universities have established planning offices which have re-

For notes see pp. 93–113.

sponsibility for planning tasks, and many institutions have offices of institutional research, which collect and analyze data necessary for the planning and evaluation process. These activities are most advanced in the United States where academic administrative structures are largest and where there is a tradition of planning by individual academic institutions. In recent years, as public universities have been joined in large complex multi-campus systems, planning has taken on an increasingly important role.[109] The literature on individual institutional planning is relatively sparse and it is very difficult to obtain relevant data because only a small amount is published. The multi-volume study edited by Victor Onushkin is a good source for institutional planning for individual universities as well as for academic systems.[110]

National and regional planning has been undertaken in many nations, usually by governments but occasionally by private agencies, foundations, individual universities or international bodies like UNESCO. The plans vary substantially in quality and scope, and range from brief considerations of quite specific issues, such as the development of student services, to documents of hundreds of pages reflecting a broad approach to higher education and a concern for effective long-tange planning. Some nations with an ideological commitment to planning in all aspects of society have, not surprisingly, included higher education in the general social planning process. These nations include most notably the socialist countries of Eastern Europe.[111] Other countries have varied in their use of formal planning in higher education. Most planning documents relate to particular problems raised by governments, universities, or simply the force of events. The British Robbins Committee, for example, was established when government and universities foresaw academic expansion and wished to devise ways of dealing with it.[112] Similarly, perceived difficulties led to the appointment of a high-level commission by the Government of India, which drafted a plan for all Indian education, including the universities.[113]

Demands for expansion force the academic community reluctantly to increase the size and/or number of universities. A commission is set up to consider the most effective way of doing this, and the result of this commission is a plan for higher education in that particular country (or state or region). The seemingly straightforward problem of how to deal with expansion becomes complicated when such implications of expansion as long-term manpower needs, the consequences for the academic profession, the implications for ancillary services such as student housing, and others are considered. As a result, these plans often become more complex and far-reaching than the original seemingly simple 'problem' reflected.

Student activism in recent years has stimulated the planning process in a number of countries including the United States.[114] Official commissions set up to look into the causes of student activism often make recommendations for various changes. Increasing government concern over the size and effectiveness of educational expenditure has also contributed substantially to the planning process. For the most part, documents are prepared by government agencies or with government financial support. In the United States, with its decentralized educational system, some planning has been done with federal government initiative but the bulk has been accomplished by state and regional bodies and by private groups.[115] The Education Commission of the States, the American Council on Education, and similar agencies have participated in university planning and have provided data to agencies concerned with higher educational planning. The Carnegie Commission on Higher Education has had significant influence on national policy as well as on the decisions of individual institutions concerning their future programs. The Commission's multi-volume research reports and its recommendations in areas ranging from dental and medical education to curriculum reform in the arts, have had widespread influence, although the Commission itself had no official government sanction. Many states, especially New York, California, Wisconsin and some others, have engaged in extensive planning efforts.

Canada and Great Britain are similar to the United States not only in language and culture, but also in their academic ethos. This is particularly true for Canada, which has closely followed American academic trends, and has expanded its higher education system into a 'mass' system, while building on a British model. Several useful reports have dealt with Canadian higher education in a period of change. The influential Duff-Berdahl report dealt specifically with problems of university government.[116] Most of the Canadian provinces have produced planning documents. One of the most important was issued by Ontario in 1972.[117] With the exception of Quebec, most of the Canadian provinces have 'Americanized' their higher education systems to a considerable degree, and a debate concerning the impact of foreign models in Canada has occurred.[118]

One of the most influential commission reports of the post-World War II period is the Robbins Committee report, which made recommendations for sweeping changes in British higher education and paved the way for British university expansion in the 1960s. The Robbins Committee's multi-volume report is a model of thoroughness and included materials on topics related to expansion but not directly concerning it. The British have made effective use of blue-ribbon commissions to investigate aspects of higher education, and these reports have had wide influence on policy and practice.[119] Recently, a Commission headed by Lord Rothschild dealt with science policy and another chaired by Lord James made wide-ranging recommendations concerning teacher education.[120] One particularly good analysis of the impact of the Robbins Committee was edited by Richard Layard, et al.[121] Other analyses of the effectiveness of planning in Britain can be found in a volume edited by Tyrrell Burgess and in several incisive articles.[122]

Gareth Williams, a highly-regarded economist of higher education, has written extensively on the economic aspects of planning in British higher education, and his work has relevance to other countries as well.[123] Indeed much of the literature on the applied economics of higher education is directly related to problems of higher education planning. Several journals devote considerable attention to the inter- section between planning and economics. In the Anglo-American context, the *Journal of Human Resources* has devoted attention to manpower questions as they affect higher education, and the new publication, *Higher Education Bulletin*, issued by the Institute for Research and Development in Post Compulsory Education at the University of Lancaster in England, has focused attention on the broad implications of planning, mainly in the British context. Two recent books relating economics to education planning are a volume edited by Keith Lumsden[124] and a study by Donald Verry and Bleddyn Davies.[125] Brian MacArthur wrote generally of prospects for British higher education in the 1980s, taking into account economic and other trends.[126] Several case studies of the results of university planning have also appeared in Britain, Among these are volumes by Michael Beloff[127] and by David Daiches.[128] Douglas Windham has written a useful overview of the field of econ- omics of higher education.[129]

Following the British model, a number of the Commonwealth countries have engaged in academic planning excercises through of- ficial commissions, often with the assistance of British academics or technical personnel. An Australian commission produced an in- fluential report in 1957, and other more recent efforts have also taken place.[130] Several Canadian studies have already been mentioned.

The former British colonial countries have been especially active in higher education planning, since they have had, for the most part, to build up university systems from very small beginnings. While the British permitted higher education to expand in India during the colonial period, they were very cautious in Africa.[131] Countries such as Ghana, Nigeria and Kenya, had rapidly to expand their higher edu- cation systems, and they all attempted to plan this expansion ration- ally.[132] India has also engaged in many official planning efforts, few of which have been very successful.[133] The major Indian planning docu- ment of the post-Independence period is the Education Commission's 1964 report, but this is only one of many documents.[134] The Indian ex- perience shows that even with adequate data, imaginative thinking, and clear understanding of the relevant problems, the implementation of educational plans is a difficult process. The reality of African higher education in many countries does not relate with the educational plans prepared for these countries.[135] The reasons for the failure to implement plans are manifold—expense (particularly for Third World nations), political factors, inertia or opposition from elements of the academic community, and others. Some plans have been sucessfully implemented and careful study of the reasons for these successes would yield useful results. For example, many of the recommendations of the Robbins Committee were implemented, and the Ashby Commission on higher education in Nigeria was largely put into effect by the Nigerian government.[136]

Other efforts at academic planning are outlined in Onushkin's multi-volume study, which features case studies of academic institutions in countries as diverse as the German Democratic Republic, the United States, Britain, France, the Soviet Union, and others.[137] Japan has been active in university planning, and indeed started its university system by analyzing the experiences of other countries. Michio Nagai has provided an overview of Japanese academic developments,[138] while John Blewett discusses the immediate post-World War II period.[139] William Cummings analyzes the most recent period in university planning in Japan.[140] The Japanese universities prior to World War II patterned themselves largely on the German model but after the war many elements of the American system were imposed on them, and gradually were accepted as part of the academic system. The impact of post-war expansion, major alterations in the curriculum, and a shift to a more American, 'practical', orientation from the former German model has been crucial to academic life in Japan.[141] A recent O.E.C.D. report analyzed Japan's educational system from a broad perspective and indicates how planning has worked over a period of several decades.[142]

The literature on planning varies from the most far-reaching considerations taking such factors as social indicators and future societal currents into account as well as the usual statistical variables to narrow institutional plans. The emergence of a sub-profession of planners has without question increased the sophistication of the planning process, but also has established planning methodologies which sometimes limit the imagination of academic planners. Of course, nations or even individual institutions approach the planning process with ideological and other preconceptions which will in many ways dictate the nature of the outcomes. The American decentralized educational system and American commitments to 'market forces' in education as well as in the economy generally affects the nature of the outcome of planning. The Socialist countries of Eastern Europe, with their firm commitment to a regulated economic system, make detailed predictions concerning the need for certain kinds of graduates and then impose academic policies which provide the appropriate numbers of trained individuals.

As C. A. Anderson has pointed out in a number of contexts, educational planning is, at best, a very inexact science, or perhaps even an art with very few skilled practitioners.[143] In most academic systems, there are too many variables, too large an ingredient of politics and too complex a university environment to effectively provide detailed plans. Data is often missing, unreliable or out of date. Elements of the academic community, seldom consulted in the planning process, often oppose aspects of an academic plan and are sometimes in a position to sabotage the plan. The fact that planning has become, for the most part, a 'technical' undertaking with economists providing the major expertise has created problems as well.

Without question, planning in higher education is now established. As systems grow larger and as funding agencies demand rational expenditure of money, academic systems increasingly perform their functions according to prearranged plans. The literature on academic planning indicates some of its possibilities and also its problems. Technical expertise is, of course, necessary in any complicated process, but it is clear that planning for institutions of higher education demands more than technical expertise. It demands an understanding of entire systems and how they fit in with key elements of society. Academic planning cannot be done without an understanding of the 'crisis' discussed earlier in this essay.

B The professoriate

Professors are at the center of the academic equation. They have traditionally had basic control of the curriculum, of the internal governance of universities, of requirements for academic degrees, and over the examination of candidates for degrees. If academics have low morale, the internal life of the universities will necessarily be affected. If they are not well-qualified, the standards of the universities will be low regardless of the funds available or the ability of the students. If professors give only part of their attention to the university—as was the traditional pattern in Latin America until recently—the universities will not be fully effective.[144] Without question, the professoriate's qualifications, attitudes, orientations toward academic work, politics, and economic and social status, directly affect the functioning of any institution of higher education. Further, professors tend to be the most permanent part of any academic institution—their careers in higher education are usually longer than those of administrators, students, or others involved with universities.

Since academics are so important to universities, one would expect there to be a considerable literature on the academic profession. Yet, for most countries, the data and analysis available concerning academics is very limited. Even in the United States, where the literature is by far the most extensive, the number of citations concerning the academic profession is smaller than for students, academic administration, and many other topics related to higher education. For many nations, there is virtually no analysis of the academic profession. Key aspects of the profession, such as patterns of academic work, have not been studied in most countries.[145] One of the few cross-cultural analyses of the academic profession is a recent volume edited by P. G. Altbach, which provides case studies of eight different countries.[146]

There are reasons for the lack of research on the professoriate. For one thing, the mystique of the academic profession is strong and many have felt that teaching at the university level was somehow above the scrutiny of the social scientist. There has been some reluctance to discuss dispassionately the often rather privileged working style of the academic for fear of generating criticism. For a long period of time, professors have been virtually autonomous in their academic work. The concept of academic freedom in many nations extended from the freedom to teach one's subject without interference to virtual autonomy over most aspects of academic work and to freedom of political expression as well. The strong traditions of the university helped to maintain this rather unique autonomy. As a result, no outside agencies were responsible for the activities of the professoriate, and no one took much interest in their work, life styles, or other aspects of professorial existence. Since universities were small, played relatively little direct role in societal affairs, and were fairly inexpensive, their activities did not attract major government attention. This suited the academics very well.

In recent years, this situation has dramatically changed. As higher education has expanded, the number of professors has concomitantly grown. They are, in general, better paid than in former times. Professors have assumed positions of considerable importance in society, not only because the universities themselves have become more crucial as a means of social mobility and advanced training, but also because professors now carry a significant part of the research burden so crucial to industrialized societies. In a number of countries, particularly in the Third World, academics play important political roles in society. They are not only involved in government service, but some academics are key oppositional figures. Thus, universities and the individuals involved in them have become more important in their societies, and it is not surprising that there has been more interest in understanding both professors and students.

This section will highlight some of the best studies on the academic profession, focusing largely on materials based on social science research. Most of the relevant literature is in the social sciences, and a limited number of countries seem to have published the bulk of research studies on academics. The United States probably has produced twice as many studies on academics as all other nations combined. West Germany, Britain and Japan have also been active in researching academics, but the literature for most other nations is very limited, usually with only a few studies concerning any particular country. There is no useful bibliography on this subject currently available, and this discussion features only a small number of the relevant studies, and omits many key writings which are not in English, French or German.

While there are as yet no accepted 'classics' in this field, there are a few volumes which provided excellent analysis and/or fairly wide geographical coverage. A. H. Halsey and Martin Trow's *The British Academics* provides a comprehensive sociological study of the British academic profession.[147] In the United States, the Carnegie Commission on Higher Education has sponsored a series of large-scale studies of American academics as well as graduate and undergraduate students. Several of the reports of this research provide excellent data on the attitudes and demographic variables of the American academic profession.[148] Walter Metzger's recent edited volume brings together many of the most useful American studies on academics.[149] The medieval European academic profession is discussed in the classic studies by Rashdall[150] and Haskins.[151] Without question, the power and authority of the professor was established in medieval times, and many of the traditions of academe stem from this period. There are few detailed accounts of the academic profession between the medieval era and the 'modernization' of the university in Europe under German leadership in the early nineteenth century. One of the few such analyses is Howard Kaminsky's study of the Czech universities during the Reformation.[152]

The British academic profession received historical attention in analyses by Arthur Engel[153] and by Sheldon Rothblatt.[154] The current status of the British academic profession has been admirably analyzed in several volumes. Halsey and Trow's sociological discussion is based on detailed questionnaire data and is able to present a statistical portrait of the British academic profession prior to the recent crises.[155] Williams, Blackstone and Metcalf's analysis of the academic labor market in Britain discusses another key aspect of the socio-economics of the profession.[156] Harold Perkin's case study of the Association of University Teachers provides data on the most important representative of teachers' opinions.[157] Hornsby-Smith's useful article on working conditions in British universities helps to round out our knowledge of the British professoriate.[158] A general impression from these analyses is that the British professoriate owes much to the élite traditions of Oxford and Cambridge, and has been able to retain much of its autonomy despite many changes in the academic system and the expansion of recent years. British academics seem basically satisfied with their professional roles, and seem somewhat less pressured to 'publish' than their American counterparts. It should be added, however, that these studies do not take account of the recent difficulties of the British universities which have directly affected academics, nor do they consider in any detail the growing number of teachers in the non-university segment of the post-secondary educational system.

Germany has received quite a lot of attention from analysts of the academic profession, in part because the German university of the nineteenth century provided an important international model. The German model was especially important in the academic development of the United States and Japan.[159] An excellent discussion of the early reform efforts in Germany is Turner's article on reformers and scholars prior to 1806.[160] Busch[161] has written of one aspect of the academic profession and Fritz Ringer's excellent study of the later period of German universities provides useful data and analysis.[162] Max Weber's comments on the political and moral dilemmas of the German professoriate add a dimension to the study of the German academic profession.[163] Hans Anger's recent sociological study of the German professoriate[164] provides data on current conditions as does H. Plessner's three-volume study.[165] Alexander Busch's article on the problems of junior academic staff in Germany provides an added dimension to the German academic scene.[166]

The German academic profession and especially the chairholding professor, has traditionally held a position of considerable prestige and power. The professors were responsible for the development of the academic disciplines in Germany, and had almost total control over the curriculum and internal governance. The very recent period has seen considerable reform, and the power of the full professors has been severely limited although long-term impact of these changes on the professoriate is as yet unclear.

Other European countries have also received some attention from analysts, although the literature, especially in English, is much more limited. The very serious crisis in the Italian universities is described by Martinotti and Giasanti.[167] Burton Clark also considers the role of academics in his book on Italy.[168] Lammers discusses the Dutch situation.[169] Daalder, in his discussion of recent developments in Dutch universities points out that the professors in Holland have lost much of their power.[170] The French academic profession seems to have received only limited attention despite the recent substantial changes in the

French universities. Gaussen's article discusses the problems of an overproduction of university teachers.[171]

Several general discussions of the situation in Europe are relevant to a consideration of the academic profession. Stephen Lofthouse[172] has written about the general issue of research and publication in academic life and Eric Ashby has written a general overview of the academic profession.[173] These articles deal with general and philosophical questions relevant to the academic profession in most countries. Three other studies of the conditions of academics in Europe provide some useful comparative perspectives.[174] They also provide some comparative statistical data. A recent study by the O.E.C.D. provides some particularly useful statistical information on the expansion of the academic profession in O.E.C.D. nations.[175]

The Japanese have taken an interest in the study of the academic profession, but most of the relevant literature is in Japanese. Not only has the Japanese university seen rapid expansion in recent years, but since it is based on the German model, its professoriate has held considerable power and continues to wield much authority over internal academic governance and has high prestige in society. Michiya Shimbori has written several articles on the Japanese professoriate,[176] and William Cummings and Ikuo Amano[177] have written perceptively on the academic profession as well.

Third World nations have received little attention from analysts, and most of these nations have seen literally no analysis concerning the academic profession. India, in part because of its large and active academic community, has received considerable attention from researchers. Altbach[178] and Chitnis[179] have written about college teachers, while Gilbert[180] has written perceptively of the history of the Indian academic profession. Thomas Eisemon has written about engineering professors, providing some data concerning academics in an applied field.[181] Edward Shils has written the most comprehensive article on the Indian academic profession, in which both historical and contemporary data are provided.[182] These analyses indicate the problems of establishing strong academic traditions in nations which have severe economic problems and no history of Western-style universities. The Indian professoriate has expanded dramatically in recent years, but the universities have not been given adequate funding, and academic salaries, and general standards of higher education have suffered as a result.

Africa stands in sharp contrast to India, as Van den Berghe has perceptively analyzed. African universities have not expanded as dramatically, and they have maintained high academic standards and considerable élitism.[183] The Latin American universities seem to stand somewhere between the democratization and expansion of the Indian system and the élitism of Africa. Pelczar[184] and Socolow[185] have written about the problems of the Latin American professoriate. The Latin American academic profession is undergoing major changes as it shifts from a part-time occupation to a full-time profession with increased emphasis on research and publication.

It is difficult to generalize about the problems of academics in the Third World, although their situation is different than in the industrialized nations, and for the most part, more difficult. The lack of an established university tradition rooted in the society makes the maintenance of university autonomy difficult. The problems of development and modernization coupled in most cases with a lack of financial resources, increases pressure on academics to perform a variety of tasks without adequate resources. Norms of academic life are often not well established, and procedures and requirements for promotion are in many cases unclear. Some of the most able academics are pressed into government service and are unavailable to help in developing the universities. In some countries, academics are involved in oppositional, intellectual or political activities, and this creates some suspicion of the universities in government circles. Third World academics have to translate an international knowledge system in the sciences and social sciences to societies which retain many elements of tradition.

While it is almost impossible to generalize from the diverse literature on the professoriate which is reflected in this essay, it is possible to delineate some trends which are evident in the current period:

*'Academic drift', as Grant Harman defines it, is a theme of many academic systems.[186] Academics seem to accept the various and often conflicting demands placed on their institutions without much debate or objection. As long as the new demands resulted in added resources, they were accepted without a clear understanding of the long-term consequences.

*Numerical growth in the academic profession has resulted in a loss of community, broadening of the social-class base of the profession, increased differentiation by discipline or speciality, and in general a weakening of common interests.

*The professoriate has tended to oppose reforms which change the traditional patterns of university governance, curriculum, or other elements that affect working conditions and privileges. The profession has tried to deal with increased numbers of students and new academic functions without changing organizational patterns.

*The professoriate has had mixed success in protecting academic autonomy from governmental and other demands for accountability, and from the growing power of administrators.

*There has been a trend toward democratization of the professoriate by extending participation in governance to junior ranks and upgrading some academic staff (such as librarians and research personnel) to professorial ranks. This democratization has often been opposed by senior professors, but in general this opposition has not prevented change.

*Because of expansion during the 1960s, the average age of the professoriate has temporarily declined. This had led to some generational conflict and tension between established academics and their younger colleagues.

*There is an international trend towards emphasis on research and publication as criteria for academic advancement, at least at the university level. This is changing academic systems, especially in the Third World, that had not traditionally stressed the research function.

*There are significant national differences in the traditions, roles, remuneration, working conditions, and other variables concerning the academic profession. Attitudes, values, socialization patterns, and responsibilities vary. Even within national academic systems the profession may be segmented by institution, discipline, or function. These variations make generalization difficult and have mitigated against the emergence of an international academic consciousness.

As is clear from this summary of the literature on the academic profession, the available material is incomplete, lacks comprehensive geographical coverage, and even for those countries where studies do exist, there is seldom full data available concerning the topic. Thus the need for research on almost all aspects of the academic profession is great, both from the viewpoint of individual countries and from a cross-cultural perspective. Given the key role that academics play in the university, the need is not only to fill a gap in the literature, but a pressing requirement to understand an important part of higher education.

C Governance

Without question, the organization of universities has much to do with their effective functioning, their role, and their ethos. Recently, the term 'governance' has been used to describe the ways in which universities are managed and organized. Such factors as the structures of decision-making within an academic institution, the roles of the various participants in the academic community, and the pattern of administrative control are all related to institutional effectiveness and are included under the theme of governance. As with some other aspects of higher education research, consideration of governance both from a theoretical viewpoint and in terms of practical proposals for change have been pioneered in the United States. Most of the American literature has no mention at all of non-American situations, although the Carnegie Commission's report on governance does have an appendix that discusses some recent reforms in Britain.[187] Much of the literature on governance of individual universities can be found only in documents very difficult to obtain, as many interesting reports are published for private circulation by individual universities or government agencies. This literature is not reflected in this essay or in the bibliography which follows.

Some of the writing on university governance is related directly to university reform and these references are listed in the section on reform. Further, the study of university governance is approached from a number of disciplinary perspectives, notably political science, history, and sociology. Because of its inter-disciplinary nature, the literature on governance cannot be easily categorized in terms of its theoretical background, and much of the writing tends to be descriptive. If there is any 'theoretical' base for the study of university governance, it probably comes from political science and public administration, fields which have as their concern the formal operation of institutions. Sociologists are also concerned with the functioning of social institutions. It is significant that no well known political scientists in any major nation have tried to build a model of university governance. Several sociologists have attempted to analyze the operation of universities, but these efforts have not focused mainly on questions of governance but rather are general analyses of universities as institutions. Among the most significant of these analyses is one by Talcott Parsons and Gerald Platt.[188] The most comprehensive effort to understand the organization of universities can be found in a volume edited by James Perkins. This volume includes a chapter focusing on cross-cultural issues, although it is generally concerned with the United States. Perkins has also edited another volume which is more directly comparative in focus.[189] This book features essays on a number of different nations. Sociologist Alain Touraine has written a book on the American university which considers organizational factors.[190]

Several general analyses of university governance are useful in thinking about some of the inherent political and sociological issues involved.[191] Most of these considerations are based on the American experience, but also attempt to deal with theoretical issues. J. V. Baldridge has written an analysis of internal decision-making at one American university which discusses the political issues involved.[192] Two recent books edited by Baldridge also focus on university governance issues in the American context.[193] Leon Epstein, a political scientist, has written a book on university governance from the viewpoint of the typical American large state university.[194] John Corson's classic study of academic governance deals with both the practical and theoretical aspects of academic organization.[195] None of these volumes provide a full satisfactory theoretical framework useful in a cross-national context.

Several analysts have dealt with university governance and organization from a cross-cultural perspective. Eric Ashby[196] has written in general terms about the challenges to university organization in a period of change, and Barbara Burn has contrasted systems of governance in four European countries.[197] The International Association of Universities[198] sponsored a volume on university administration. An article by Clerk and Debbasch[199] deals with student participation in university governance in several European nations. These studies have the advantage of taking an international perspective, and one can find in them a feeling for the complexities of comparative analysis.

Several useful British studies have also appeared which deal with the organization of higher education. Among these are volumes by Hugh Livingstone,[200] Colin Flood Page and Mary Yates,[201] and Grame Moodie and Rowland Eustace.[202] The last two volumes provide the most detailed discussion. Janice Beyer and Thomas Lodahl have written a comparative article on the politics of American and British universities.[203] Bruce Williams' article considered the values of academic organization in the British context, and has some cross-cultural relevance as well.[204] Several detailed studies of Canadian academic organization have appeared, including the influential report by James Duff and Robert Berdahl.[205] Ross[206] and Halliday[207] have criticized recent trends in Canadian academic organization, feeling that there has been too much 'democratizing'. Two studies from India highlight some aspects of governance as they apply to Third World nations. The problems encountered in nations like India are especially difficult, since universities generally enjoy less autonomy and have very limited resources. S.C. Malik's[208] volume combines some analytical discussion with some suggestions for change in Indian universities, while Susanne and Lloyd Rudolph's[209] excellent portrait of a single Indian university provides analysis of some of the underlying factors of academic administration. A.K. Rice, using Indian data, has written one of the very few comprehensive models for university reorganization focusing mainly on governance issues.[210]

Academic governance is not a question that can be considered in isolation from other key issues. For example, much of the literature on university reform, discussed later in this essay, is directly related to governance. Reformers have often failed to successfully change the mode of academic organization so necessary to the implementation of reform plans. In addition, the following section on university-society relations relates directly to governance and organization. The internal life of an academic institution does not exist in isolation from the wider society. Those external elements which provide funds and, increasingly, demand 'accountability' for academic programs and activities loom large in the university equation. The literature discussed in this section reflects only a small proportion of the available material. There is a good deal of writing in Spanish on questions of university organization, but much of this work is of a very general nature. In addition, material in German and French is not reflected here to any extent because of its lack of availability to this researcher. Despite these omissions, it is fair to say that the literature on university governance is in a fairly early stage of development. The number of detailed, data-based studies is quite small. Few political scientists have as yet devoted themselves to this topic, and most writers who consider governance deal with it as part of a broader analysis of the university. For example, an excellent recent book on higher education has one chapter of about thirty pages devoted to academic governance.[211] While the internal arrangements of a university are clearly related to other aspects, there is a definite need for more detailed analysis of this specific issue.

D University-society relations

If there was ever a 'golden age' in which universities were truly autonomous and able to conduct their affairs without interference from outside authority, that time is long past. Indeed, the history of higher education indicates that universities were in fact never free of contact with society, and were always to some extent under societal influence. Even in the Middle Ages, universities found themselves in the midst of theological and other disputes.[212]

In the modern period, universities have moved more to the centers of their societies and have become institutions of considerable importance for continued technological development and have also taken up increasing amounts of funds. Precisely because universities have assumed new functions—albeit thrust upon them by government demands in many cases—they have come under increasing scrutiny by the societies which increasingly depend on them.[213] And since most university systems depend on funding from government, it has been the government which has taken most interest in the operation and performance of higher education. This development has been called accountability, and in general it means the demands for detailed responsibility for how funds are spent and the measurement of the outcomes of university programs and projects. Even in academic systems, like that of Britain, which have traditionally been carefully insulated from direct government involvement and scrutiny, there have been pressures for accountability, and the traditional role of the University Grants Committee has been vitiated to some extent.

In many other countries, especially in the Third World, traditional concepts of the autonomy of universities have been virtually destroyed in part because of often well-intentioned demands by government for accountability for expenditures.[214] It is clear that notions of academic autonomy, long considered necessary for the effective functioning of universities, have been called into serious question by demands for accountability. It is still unclear how the tension between accountability, which is generally accepted as a legitimate demand of funding agencies, and academic autonomy and traditional governance patterns will be resolved.[215]

The problem of accountability is linked to other elements of the university crisis in that increased expenditures and the expansion of roles have led directly to demands for accountability. The public has taken a greater interest in the operation of universities in many countries because higher education serves a larger proportion of the population and is especially important as a means of social mobility and status for the articulate middle classes. The public has been willing to devote larger amounts of money to higher education, but at the same time it has demanded more control over the operations and goals of universities.

There is little question but that public authority—government—is winning the 'struggle' for accountability and that universities throughout the world are adjusting to demands for data, and increasingly for participation in academic affairs. Indeed, many of the reform efforts of recent years have included expanded participation in governance, not only by students and others within the academic community but in some cases by representatives of the public. New computerized accounting procedures have given governmental authorities more and better data concerning university expenditures. Academic institutions have increasingly been called on to make their own plans within the context of often constraining government policy guidelines. In other words, the traditional right of the university to define its own academic goals, to maintain autonomy in terms of internal governance, and to expend its funds essentially without scrutiny from the outside have all been called into question, and the universities are quickly losing some important elements of their autonomy. The issue of university-society relations, in all its sometimes subtle manifestations, is one of the most perplexing for higher education in the current period.

The issue of university-society relations has been discussed in a general way by a number of writers, and indeed most analyses of higher education include some discussion of this issue regardless of the basic focus of the study.[216] Several writers have dealt with the historical relations between university and society, pointing out that throughout history there has been a tension between the university and its surrounding society. Lawrence Stone's two-volume edited study has examples from both Europe and the United States[217] while Baldwin and Goldthwaite[218] concentrate on the late Middle Ages in their edited book. Two studies sponsored by the International Association of Universities focus attention on university autonomy and university-society relations.[219] These volumes consider these questions from a quite general perspective and largely in the European context. A. H. Halsey has written an excellent article focusing on university-society relations which provides a sophisticated discussion of the issue,[220] and both Sydney Caine[221] and T. R. McConnell[222] have written on the topic from a fairly general point of view. Halsey and McConnell are in general more accepting of the role of the state in higher education than is Caine.

The issue of university autonomy has been a key focus of discussion about university-society relations, since internal autonomy has been an important traditional value of the university. The amount and nature of university autonomy differs from country to country. The traditional German university, for example, had considerable autonomy in terms of internal governance and the shaping of the curriculum, but relatively little concerning politics. In addition, professors were state civil servants, and various restrictions were placed by government authorities from time to time on the appointment of professors.[223] In the United States, different types of universities enjoy different levels of autonomy. The prestigious private universities typically have most internal autonomy, with the great state universities with powerful faculties coming close to the private institutions. The community colleges and many four-year colleges have much less autonomy and tend to be tied to local or state government policies and fiscal oversight. Traditional concepts of university autonomy are not influential in the universities of the Soviet Union or Eastern Europe, where government policies guide academic planning and where political loyalty is usually strictly enforced.[224] However, even in these nations, universities often have more leeway in dissent and in setting their own goals than other segments of society.

Third World nations typically allow their universities less autonomy than is customary in the West. This is due in part to weaker historical traditions of autonomy, but also to the great pressures on the universities to contribute to urgent development tasks. In India, for example, the universities are under the jurisdiction of the state governments, some of which permit considerable autonomy but others impose rigid control even on small policy matters. Ashby has summarized the historical development of Indian universities,[225] while Dongerkery[226] and the Rudolphs[227] have discussed the current situation. Direct government funding of higher education, a tradition of academic involvement in politics, and massive public demands on universities all contribute to the lack of autonomy. In Ghana, the British tradition to some extent protected the universities from direct political involvement but there has nevertheless been considerable government interference in academic affairs, both during the Nkrumah regime and later military governments. Ashby and Anderson[228] have written generally of the situation in Anglophone Africa, while Dennis Austin has discussed the more recent situation in Ghana.[229]

Latin American universities traditionally had a good deal of internal autonomy, but recent political currents have limited that autonomy in many nations. Of special importance was the tendency of the university to be anti-establishment. As military governments have come to power, political authority has been increasingly unwilling to permit oppositional activities from the universities. Recent trends in Latin America have in many respects improved academic quality but have weakened autonomy.[230]

A number of countries have tried to protect university autonomy through various policies, but with increasing financial stress and political involvement these instruments have been under great pressure. One of the most successful is the British University Grants Committee (U.G.C.).[231] The U.G.C. was devised as a means of providing government funds to the universities while preserving virtually total autonomy in the expenditure of those funds. There was, in Britain, a consensus that academic decisions should be insulated from the day-to-day considerations of governmental policy, although overall government education policy should have some role in shaping the universities. Robert Berdahl[232] has written a detailed analysis of British government policy and higher education, focusing on the functioning of the U.G.C., while Edward Boyle has also written on this general topic.[233] Eric Ashby's[234] article has attempted to reinforce the basic concept of the U.G.C., for the agency has come under considerable criticism in recent years, as funds for education have grown more limited, and parliament and government ministers have demanded more direct participation in the expenditure of funds so that the link between fund allocation and policy implementation would be closer. The financial crisis in Britain in recent years has severely strained the U.G.C. concept, and some commentators have argued that it has been irreparably weakened.

The U.G.C. model has been adopted by other countries, especially in areas which were formerly under British colonial control. The Indians adopted a modified U.G.C. about twenty years ago, and have had limited success with it.[235] The Indian U.G.C. has only limited jurisdiction over the allocation of funds to higher education, and it is clear that it has not provided an effective buffer between politicians and academics.[236] In addition, Ghana, Nigeria, some Canadian provinces, and several other parts of the world have experimented with the U.G.C. idea with varying degrees of success. Despite the fact that the U.G.C. is now under pressure in Britain itself and has had its problems in other countries, it has proved to be one of the most successful means of maintaining a degree of separation between government and the universities.

The 1960s brought an increasing concern about the relationship of the universities to societal politics. The political turmoil of the sixties often involved the universities, and especially student movements, and in many cases government authorities became concerned about the political loyalty of institutions of higher education. These political concerns, combined with the growing demands for accountability and desires to have more impact on academic policies led to unprecedented confrontations between political authorities and the universities. It is fair to say that the universities are themselves almost powerless in such confrontations. Their power is that of tradition and history, and of the impact of moral authority, and in a time of tension and confrontation these elements have only limited power.

Conservative analysts have pointed out that the 'politicization' of the universities is not solely a matter of governmental interference in academic policy, but also includes the involvement of the universities themselves and/or a significant segment of the teaching staff or students in oppositional politics. It is argued that the involvement of the universities in politics has severely damaged academic independence and autonomy, and is not in keeping with the best traditions of higher education. Further, some recent reforms which have expanded participation in university governance to students and even to non-university groups, further damages traditional autonomy. Paul Seabury's edited volume represents this position and presents a number of case studies of increasing political involvement of universities.[237] Edward Shils has discussed current developments in higher education from this perspective and has decried what he sees as a decline in academic norms due to increasing politicization in the universities in the West.[238] Henry L. Mason[239] has written two case studies with similar themes concerning the Netherlands and West Germany and Hans Daalder has written of the political results of recent academic reforms in the Netherlands.[240] These analyses generally argue that traditional values of the university are what is important and that most recent reform has been motivated by elements within the universities uninterested in academic standards and by government agencies which do not understand the true nature of higher education.

Traditionally, radicals within universities in most countries were few in number, and they took relatively little part in internal academic affairs. Universities, as institutions, remained aloof from direct societal political involvement but were implicitly involved with mainstream political currents because of the sources of their funding, their research roles, and the social class backgrounds of both faculty and students. Crises arose when academic institutions became home to increasing numbers of radicals during the 1960s and when, in a few cases, there was considerable pressure within universities for institutions to take anti-Establishment stands on major social and political questions. Conservatives argued that universities should take no political stand, while radicals pointed out that institutions of higher learning had a responsibility to speak out on key social questions, and were in any case inherently involved with key social institutions and were not truly non-political.

Student movements used universities as a base for social protest, and in some countries academic institutions became a key launching-ground for dissident political activism, in some cases resulting in major societal disruption. Considerable pressure from governmental authorities was placed on academic institutions to limit their involvement in political dissent. Debate raged within institutions, among both faculty and students, concerning the political nature of the university and its proper role in society. While much of the direct political involvement of universities evident in the 1960s has disappeared, the debate concerning the role of the university in politics continues, and it is clear that institutions, with their large size and increased resources and their place at the center of modern societies, have an intrinsically larger political role than was the case in previous periods, and that the traditional tranquillity of higher education has been ended forever.

A number of analyses have been made of the political role of universities and the interaction between university and society. Henri Janne[241] has written of the European university in society, discussing the necessary relationships that exist, and Julius Gould[242] has discussed the British situation from a critical perspective.

A special issue of the *Journal of Social and Political Ideas in Japan* was devoted to 'university and society', focusing on a country which has debated these issues at length and in which the government plays a considerable role in higher education policy.[243] Two excellent studies concerning the involvement of the government university affairs in Singapore have appeared.[244] These articles document how the government has virtually destroyed academic autonomy in Singapore. Several other Third World nations have also been analyzed in terms of university-society relations, and there is no question but that the problems of the Third World in this area are especially difficult. R. C. Pratt[245] and M. Crawford, *et al*[246] have discussed the situation in Africa, while Joseph Fischer[247] has considered South-east Asia. Several of the essays in the volume edited by Amrik Singh and P. G. Altbach discuss aspects of the Indian situation.[248]

European nations have received considerable attention, not only in scholarly journals and in books, but also in the daily press, which has from time to time, and especially during the turbulent sixties, been very much concerned with higher education. Michelle Patterson[249] has dealt with one aspect of French higher education and politics, while André Philippart[250] has considered the Belgian situation. The German literature on university-society relations is very extensive, as the re-current crises in the West German academic community have all been related to this issue, in part because the government has so direct a role in academic affairs.

There are a few common threads in this literature. The crisis of the sixties was especially difficult for European nations and placed grave strains on traditional university structures and on autonomy. Although the 'crisis' has subsided in most countries with the end of the student activism and general social unrest of the sixties, the issue of university-society relations remains crucial because of the new demand for accountability. Political dissent has been replaced by fiscal constraints as the flashpoint of the debate, and both are powerful forces against traditional ideas of academic autonomy. It is fair to say that in almost all nations strong pressures exist and the question of the proper relation-ship between university and government is under consideration but that few solutions have thus far been found. It also seems that in few cases do the universities have much power to affect emerging public policies. And in many instances, the universities have themselves been fighting a 'rearguard' action trying to protect their interests by holding firm rather than developing new solutions to problems.

E Student activism

Students are, of course, a major part of any academic system. In a sense, universities exist to serve students by providing them with edu-cation, knowledge, and increasingly, various kinds of ancillary ser-vices. Along with the faculty, students are a major 'estate' of the university. In most university systems, students do not have much power or even input into the internal life of institutions. A major exception here has traditionally been the Latin American university, where since 1918 students have held power in major decision-making academic bodies.[251] But in many Latin American nations these insti-tutional arrangements have been eliminated in the interest of political quiet by academic 'efficiency'. In the past decade, a number of national university systems have begun to include students in academic governance and in other decision-making areas, and such reforms will be discussed briefly in the section on reform. In general, however, students have gained relatively little power within universities, and even in those systems which included students in governance, such as West Germany and France, the trend has very recently turned away from such participation.

The literature on student activism is very large—much larger than for the other major constituent of the university, the teachers. Several bibliographies outline the scope of this literature in the United States and in other countries.[252] Student activism is not the only element of student life that has been studied. In the United States, analytical attention has been given to many student-related topics, from extra-curricular life to the effects of the university experience on students.[253] Research on psychological and other aspects of student life is much better developed in the United States than in other countries, due in part to the long tradition of concern with the extra-curricular life of students, expressed in the concept of *in loco parentis* and in part because of a concern with educational research and the larger number of researchers working. Until recently, most European universities took no interest in the non-academic lives of their students, feeling such matters to be beyond the scope of their responsibility. Thus, little research has been conducted on aspects of student life. This situation is now changing as student numbers have increased and universities have begun to take more responsibility for students. We concentrate here on student activism, not only because it is one of the most dramatic and important elements of the university 'crisis' of recent years, but also because the literature on this topic is quite extensive and often has relevance for understanding the politics and sociology of higher education.

The literature on student activism is extensive for several reasons. The most important, of course, is the fact that students, especially in the 1960s, proved to be one of the most disruptive forces in higher education. In many nations, from France and West Germany to India, Japan, Thailand, Ecuador, and South Korea, students had a major role in precipitating societal political unrest and in several nations were instrumental in bringing down governments. In the United States, the student movement was a key force against the Vietnam war and in favor of civil rights for blacks. And while the major international thrust of student activism has been directed at broader political issues, such as racism, war, political ideologies, and others, student movements have also had an effect on internal university matters. In a few countries, students have pressed demands for university reforms, and these have in a few instances been influential on policy.[254]

The literature on student activism grew most rapidly during the

1960s, when the major industrialized nations were rocked by student dissent, and the amount of literature has diminished dramatically recently. Student activism remains an important force in many nations, however, although with the exception of Italy, it has largely subsided in the West. In 1977, major student dissent occurred in such nations as South Africa, South Korea, Thailand and Brazil, but this activism has not attracted much interest from social scientists and other analysts. During the 1960s, social scientists became interested in students as they moved to a position of considerable importance in society, and funds became available for research on student movements. Thus, while a modest literature did exist prior to the upsurge of the sixties and some work continues to be done at present, it is fair to say that much of the literature that is reflected in this essay was stimulated by the sixties.

This section will deal with two aspects of the literature on students. It will first discuss some of the 'theoretical' or general studies of student activism—writings which attempt to place student movements in a broader theoretical context. We will then present some of the more significant studies of student movements in particular national or regional settings. In this discussion, stress is placed on studies which have some theoretical contribution rather than purely descriptive material.

The cross-cultural analysis of student activism is a difficult undertaking, since so many variables are involved. Not only do academic systems differ, but the political atmosphere in individual countries varies and this naturally affects student activism. In a country with a relatively open political system and with a historical tradition of student political involvement, it is more likely that student activism will occur and have an impact than in a country without such traditions or with a severely repressive regime. In addition, such highly complex factors as the role of the family, child-raising practices, and the norms and values instilled by both the school system and the political culture, all affect student activism. At present, there is no satisfactory 'theory' of student political activism which covers a variety of national settings, despite several efforts by social scientists to create such a theory. In addition, most social scientists bring their own methodological perspectives to the study of student activism, and thus the literature reflects a range of methodologies and different perspectives. Many analysts also bring their own political views to their analysis of student activism. It is not suprising that conservative analysts tend to be more critical of the student movement than radical commentators. For example, Lewis Feuer's study of generational conflict is highly critical of student activism.[255] Feuer himself was opposed to the activist movements which he encountered at the University of California during the 1960s, There is a high correlation between the political orientation of the analyst and the nature of the analysis. Thus, when considering the writings of analysts of student activism, one must keep these limitations in mind.

There are several generalizations which are evident from the literature on student activism. These are by no means all the insights that might be indicated, nor are they universally applicable. Nevertheless, they may be useful in thinking about the nature and function of student movements in the modern world.

*Student activism is in almost all cases a minority phenomena. Only a small proportion of the student population is involved in activist movements, usually even during periods of crisis. Despite this fact, these minorities often have widespread support in the student community and sometimes speak for other segments of the population as well.

*Student activists are not randomly distributed in the student population, but come disproportionately from the social sciences, from students who are successful in their studies, and from among students in the most prestigious and centrally located universities. In some countries, activists tend to be selected from upper income groups among the students and from among identifiable religious or ethnic groups.

*Student activism is in general stimulated by broader political questions in the society rather than by campus events although campus crises are often used to generate support for movements or can help to provide the catalyst for mass action. There are, however, some regional differences in this area.

*Student activist movements tend to be more 'successful' in terms of overthrowing governments or producing massive political change in Third World nations, where political infrastructures are relatively weak and where students may wield political influence beyond their relatively small numbers.

*Student activist organizations and movements are generally of relatively short duration. They find it difficult to sustain either organizational or political momentum, due in part to the difficulty of maintaining a high level of struggle and in part to the basically transitory nature of student generations.

*There seems to be relatively little evidence of 'generational conflict' in student activist leadership or in the demands and issues of concern to student movements.

*Student activism in the post-World War II period has been almost exclusively leftist in its orientation, although this has not always been the case historically.[256]

*There is little 'international consciousness' among student movements. While foreign policy questions are often of interest to movements, there is little evidence of an international student movement. Student activist movements seem to be basically national in nature and orientation.

A number of edited volumes appeared during the 1960s, stimulated largely by the wave of activism at that time, which provide an overview of student movements in various countries. These volumes are, in general, well written and are very useful in obtaining a general picture of student movements in an international perspective. They do not, in general, deal theoretically with student activism, but the data presented may yield some useful general comparisons. S.M. Lipset has been especially active in research on students, and his edited volume is a valuable source of data.[257] Lipset and Altbach have also compiled a useful volume.[258] Both these books provide some theoretical chapters as well as case studies of various nations. M.S. Archer's edited book includes detailed essays on major West European nations, and its chapters combine a consideration of student activism with some general analysis of the university systems.[259] Edited collections by Cockburn and Blackburn,[260] Nagel,[261] and McGuigan[262] all include cross-cultural data and are quite useful. Two excellent volumes concerning Third World nations have also been published. Donald Emmerson's[263] volume includes coverage of all Third World regions while W. and J. Hanna's[264] book is concerned with Africa.

As indicated above, the amount of 'theoretical' material concerning student activism is not very large, nor has any widely accepted framework been posited as yet. Lewis Feuer's generational conflict hypothesis has been widely discussed, but is not generally accepted among scholars.[265] Kenneth Keniston, dealing mainly with American students, has argued that dissenting students are usually very much in tune with their parents.[266] Michael Miles, again arguing from an American perspective, states that the student activism has a clear logic which is related to societal politics.[267] Cohn-Bendit, one of the leaders of the French student revolt and a Marxist, has written a theoretical volume attempting to explain student unrest.[268] Alain Touraine, a French Marxist sociologist, has analysed student activism from a Marxist perspective, largely dealing with the French situation.[269] S.M. Lipset has written a theoretical paper on students in developing countries,[270] and P.G. Altbach has analyzed some of the general issues relating to student activism.[271] Frank Pinner's analyses of student activism in Western Europe also have general relevance as his categorization of various types of student movements is original.[272] While Pinner explored student activism from the viewpoint of a political scientist, Ian Weinberg and Kenneth Walker[273] have written a sociological analysis of the nature of student movements, and P.G. Altbach[274] has explored some of the historical implications in the Asian context. G.A.D. Soares has explored the limited scope of Latin American student movements in his article, and he discusses the opinions of student activists.[275] Finally, E. W. and M. S. Bakke have written a volume devoted to the various theories of student activism.[276]

American student activism has received the largest amount of analytic attention from scholars and others. During the 1960s alone, more than fifty volumes and hundreds of journal articles on American students were published. It is not possible to discuss the American literature in any detail, and thus only a few of the most significant volumes will be mentioned here. A more complete listing can be found in the bibliography by Altbach and Kelly.[277] Several historical studies of American students have appeared, and these shed valuable light on the traditions of student activism in the United States. Altbach's[278] volume provides the widest overview, while S. M. Lipset[279] includes several historical chapters in his book on American students. Steven Novak has written about American students during the early period of United States' history.[280]

In addition to the volumes mentioned above on American student activism, several others stand out as important, and as indicative of currents in the literature. Richard Flacks, a sociologist, was one of the first analysts to point out that generational conflict was not a readily apparent factor among American student activists. Flacks has also sympathetically discussed the student movement in his volume.[281] Relatively few analysts have discussed the demands and concerns of the student movement in any country. One of the few volumes that does this is Wallerstein and Starr's two-volume collection of writings related to the demands of the student movement and in general to the university crisis of the 1960s.[282] Kirkpatrick Sale[283] has written the definitive history of the S.D.S., the main American activist organization of the sixties, and James Wood has provided a sociological study of the background of American student activism.[284] His volume is a compilation of attitude and other surveys, and it paints a portrait of the attitudes and values of activists. Sampson and Korn have edited a useful volume, mainly presenting psychological aspects of analysis of American student activism.[285]

European students have received a great deal of analytical attention from scholars and commentators, particularly during the period of unrest of the 1960s. It is not surprising that France and West Germany, the two countries which experienced the most dramatic student movements, have received the most attention. The material on student activism in French and German, both books and articles, is very extensive and is hardly mentioned here. Any serious student of European student activism must examine the scholarship that exists in the various European languages. These comments, and the bibliography that follows this essay, are mainly concerned with a small sampling of materials largely in English.

France and West Germany were most shaken by student activism during the 1960s, and both countries not only experienced political crisis, but students were instrumental in engendering academic reforms of various kinds. The French 'events' of 1968 came very close to toppling the government, and convinced the ruling authorities that university reform was necessary. Alain Schnapp and Pierre Vidal-Nacquet[286] have presented a collection of documents, while Alain Touraine has written an analysis of the 'events' from a broader perspective.[287] Both these volumes treat the May Movement sympathetically. John and Barbara Ehrenreich[288] have written a general survey of European student movements, focusing on France and West Germany. An article in the French journal *Esprit*[289] provides a good summary of the crisis and several reports in *Minerva* include an excellent factual summary of both the political and the educational factors which contributed to the student movement in France.[290] While the French students severely disrupted French politics and speeded the process of university reform, they had little role in designing the reform and many were in fact opposed to the final reform plans of the government. In addition, once the dramatic events of May 1968 receded into the background, the movement never regained its strength, and even the leadership groups experienced splits and indecision.

The West German student movement was more successful than the French in stimulating university reform, although it was never a serious threat to the established political order. The most important center of student unrest in West Germany was in West Berlin. Richard Merritt[291] has analyzed the situation in Berlin, while several social scientists have attempted to provide some sociological analysis to the student movement. Among the best-known of the sociological analyses are those of Jurgen Habermas[292] and Ludwig von Friedeberg.[293] Several documentary reports in *Minerva* provide a good summary of some of the activities of this period of intense activism.[294] Finally, Uwe Bergmann *et al*, have written a volume clearly stating some of the motivating factors for the student revolution from the viewpoint of the students themselves.[295] Without question, the West German student movement was successful in stimulating university reform, particularly in those states controlled by the Social Democratic party, but as in France the student movement was unable to maintain itself in a coherent form after the period of activism was over. It is curious that despite the fact that the German student movement in fact was less of a threat to the political authorities, it had a major impact on German higher education and on German public opinion.

Other European countries were less directly affected by student activism than France and West Germany, but most had some upsurge of activism during the 1960s, and this stimulated research and commentary. The British universities were only marginally affected by activism generally, although there were a few severe local agitations. Halsey and Marks[296] have provided a good overview of British student politics, and Blackstone and Hadley[297] have compared British students with those in the United States. The Italian universities have seen almost continuous disruption and activism for more than a decade, related mainly to the very poor conditions in these institutions. Despite student pressure, there has been little reform in Italian higher education, nor has the political system been very much affected by the activism. Martinotti[298] has provided several analyses of Italian students and Frederico Mancini has written a general description of the Italian student movement.[299] E. T. Galvin has written of the Spanish student movement in the sixties, although the Spanish situation has dramatically changed since the end of the Franco régime.[300] Although students in the socialist countries of Eastern Europe have not directly participated in major activist movements—with the exception of student participation in the Hungarian revolution of 1956—they have received some analytic attention, since university students have been vocal on political issues from time to time. Richard Cornell[301] has provided a general analysis while David Burg[302] has concentrated on students in the Soviet Union. Aleksander Gella has written of Polish students.[303] Finally, G. Statera[304] has written a post-mortem of the European student movements in a volume which discusses a number of Western European nations.

Japanese students have been very active and came close to overthrowing the government in 1960, and caused severe disruption of higher education during the sixties. Unlike West Germany, where students had impact on changes in university structure, Japanese students had little impact on reform and the curriculum, and also had little lasting political impact in the society. The Japanese student movement has received much analysis by scholars and others. The literature in both Japanese and English is quite substantial.[305] Stewart Dowsey edited an excellent volume which provides information on the various Japanese student organizations involved in the movement.[306] This volume also indicates the political orientations of these groups. Ellis Krauss has written a study of the attitudes and values of student radicals, bringing together much sociological and political analysis.[307] Michiya Shimbori, a Japanese sociologist, has written several articles dealing with various aspects of the Japanese student movement.[308] His work combines sociological and historical commentary, and presents a fairly complete analysis of the context of Japanese student activism. Finally, Kazuko Tsurumi has painted several portraits of Japanese student activists and has discussed the movement generally.[309]

Her work presents useful insights concerning psychological aspects of Japanese student activism.

The Third World nations have experienced much student agitation. Indeed, as indicated previously, it has only been in Third World nations that students have successfully overthrown governments. Thus, students are not only a force on the campus, but they have very real potential to precipitate political change. It is also significant that in no nation have student movements been able to hold power once they have achieved initial success. Others, often the military, have moved in quickly to assume control. There are many reasons why students in the Third World have considerable potential political power. One is that there are fewer competing political forces in society, and student activism assumes large proportions in the existing political structure. Much of the political life of Third World nations is concentrated in the capital and among relatively small urban groups. Universities are prominent institutions in Third World capitals, and it is easy for students to mobilize demonstrations. Students in the Third World often speak for segments of the educated middle class, and articulate their feelings. Thus, their impact goes beyond their own usually relatively small numbers. Students are often considered a future élite, and they have a certain 'moral' force. Finally, in many Third World nations there is a strong tradition of involvement by students and intellectuals in independence struggles and other movements, and it is informally expected that students will participate in politics and there is a certain legitimation for such participation. All these factors have contributed to the potential—and in some cases actual—power of student activism in the Third World.

Asian students have been quite active for long periods of time. Altbach has examined the historical roots of Asian student movements in an effort to find some common elements among activist movements in the region.[310] China and India have strong traditions of student activism, and students in both countries have been active in political and intellectual movements for more than a century. John Israel has written several excellent studies of Chinese student movements, indicating that the activist tradition is a long one and that it links up with such recent episodes as the Red Guards of the 1960s.[311] Victor Nee[312] has written of the important Cultural Revolution, itself at least in part a student movement, and Bruce Larkin has written a broad survey of Chinese student activism.[313] Chinese students were active in the May 4 Movement in 1919 which paved the way for the emergence of the modern Chinese state.[314] They continued their activism up to the time of the Communist revolution in 1947. And as indicated by the role of the Red Guards and the continuing impact of the universities on Chinese politics, the students and the intellectual community continue to play an active role in Chinese politics, even under a highly controlled political system.

The other major Asian nation, India, also has a long history of student involvement in politics. P. G. Altbach has edited a comprehensive volume on Indian student activism which provides both historical and contemporary analysis.[315] Indian students were active in the independence struggle, and have been involved in agitation and politics since 1947 as well. Indeed, students have been instrumental in the downfall of several state governments in India, and their continuing agitation, often concerning local campus questions, has caused serious disruption of the educational system.[316] Aileen Ross has written a broad sociological overview of Indian student attitudes and values, in which some of the underlying reasons for student political activism are discussed.[317] Indian students, who study under poor conditions and who are faced with very serious employment problems after graduation, are often involved in 'indiscipline' or sporadic student unrest without a clear political or even educational motive.

Other Asian nations have had active—and highly effective—student movements. Governments have been overthrown by students in South Korea, Thailand, and Indonesia, and several excellent analyses have been written concerning these nations. In Indonesia, student agitation favored the 'right' in the major agitation of the early 1960s, and students helped to oust the Sukarno regime.[318] Robert Zimmerman[319] has written of the Thai student movement, while R. Heinze[320] has provided an account of Thai student involvement in anti-government agitation. William Douglas[321] and Princeton Lyman[322] have written of Korean student activism focusing largely on the early 1960s, when Korean students were involved in major anti-government activities.

There are perhaps more similarities between student activism in different African nations than is the case for Asia. Student populations in Africa are smaller, and universities were until very recently élitist institutions. Academic conditions are in general better in Africa than in Asia. By and large, African students did not play as large a role in nationalist or independence movements and there are weaker traditions of student political involvement. On the other hand, African students are seen as a future élite group and in many countries are taken quite seriously by government officials. African student movements have been less successful than their Asian counterparts in overthrowing governments, and have had relatively little impact on shaping university policies. Indeed, students have opposed government-sponsored reforms in Tanzania as they viewed these reforms as diminishing their privileges.

The most comprehensive volume on African student activism has been edited by William and Judith Hanna; it includes a theoretical essay on African students and a number of analyses of individual countries.[323] Dwaine Marvick has written a perceptive essay on African students as a 'presumptive élite' in which the argument is put forward that students are treated with respect because of their future élite status.[324] Joel Barkan is the author of a detailed comparative study of student attitudes in Ghana, Tanzania, and Uganda.[325] This study links student attitudes on a number of issues, including politics, economic and social development. In addition, several of the essays in Emmerson's collection on student politics deal with such African countries as Zaire, Ghana, and South Africa.[326] Ghana has received considerable attention from analysts, and is one of the most thoroughly studied African countries.[327] Despite the relatively small number of research studies on African students, the quality of much of this writing is high, and it is possible to obtain some very useful generalizations from the available material.

Latin American nations have a unique tradition of student activism dating from the famous reform movement of 1918 in Argentina. This movement, well analyzed by Richard Walter, transformed much of Latin American higher education by pressing for reforms which included students in major structures of academic governance.[328] This movement built up a tradition of activism. In the past two decades, as Latin American universities have moved to professionalize themselves, to hire full-time staff in place of the traditional part-time professor, and as many Latin American nations have become military dictatorships, students have been removed from their decision-making roles. In addition, student movements have been severely repressed, and at present students have neither a key role in governance in most Latin American countries nor are activist movements especially active. The potential for activism, however, remains strong.

The literature on Latin American student activism is quite diverse. Cuba, where students were an important element in the revolutionary movement which brought Fidel Castro to power, has been analyzed by Jaime Suchlicki.[329] His historical treatment provides useful background to understanding the student role in Cuban politics. Frank Bonilla and Myron Glazer have written a useful book on Chile, another Latin American nation which has seen considerable activism.[330] Two volumes based on large-scale attitude surveys of Latin American students have been published which report on the surveys as well as provide some general overviews of student activism in a number of Latin American nations. Liebman, Walker and Glazer have studied students in six nations and have reported on their attitudes toward education, politics and other variables, as well as placing these attitudes in the context of the institutional setting of Latin American universities.[331] David Smith has also studied student attitudes, and has provided a sophisticated analysis of a range of attitude variables.[332] A number of writers have provided general analyses of student activism in the region, and these are quite useful to obtain a general picture. Orlando Albornoz, a Venezuelan sociologist, has written two articles, one focusing on academic freedom and the other on activism generally.[333] Kenneth Walker has examined university reform movements in Argentina and Colombia, two nations which have been actively engaged in such movements.[334] Alastair Hennessy[335] and Kalman Silvert[336] have written in general of Latin American students, focusing on their political activities. Finally, Dani Thomas and R. B. Craig[337] and John Peterson[338] have written about research currents regarding Latin American students and have comparatively analyzed Latin American student politics.

This discussion has reflected only the literature in English on Latin American student activism. There is also a substantial amount of material written in Spanish and Portugese on this topic. Much of the Spanish-language material is of a general or philosophical nature, and the number of research-based studies is fairly small. Students in Latin America have been quite important politically since 1918. They have generally been leftist in their orientation. Because of the tradition of the sanctity of the university campus, universities have been hotbeds of anti-government activity throughout the continent since it was more difficult for repressive political authority to enter the campus. The tradition of student political involvement is in general well-established —students have been political actors for many years and their involvement is expected.

Students have been instrumental in political affairs. For example, they have been actively involved in Brazil prior to the current military regime, have been involved in overthrowing regimes in Ecuador and Peru, were a key intellectual support for the Cuban revolutionary movement, and have been sporadically active in Venezuela and Mexico. Students have been almost constantly active in Argentina, where the 1918 movement began. The general trend of leftist student activism has at least been temporarily broken in recent years. Military regimes have been increasingly willing to enter the campuses, arrest students and others, and in general to impose repression. The universities have also been undergoing change which has diminished or eliminated student involvement in governance.

F Higher education in the Third World

This essay is not organized according to geographical regions or countries, yet it seems justified to consider the specific problems and conditions of higher education in the Third World. The Third World comprises most of Asia, Africa, and Latin America, and contains the large majority of the world's population. There are, of course, major differences in terms of politics, economic conditions, and educational traditions and realities among Third World nations. Nevertheless there are sufficient common problems and issues that it is worth while to understand some of the specific generic problems of Third World higher education. The literature concerning these countries is much more limited than that for the industrialized countries, and many of the existing studies have been written by scholars from the industrialized nations. Thus, the available research and writing is of a somewhat special nature. Only materials which indicate some of the generic issues concerning Third World higher education are considered and there is no effort here to provide complete geographical coverage.

Third World universities face special problems and challenges. While it is difficult to generalize about many different nations, some common elements are evident. But even here national variations are common. For example, in general Third World universities are newer than those in industrialized nations and have weaker academic traditions, but the universities in Mexico, Peru, and Guatemala are older than any in North America. Many Third World universities come out of a colonial tradition and retain the mark of the colonial past. Yet nations like Japan, Thailand, China, and others were never formally colonized. Nevertheless, despite the variety of Third World reality and the possibility that some generalization will have only limited validity, it is useful to think broadly about the Third World:

*Universities do not, with a handful of exceptions, have indigenous roots. They are institutions imported, voluntarily or not, from the West and implanted in societies far different from those in which European universities developed.

*Third World universities, without exception, are based on Western models. Indigenous institutions, which existed in many parts of the Third World, have virtually disappeared. Even those Third World nations, such as China and Tanzania, which have sought to break with the political, economic and social patterns of the industrialized nations have maintained academic structures which are not very different from those in Europe or North America.

*Most knowledge is produced in the West and distributed through Western channels. Third World nations are basically consumers of knowledge, especially in the sciences and technology. The bulk of research funds are spent in the industrialized world, and the means of transmitting knowledge, such as journals and publishing houses, remain under the control of the industrialized nations. Third World nations lack control over knowledge, production and distribution.

*Western languages remain crucial throughout the world for higher education and research. Many Third World universities continue to use Western languages as the sole medium of instruction. Others have shifted in part to local languages, but even in such cases some textbooks and virtually all scientific monographs are available only in Western languages, and therefore the reliance on these languages continues to a considerable extent. There is no question that the continued use of Western languages has a key impact on many aspects of academic life.

*Third World universities are generally less autonomous than their counterparts in the West. Traditions of autonomy are weaker, the pressure to 'serve national needs' are much greater and the political involvement of institutions of higher learning often substantial. The establishment and financing of universities has been almost totally a government responsibility, and few means have been established to maintain some distance between government and university. All of these factors have tended to limit autonomy.

*Research is generally less important as part of the university environment than it is in many Western universities. Universities have been pressed to contribute directly to the process of development, to train large numbers of students, and to provide expert assistance to government and other agencies. In addition, research facilities are often limited, particularly in the sciences.

There is no question but that universities in the Third World are at a distinct disadvantage in comparison to their counterparts in the industrialized nations. In a world dominated by inequalities, they are weak and given the current trends of research expenditure and other factors are unlikely to attain equality in the near future. In a sense, Third World universities are dependent on institutions in the industrialized nations for scholarly advancement and are in general part of an international knowledge system which places them at a considerable disadvantage.[339] The major factor is basic inequality in the world of knowledge, but the situation is to some extent exacerbated by some foreign assistance policies of the industrialized nations which tend to maintain unequal relations and reinforce patterns of dependency.[340] The point here is that Third World universities exist in a world on inequalities and that their historical roots reinforce the pattern of dependency which still exists in many parts of the globe.[341]

For the most part, the history of universities in the Third World is a recent history. Only in a few Latin American nations are modern-style universities well over a century old.[342] In Africa, most universities are less than two decades old, and in Asia the situation varies from India, where universities date from 1857 and some colleges prior to that, to the Arab World, Iran, and many other parts of the continent where modern universities are less than fifty years old.[343] A number of writers have reflected on the historical traditions of Third World universities and the impact of these traditions on current conditions. Robert Koehl[344] has written on the history of Nigerian universities, as has A. B. Fafunwa.[345] Indian universities have received a good deal of historical attention, in part because India was among the first colonial nations to develop a sizeable educational system, and in part because the Indian example was very influential in other British colonial areas. Aparna Basu[346] has written of the link between educational policy and educational development under colonialism, while B. S. Goel[347] has discussed the changing organizational structure of higher education under colonialism. The question of adaptation of Western universities in the Third World has been considered by a number of writers. Audrey Richards[348] has written of the situation in Africa while J. Lockwood has discussed university 'transplantation', also in the African context.[349] Eugene Lubot has discussed the historical development of Chinese higher education and has stressed its relevance to recent history.[350] These analyses have concerned the development of higher education under colonialism for the most part. Thailand and Japan are nations which established educational patterns, largely of a Western type, free of colonial rule. The Thai case is discussed in David Wyatt's excellent book,[351] while Japan has received attention in Michio Nagai's volume.[352] These cases of 'independent' development are an interesting contrast to the more usual cases of colonial dominance. It is also interesting that in all cases there was necessarily a degree of interaction between the colonizer and the colonized in the nature of the institutions established and their function in the society.

A number of general studies of Third World higher education provide an overview of a system or institution in a country or region. These analyses are especially useful for gaining a broad perspective, which is necessary for more detailed study. Two recent books on African universities are especially useful in this regard. These volumes are by Pierre van den Berghe[353] and T. M. Yesufu.[354] Robert Arnove[355] has surveyed the literature on Latin American higher education and Darcy Riberio[356] has written cogently about the problems of higher education on the continent.

Asian countries have seen substantial analysis. India, especially, has been the subject of considerable research and writing. Robert Gaudino's[357] volume provides an overview of the Indian universities. S. R. Dongerkery,[358] an experienced Indian educator has also written a general volume on Indian universities. Amrik Singh and Philip G. Altbach's edited volume[359] provides detailed analyses of a number of key issues facing Indian higher education. P. G. Altbach has written a factual survey of the Indian scene and a case study of an Indian university.[360] Joseph DiBona has also written a useful case study.[361] *Minerva* has devoted considerable attention to Indian developments as well.[362]

Other Asian nations have also been considered in the literature, although there is no question but that India has been analyzed at greatest length.[363] China has received some attention in the literature. Theodore Chen has written a general book on educational policy in China which also considers higher education.[364] R. C. Hunt's recent article discusses Chinese higher education since the Cultural Revolution.[365] Joseph Fischer[366] and T. H. Silcock[367] have written books on the university in South-east Asia which provide overviews of the nations of the region although both volumes are now somewhat out of date. J. J. Waardenburg is the author of a two-volume study on higher education in the Arab countries, one of the very few studies of higher education in this important region.[368]

One of the most widely discussed questions concerning the Third World is that of development. We cannot deal here with the very complex and often controversial issues related to the definition of development and the various strategies to achieve it. The role of the university in contributing to the development or modernization process, however defined, has been an issue of great debate since World War II. For a time, it was widely thought that higher education unlocked the doors to modernization and much emphasis was given to building up universities in the Third World. More recently, there has been some criticism of the role of the universities in development, and funds have been shifted to other segments of the educational system or to other fields. Kenneth Thompson's[369] two-volume study considers some of the issues raised by the challenge of development, as does an important volume edited by F. C. Ward.[370] These two volumes directly contribute to the current debate on the role of universities in development and raise some questions about this role.

A number of studies have dealt with higher education and issues of economic growth, employment, and development in specific national contexts. The work of the International Institute for Educational Planning in Paris is concerned in part with questions of development, and the I.I.E.P. has taken a strong interest in Third World nations. Bikas Sanyal has authored three studies concerning higher education and employment issues in African nations.[371] These volumes indicate the problems of articulation between university policies and job markets in the Third World. A. Tapingkae of the Regional Institute for Higher Education and Development (R.I.H.E.D.) in Singapore, has edited a volume dealing with economic growth and higher education in South-east Asia.[372]

The R.I.H.E.D. in Singapore has taken an active interest in issues of development and higher education in its region—South-east Asia— and has sponsored a number of excellent publications. The massive report of the Education Commission of the Government of India, issued in 1966, deals in part with post-secondary education and is without question one of the largest studies of the role of education in general in development and modernization.[373] David Lim[374] has discussed the role of the university in development planning in Malaysia, and J. N. Kaul has written on India.[375] A fairly early study, sponsored by UNESCO and the International Association of Universities looks at problems of higher education and development in South-east Asia.[376] Immanuel Hsu has looked at higher education and industrialization in China, a topic related to questions of development and modernization.[377] Finally, F. X. Sutton[378] has looked at the situation in Africa and Darcy Riberio[379] has analyzed the role of the university in social development in Latin America.

The internal planning of universities in the Third World has also generated some analysis, and is a topic of considerable importance. Questions such as the appropriate level of financing for universities and the relation of university growth to employment requirements are very complicated. Further, in the Third World, there is a notable lack of adequate statistical data and few established procedures of resource allocation to assist in such matters. Many Third World nations are faced with a lack of resources, financial and otherwise, and find it difficult to allocate adequate resources to the many competing institutions and functions demanding them. Thus, the proper level of financing for higher education and a well-developed plan regulating the allocation for resources is quite important to assure efficient use of limited resources. It is fair to say that there is no widely accepted model for university development. The four-volume study edited by Victor Onushkin for the International Institute for Educational Planning has some relevance to the Third World, but no adequate 'model' exists.[380] Daniel Rogers has written a general discussion of university funding in the Third World, and agencies like the I.I.E.P. and UNESCO have been concerned with university planning.[381] Further, in many instances, politics, competing interest groups, and other factors get in the way of appropriate resource allocation, both in terms of government funding of universities and of internal decisions within academic institutions concerning funding.

The following references indicate some of the literature for the main geographical regions and certainly do not reflect the total amount of material. Two studies deal with the process of planning in Africa. John Hanson[382] has written a case study of the development of the University of Nigeria, while E. F. Godfrey[383] has written on the economics of an African university. An Indian study by J. L. Azad focuses on problems of financing and resource allocation in higher education.[384] Amnuay Tapingkae[385] has dealt with problems of university expansion in the South-east Asian context, and Richard G. King has discussed the growth of the provincial universities of Mexico.[386]

A topic of considerable interest is the relationship between politics and higher education in the Third World. As was indicated earlier, Third World universities are often politicized. They are at the center of intellectual and political thought in their countries because of the lack of other, competing, institutions. They are often located in the capital cities, and there is considerable movement of staff from the university to government ministries. The traditions of academic autonomy and of institutional neutrality are in some cases not well-developed and there is more pressure for institutions to become involved in external politics. Governments are in some cases willing to interfere with the functioning of universities in order to assure political stability.

The university and societal politics has been a frequent topic of analysis. Latin American universities have long been involved with national political affairs. Since the reforms of 1918 they have actively participated in political events. Students have been active, and staff members have also been politically involved. Jerry Haar[387] has written on Brazil, while John P. Harrison[388] and Margaret Goodman[389] have written in general about the role of the Latin American university in politics. It is clear that while the Latin American university at one time had considerable autonomy, authoritarian régimes in recent years have prevented this kind of political involvement, often by changing university laws or by applying repression to students or staff. Two African case studies are also worth mentioning. Davidson Nichol[390] has written in general on African universities and politics while A. A. Mazrui and Yash Tandon[391] have written on East Africa as a case study. Susanne and Lloyd Rudolph[392] have edited an outstanding volume on the Indian educational system, which includes several case studies of the role of politics in the internal affairs of educational institutions as well as on how governments relate to higher education in India. G. E. von Grunebaum has written on the political role of the university in Egypt.[393]

While this section has considered only a few topics concerning higher education in the Third World and a very small proportion of the relevant literature, it is clear that the subject is an important one and that a significant amount of material of high quality is available. As indicated, much of the literature is virtually unavailable to the scholar because it has been published in journals which have little circulation outside their own countries or even their university. Bibliographical tools and other reference aids concerning the Third World are, in general, quite poor. Thus, research on the Third World is more difficult than it is on the industrialized nations.

Higher Education Reform:
Key Issue for the Seventies

University reform is among the most controversial and important issues facing the academic community. Not only do differences exist among the various constituencies of the academic community concerning the desirability and nature of reform, but the formulation of workable reform plans has been a challenge of major proportions. Most countries have had to grapple with the issue of university reform, although relatively few have been able to implement successful reform plans.

The process of university reform—or planned change in education—faces quite specific problems and it is difficult to generalize about the process from one country or even one institution to another. Nevertheless, there seem to be some common elements which are evident, and it is the purpose of this section to note some of the common problems as well as to discuss some of the specific reform proposals which have been made in various nations. As noted earlier, it is probably impossible successfully to 'transfer' reforms from one country to another, but there is much that can be learned from the successes—and failures—in the field of university reform.[394]

Some historical eras have seen more academic change than others. One such period was the period of 'Germanization' in Europe and the United States during the late nineteenth and early twentieth centuries, when universities adopted the research function and took a greater interest in the affairs of society. Universities gradually became quite important for the technological progress of modern societies and became key training institutions for scientific élites as well as for the traditional upper classes. Academic institutions underwent major changes during this period, assuming new functions and reorganizing their patterns of governance. Professorial roles changed, and in most countries academic governance changed to adapt efficiently to the new research and advanced training functions of academic institutions. In some nations, new universities were established which provided new models. This occurred in the United States and Britain, although in the United States established universities also gradually changed.[395]

It is not surprising that the period of the 1960s proved to be a period of pressure for change in universities in many nations. In a previous

For notes see pp. 93–113.

section, the 'crisis of the university' was discussed in some detail. Many of the elements indicated in that discussion contributed to demands for change in higher education. Perhaps the key element was expansion of enrollments and functions, a process that began at different times in Europe, the United States and the Third World but which reached considerable proportions during the 1950s. Academic systems were simply unable to handle this expansion effectively. There were too many professors, too many students, too many new functions, and in a sense, too much money. Outdated administrative structures could not cope, and students recognized that the quality of their experience was suffering. Academics felt an anomie about their roles in the universities, and many resisted the new pressures. Most institutions simply tried to adjust to new circumstances by modest tinkering with existing structures, and this 'growth by accretion' worked for a while but the systems which evolved proved to be rather ineffective in dealing with crisis.

The 1960s were a period of rapid growth, of political crisis in a number of countries which involved elements of the university system, and of the beginnings of financial crisis for higher education. Without going into the details of the crisis—which varied in any case from country to country—one of the results was a demand that the universities change so as to deal with new circumstances more efficiently. The demands for change came from various sources; students expressed their discontent with universities through demonstrations and activism. In a few countries, they pressed for university reform, and in at least one—West Germany—students had a major input into the reform process.[396] A very powerful force for change in higher education was that of government authority. As expenditures for higher education increased and as the 'university crisis' spilled on to the front pages and resulted in serious institutional disruption and political unrest, governments sought to stimulate—or at times to force—reforms that would permit universities to function efficiently or at least to remove the immediate causes for unrest and disruption. Significantly, the faculty itself was seldom the source of pressure for change, and in fact the professoriate often opposed reforms that were proposed by others.

There are relatively few cross-cultural generalizations that can be made about the reform process in higher education, but the literature does yield a few common elements which can be at least tentatively discussed.

*Reforms usually have to be stimulated by major crises and be carried through by forces outside normal academic decision-making systems. This concept has been called the 'big bang' theory of university reform by Kitamura and Cummings who were writing specifically about Japan but whose idea seems to be applicable in other countries as well.[397]

*Students, despite their vocal activism on political matters and occasional inchoate discontent with universities, are seldom key factors in the reform process. They may, by their activism, stimulate reform efforts, but they seldom play a role in the process itself.

*Professors are in general opposed to reform efforts, particularly those that are perceived to weaken the prestige of the professoriate or to adversely affect working conditions. Further, the professors are often able to sabotage reforms that are legislated by refusing to fully implement them.

*Many of the reforms of the past decade have been aimed at democratizing higher education by increasing access to places in the university. Efforts have also been made to increase the efficiency of academic governance, although increasing participation does not usually lead to efficiency. Some efforts at making the universities more 'accountable' to students, government authorities, or the public, have also been undertaken.

*The traditional academic values of institutional autonomy, the authority of the senior academic staff, stress on high-level basic research, and on graduate education, have all been under attack and all have, in general, suffered to some extent where reforms have been instituted.

*Reforms have not been overwhelmingly successful in most countries. Implementation has been difficult and political reality has often forced compromise or has limited the effectiveness of the reforms.

*Reforms tend to be expensive, and their cost has on occasion prevented their implementation or circumscribed their scope.

There are, of course, many kinds of academic reforms. This discussion is generally focused on 'large' reforms in the structure of institutions, in broad participation issues, and the like. Many academic reforms are on a much smaller scale, such as the adoption of new curricular directions in limited areas of the university, or the amalgamation of small administrative units in a single university. Single institutions occasionally reorganize themselves effectively based on a local reform plan. These local or limited reforms have a better chance for success than large or system-wide efforts. Unfortunately, there is relatively little literature that considers the process of these micro-reforms. Three studies sponsored by the O.E.C.D. concerning Britain,[398] France,[399] and West Germany[400] do provide analytical attention on changes made at the level of individual institutions.

It is surprising that relatively few writers have written in defense of the traditional values of the university and in opposition to reform, since many scholars hold a traditional view of the university, and most reform proposals engender widespread criticism. Edward Shils[401] has been one of the most vocal critics of some of the basic thrusts of the reforms of the past decade. Robert Nisbet,[402] an American sociologist, has also written in opposition to much recent reform in his volume. Paul Seabury's edited volume also criticizes many of the reforms undertaken in Western Europe in the past decade, and defends the traditional European university.[403]

The general discussions of academic reform are, for the most part sympathetic to the need for change, although many are quite realistic about the difficulties involved with the implementation of reform. James Perkins' short essay on reform raises many of the key issues and is a useful introduction to the topic.[404] Perkins considers some of the structural and political factors involved. The O.E.C.D.[405] has presented a preliminary statement of issues involved with structural change in European universities and Jack Embling[406] has written a unique volume focusing on the usefulness of the United States Carnegie Commission's reform proposals for European higher education. Eric Bockstael and Otto Feinstein have examined university reform in Europe from the economist's viewpoint in a useful volume.[407] David Riesman has written two useful essays on the general problems of academic reform, focusing mainly on the United States and Britain.[408] Ladislav Cerych has written an excellent summary of European trends in university reform as of 1972.[409] His report presents specific information on developments in various Western European nations. These documents all provide useful overviews, focusing on both theoretical issues and on Europe, necessary to an understanding of some of the general currents in university reform. Noel Annan has written generally on some of the problems of university reform, using his British experience as a base of discussion.[410] Australian sociologist R. W. Connell has also written generally about some experiments in university reform focusing generally but using to some extent the Australian experience.[411] Most of the analyses cited above are a combination of reports from individual countries or regions and some general discussion based on these national experiences.

Several very useful publications deal in a very descriptive manner with some of the factors which have stimulated reform and with events in particular regions. Since these materials present data from a number of countries, they are particularly useful in providing an overview of experiences in different nations. Ladislav Cerych[412] has written on the impact of mass higher education on European higher education. Clearly, expansion of European universities from élite to mass systems have contributed to the pressure for academic reforms and institutional change. I. Hecquet[413] has dealt with some of the demographic changes in Europe which are influencing educational policy and change. The Council of Europe[414] has published a volume providing detailed reports of early reforms in France, the Netherlands, and Poland.[415]

Of a more theoretical nature, articles by Terry Clark[416] and Ralf

Dahrendorf[417] focus on political and sociological issues involved with the reform process. Erich Jantsch[418] has also written a theoretical paper on innovations in higher education, focusing on inter-disciplinary models. All these papers attempt to build models for university reform which are applicable in different national contexts. Although it is not clear whether these models are useful in planning actual reforms, they can stimulate general understanding of the reform process.

Governments and other official agencies have been among the key stimulators of university reform, often dragging reluctant faculties into academic change. And as Kitamura and Cummings[419] and others have pointed out, it often takes a major crisis to stimulate governmental action. There are many government reports which outline reform proposals which are quite important in understanding the nature and process of academic reform. The United States is somewhat unique in the sense that educational policy is officially a matter for the individual states and because the private sector in education is very powerful. Nevertheless, two recent documents reflect a kind of national policy direction on higher education change, since these reports came either from agencies of the federal government or from the Carnegie Council on Higher Education, a private but nationally-oriented body which made a range of recommendations for higher education during the early 1970s.[420] The Carnegie Commission's report, *Reform on Campus*,[421] had considerable impact not in terms of its own implementation but because it set the tone for discussions of change in higher education at other levels. A committee appointed by the U.S. Department of Health, Education and Welfare made a series of recommendations which have also been widely discussed in the United States.[422] Despite the lack of a formal national apparatus for policy implementation in education, there tends to be considerable informal coordination of educational policy in the United States.

Most other countries have a more centralized national means of policy formulation and implementation in education, and thus national directions concerning university reform constitute a key factor in university reform at any level of consideration. Japan, with a highly centralized educational apparatus, provides an excellent case study in national policy-making. Several official bodies have made reports on higher education reform in recent years, and there has been a general consensus in government circles on needed directions in the universities.[423] William Cummings has discussed the nature of the governmental reform process in Japan, pointing out that the conservative Liberal Democratic party, the dominant political force, has played the major role in shaping university reform.[424] It is also clear that there have been major difficulties in translating the plans of the central government to action at the level of the individual universities. Even the prestigious national universities, which receive virtually all of their funds from the central government, have not altered very much. In Japan, despite major academic crises brought on by student unrest in the 1960s and the power of the central government over educational affairs, the universities have in reality changed very little.

Sweden is in sharp contrast to Japan. Both countries are similar in that their educational systems are highly centralized, but Sweden was able, through major government initiative and pressure, to devise and implement a wide-ranging university reform plan. This plan, called the 'U-68 Reform', included the alteration of academic governance by substantially increasing participation of students and staff, decentralization of the existing universities, curricular change to reflect the employment market and needs of a technological society, and a great increase in government involvement in academic policy and administration.[425] The Swedish proposals were widely criticized in academic circles, and received considerable attention overseas. C. A. Anderson, Gunnar Bergendal and Torsten Husen have all criticized the proposals, largely attacking them for destroying academic autonomy and damaging high-level basic research in Sweden.[426] It is fair to say that most of the senior academics also opposed the reforms, and their opposition had some impact in modifying the reforms during the six-year implementation period. A highly centralized educational system, governmental authority with a strong commitment to implement its plans and the political power to do so, and the willingness of the academic community to follow constituted authority all contributed to the success of the Swedish reforms. The long-term effects of the reforms are still in question, as the full impact of the changes are only now being felt in Sweden. But the alterations in governance and curriculum are so substantial that some lasting change will result.

Chinese educational policy since 1947 shows the impact of a highly centralized decision-making apparatus. Educational decisions have been made in part because of political ideology and in part because of the perceived needs of the central government and the Communist Party. The Cultural Revolution of the 1960s, which had major effects on the educational system, was clearly the result of ideological currents in China at the time.[427] Marianne Bastid[428] has described the interplay between the economic realities and political ideology on educational policy, and Chun Wang[429] has discussed specific reforms in the universities in China. The Chinese experiences point to several realities in university reform. On the one hand, Chinese authorities attempted to use the universities for the achievement of other social changes—much as political authorities in the United States have tried to utilize higher education as a means of implementing policies of social equality for women and for racial minorities. Thus, reforms in the academic system were made which substantially disrupted the universities, changed the means of governance and altered the curriculum. Such large-scale reforms have been attempted several times during China's recent history, but after each experiment, the system returned to more 'traditional' practices. At present, it would seem that Chinese higher education is returning to a period of relative conservatism. The lesson, perhaps, is that even in a nation as centralized and ideologically committed as China university reform is a difficult process and that reforms often fail to achieve their intended results.[430]

Discussions of reform started in France during the 1950s, and there was general agreement that the major universities, particularly the University of Paris, were too large, geographically dispersed, and no longer effectively providing high-quality education to their students. A number of studies concerning pre-1968 reforms provide data on the nature of proposed changes at that time. Decentralization was demanded, increased participation proposed, and above all, an expansion of facilities—from libraries to dormitories—was suggested.[431] Authorities moved relatively slowly, however, in part because of opposition from within the universities and in part because of the large expenditures required. It was only after the 'events' of 1968 that the French government moved quickly to approve a massive reform plan and to implement it. Edgar Faure was perhaps the key architect of the French reform, and his volume on university reform reflected government policy at the time.[432] The 1968 reforms included breaking up the large universities into smaller units—this was particularly dramatic at Paris, where one university was transformed into fourteen separate institutions, each with a separate 'mission'. Participation was significantly expanded and students were for the first time included in academic decision-making. It is worth noting in this regard that the radical student organizations generally refused to participate in governance, feeling that the reforms were not meaningful. Efforts were made to diversify the curriculum, and to link academic subjects to the employment market. Attempts have been made to limit enrolments in some academic fields in order to link academic programs to available jobs and to prevent overcrowding in some fields. There has been considerable opposition to these efforts.

There seems to be little consensus concerning the success or failure of the French reforms. The highly centralized nature of the French academic system has not been broken despite giving increased participation to the new subject-oriented decision-making bodies at the local level. The government has not been fully successful in determining enrolment policy, and in many universities students have not been willing to participate in governance. The top level of the academic system, the *grandes écoles*, have been virtually unaffected by the reforms. A number of analyses have discussed the nature and scope, and have evaluated the results of the reforms of the past few years.[433] Even in a highly centralized system faced with considerable crisis, it has not been possible for the universities to fully implement reforms originated by the central government. Further, according to many observers, the reforms have generated significant 'unanticipated consequences' which have been unfavorably evaluated.

West Germany is the other major European nation that has embarked on major academic reforms in recent years. Like France, there was considerable discussion of possible reforms in higher education as early as the mid-1950s and much was written on academic change. The expansion of enrollments and the planned addition of new universities necessitated thinking about academic changes. Indeed, several 'new model' universities were established in the 1950s and it was hoped that these would provide impetus for change in existing institutions.[434] But as in France, the pace of change was slow. Several of the technical universities were upgraded to full university status, and a few new universities were established, but basically the traditional academic patterns—which were in fact little changed after the German defeat in World War II—remained dominant. If anything the German academic system is more difficult to change than the French, since education is a responsibility of the *länder* (states) and not of the federal government. Further, the traditional 'chair' system of investing considerable power in the full professors originated in Germany and was strongly entrenched there.

But the pressure of numbers, the pace of technological change and especially the major student unrest of the 1960s stimulated change and a number of the West German *länder* moved to design and implement reforms. One of the early reforms was the idea of the 'gesamthochschule' or unified university structure, bringing together the various elements of post-secondary education including teachers' colleges, technical universities and the like, in a given region, into one institution. Although a few efforts were made to implement this idea, it has not been widely accepted.[435] Because of the diverse control of German higher education, it is difficult to generalize about the nature of the 1960s, although there are some currents that seem to reflect national trends. It is in general the case that those *länder* controlled by the Social Democratic party have been more active in university reform than those under Christian Democratic control. The latter states have by and large kept to fairly traditional patterns of governance although they have expanded higher education. Thus, most of the general comments relate to the Social Democratic states.

As indicated, the basic impetus for reform has come from the state governments, which has been pressed to make changes by expansion and by student unrest. Expansion of participation in university governance has been a key element of the reforms in most states. The monopoly of the senior professors over internal governance has been destroyed. The concept of *drittelparität*, of equal participation by faculty, junior academic staff and students, has been instituted in a few institutions, although recent legal challenges have restored some power to the senior professors. The new university laws have stressed a democratization of governance. Ulrich Teichler[436] has written a general analysis of these new regulations and M. Krueger and B. Wallisch-Prinz[437] have written generally of reforming currents. Reforms have also stressed the curriculum. The concept of inter-disciplinarity has received considerable attention, and academic study has, in a few universities, been organized around working groups rather than in the traditional academic departments.[438]

These reforms have met with considerable opposition. The professors almost uniformly opposed changes, and in some cases resigned their positions rather than function in the 'democratized' universities.[439] The weight of established tradition also worked against meaningful reform, as G. Kloss has pointed out.[440]

German higher education has been substantially altered as a result of the turmoil and the reforms of the 1960s. The changes have, however, been uneven. Some states have been virtually unaffected except through the expansion of higher education. Others have made major changes. The University of Bremen, newly established in the late 1960s, was built on a new model and was expected to provide an example to other West German institutions.[441] The new university was organized around the principle of *drittelparität*, with students participating in virtually all decision-making functions. Inter-desciplinary work groups were also part of the university. A number of younger, radically inclined teachers and students were attracted to the university, which gave it a reputation for radicalism. While the Bremen model seems to have worked in the sense that the institution remains committed to its new structures, it has not been widely copied elsewhere.

The Free University in Berlin has also been substantially changed and has been the scene of considerable conflict between those who favor reform—notably students and junior staff—and the senior professors, many of whom have strongly opposed the reforms.[442] The long-term success or failure of the German reforms is unclear since the time has been short and there are many conflicting views concerning the recent changes.

The third major model for higher education reform in Europe is that of Britain. The British approach has been quite different from that on the continent. The British have expanded somewhat less rapidly than the continental university systems, and they have been committed to retaining relatively small institutions and instead expanding the total number of universities while also raising the status of some technical institutions to universities. The Robbins Committee issued its report in 1963, and this formed the basis for the expansion of the system in Britain.[443] Robbins recognized the need for expansion, but urged increasing the numbers of universities. This policy has been more expensive than expanding enrollments on existing campuses, but it has helped to preserve the ethos of the system more effectively than the European models. Further, the tradition of separation of higher education from direct government control permitted the British system to plan with more insulation from the immediate policy considerations of government agencies. The lack of a highly disruptive student movement during the 1960s also permitted a more orderly planning process. The recommendations in the Robbins report were for the most part implemented, although considerable discussion was stimulated. Richard Layard and his colleagues[444] wrote a volume dealing with the effects of the Robbins report on British education, and Charles Morris[445] discussed the nature and impact of the report in an article.

One of the major implications of the Robbins report, and a current which had been evident in Britain since the 1950s, was the establishment of new universities. David Daiches[446] edited a book on the conceptual framework for these new institutions, while Michael Beloff[447] was the author of a report on their development. The new Lancaster University has received analytical attention in an article by Harold Perkin,[448] who has also written a volume on several other new institutions.

One of the most highly publicized of the recent British reforms has been the Open University, an effort to provide quality higher education to 'non-traditional' students—individuals who are older, established in careers, or who somehow did not attend universities. The Open University's carefully planned but highly unusual organizational structure, the lack of a traditional campus, reliance on television and short-term seminars and on specially prepared books for instruction, have all attracted widespread attention. Educational planners in Japan, Iran, India, and other countries have studied the Open University and elements of its ideas are being incorporated in various parts of the world. Several American universities use O.U. books and occasionally filmed materials as well. Rodney Hartnett[449] has written of the application of the Open University in the United States, while Jeremy Tunstall[450] is the author of the widest-ranging early discussion of the institution itself. Naomi McIntosh and her colleagues[451] have discussed one of the most controversial points concerning the Open University— the nature of its student body and especially whether the university is serving a working-class clientele. This volume also considers the academic performance of O.U. students and other matters relevant for evaluating the institution's performance. John Ferguson[452] has written a volume on the Open University from the perspective of an individual involved with it from the beginning and S. B. Crooks[453] has provided a general discussion of the Open University. Finally, Jacques Fomerand[454] has analysed some of the political elements of the decisions involved in establishing the Open University.

Despite considerable expansion and the establishment of a significant number of new universities in the past two decades, the basic nature of British higher education has changed less than is the case in much of Europe. The curriculum remains virtually unaltered except at a few of the new universities, and the pinnacle of the system, Oxford and Cambridge, remain unchanged. Christopher Driver[455] has written broadly of the impact of the British reforms. The Open University does constitute a significant innovation, but it remains isolated and has not affected the mainstream. Recently, economic problems and a downturn in enrollments in some fields have led to further rethinking. For example, the James Report on teacher education has resulted in the closing of some institutions and in some changes in the general pattern of teacher education.[456] Initiative has been left to individual universities in the British scheme, instead of being legislated from a central Ministry of Education or planning body, as is common on the continent. Whether one model or another is more effective in producing lasting change in higher education remains to be seen.

Third World nations have engaged in major educational innovation in recent years, often attempting to develop new institutions where none previously existed. The progress of university reform in the Third World has varied. Virtually all reforms have emanated from governmental sources, often in the form of semi-official commissions appointed for the specific purpose of proposing reforms. India has been especially active during the last thirty years in preparing detailed reform plans but has not been very successful in actually controlling the expansion of its university system. P. G. Altbach[457] and Glynn Wood[458] have written about the reform process in Indian higher education, the first from the perspective of national policy and politics and the latter as a case study in a single state. Despite the existence of very thorough academic reform plans, such as the 1966 Education Commission's report, there has been only limited implementation of reform in India. Logistical, financial and political problems interfere, and the university system has remained virtually as it was in terms of its curriculum and orientation when the British left India in 1947.

Other Third World nations have been less hampered by the weight of tradition, but have faced serious problems for lack of trained personnel, an outdated curriculum, the use of foreign (European) languages in their universities, and similar difficulties in developing their universities. In many countries, the problem is not apparently one of reform, but rather of developing new institutions where only a few exist. But there are also problems of reform which are often unrecognized since the existing higher educational institutions are almost invariably colonial transplants which may not serve the needs of independent Third World nations. There is, as yet, only limited recognition of this situation.

Many Third World nations have been seriously engaged in the development and in some cases the reform of universities. T. M. Yesufu's[459] volume on African higher education presents a range of different experiences from Africa, and has the advantage of combining examples from Anglophone and Francophone Africa. Don Adams[460] has reported on Korea and L. S. Atanassian[461] on Iran, a nation which is rapidly expanding its universities, borrowing models from various parts of the world. Government reports from Zambia, Sri Lanka, and Nigeria provide an indication of the kind of literature available in these often quite useful documents.[462] Such government committees often include foreign experts, usually from the former colonizing power, and thus it is not very surprising that the recommendations that emerge are often not especially imaginative in terms of their adopting new academic models or sweeping innovations in curriculum or governance. It is fair to say that most of the reports have been fairly conservative in the kinds of proposals that have been presented. An Englishman involved in African higher education has written of the problems of establishing a new university in Africa.[463] The Latin American literature on higher education reform is substantial and quite valuable since the Latin American university system is old and it has engaged in thinking about reform and academic change since 1918. Gabriel del Mazo's classic study of Latin American reform focuses on the impact of the 1918 Argentine reforms throughout the continent.[464] An article in *Minerva* has brought the 1918 reforms up to the present time and Richard Pelczar has written about reform currents in Colombia.[465] C. O'Neil[466] and David Carneiro[467] have written about Brazil, Latin America's largest and one of its most important countries. It differs from the rest of the continent because of its Portuguese heritage and also because of its relatively late start with higher educational reforms.

While it is difficult to generalize about the direction of university reform and development in the Third World, much of it is clearly intended to provide more cost-efficient institutions in nations with a lack of adequate resources and a need to modernize quickly. Universities have been seen as a key to economic modernization, but recent criticism has questioned their effectiveness in actually solving problems. The colonial-based curriculum and administrative structure has also been the subject of considerable criticism as has the very high cost of academic institutions. Thus, in addition to the general problems facing universities in the industrialized world — student activism, account-ability, and the like — the Third World institutions have their own special problems. It is fair to say, however, that the solutions to these problems have not as yet been either very imaginative or notably successful.

It is possible to generalize about some of the major thrusts of academic reform efforts throughout the world. Clearly, not all of these efforts will be tried in every country, and some nations may be more thorough-going in their attempts than others, but this listing will provide an overview to the kinds of academic reforms being undertaken.

*Comprehensive universities. A number of European countries, most notably West Germany, have begun to restructure their post-secondary educational systems in order to give technological institutions, teacher-training colleges, and other schools university status, and to provide a range of different kinds of programs in university-level institutions.[468] Britain has also moved in this direction not only by 'upgrading' tech-nical institutes but by instituting the Council for National Academic Awards, which has power to grant degrees.[469]

*Open universities. This innovation, discussed earler, is indicative of trends in various countries to experiment with non-traditional forms of higher education. While the British Open University is probably the best researched and publicized effort, and has had widespread inter-national influence in its few years of existence, it is by no means the only such non-traditional experiment. Numerous efforts in the United States, such as Empire State College of the State University of New York, the University of Mid-America and others, have attempted to break with traditional academic patterns, in part to attract new stu-dents in an increasingly competitive market. An American govern-ment-sponsored agency, the Fund for the Improvement of Post-Second-ary Education, provides money to innovate academic programs, some of which are of a non-traditional nature. Other nations have also experimented with various kinds of non-traditional higher education programs, and this trend seems to be growing.

*Inter-disciplinarity. There has been considerable criticism of traditional academic disciplines as stumbling blocks to advancing knowledge in a period of rapid technological change. Criticism focuses on the organization of universities into traditional and often conserva-tive departments. Academic departments tend to inhibit change not only for organizational reasons but also because they reflect particular conceptions of knowledge.[470] In an effort to force changes in the tra-ditional disciplines and faculty organization, new inter-disciplinary structures have been created in West Germany[471] and France;[472]

Sweden and other Scandinavian countries have also become interested in this innovation as well.

*Accountability. Under the broad heading of accountability one can list a number of efforts to make education more related to public authorities in direct fiscal terms, and in terms of coordinating the university with national education policy. There is no question but that accountability is one of the most dramatic efforts of governments in the area of change in higher education. Part of the impetus is related to an increased concern with coordination and planning and the creation of more rational management techniques. Another motivation is relating academic programs more closely to employment conditions and the immediate market-demands of students. Accountability generally means more centralization of academic control, although this is not necessarily the case. Without question, accountability is in direct conflict with traditional ideas of academic autonomy.

*Administrative rationality. Related to the question of accountability in higher education has been a trend to streamline administrative structures to make them more 'efficient' and 'rational'. Modern management techniques have increasingly been incorporated into the universities to replace anarchic and often unwieldy administrative structures which have served universities for centuries. These reforms take many directions. Budgeting systems like P.P.B.S. are aimed at making units of the university account for the expenditure of funds and to develop a consciousness of the link between budgets and academic programs. Increased size and expense of universities have greatly stimulated the increased bureaucratization of academic institutions. Administrators have assumed increased power over the direction of universities in many countries, and the trend is very much in the direction of increased administrative control in order to assure a more 'rational' operation of what have become modern bureaucratic structures rather than communities of scholars.[473]

*The curriculum. Almost everywhere the traditional concept of the academic curriculum—and especially the liberal arts ideal—is being questioned or attacked. Demands to make the curriculum more 'relevant' mean different things in various countries, but relevance is a hallmark of the period. Radical students define relevance as knowledge which will help promote social change while government officials and manpower experts see relevance as training that will fit university graduates for jobs in a technological society. The faculty, which is the key element in defending the traditional curriculum, has not put up a spirited defense and in most countries there is a trend toward a more vocational curriculum. Many of the 'required' courses or subjects were dropped from the curriculum during the 1960s under student pressure. In the 1970s, difficulties in providing employment for university graduates in many countries resulted in emphasis on vocational aspects of the curriculum. At present, in many nations, there is considerable confusion concerning the nature and direction of the curriculum.

*Democratization and participation. The 1960s brought a world-wide protest against the academic aristocracy—the 'academic mandarins'—who have traditionally controlled the internal workings of the universities. Student protest movements argued that universities should be democratized and that students should have a key role in the governance process. These protests by students and some younger staff often linked with the plans of government authorities to mould higher education to the demands of technological societies since in many cases wider participation has the result of breaking down the traditional oligarchy of the university. The long-term impact of reforms in governance did not necessarily conform to the desires of radical students. Regardless of the differing motivations, substantial changes did occur in many countries which expanded participation in university affairs. This trend has gone furthest in northern Europe, where students have been included as substantial participants—in some cases achieving one-third of the votes on key university bodies. The concept of *drittelparität,* developed in West Germany, has typified this expansion of participation.[474] Students now play roles in academic decision-making in some Scandinavian nations, in Holland, and in France. Britain, the United States and Canada have not reformed their universities in this direction, although students have a greater indirect voice in that faculty and administrators seem to listen more closely to student demands. It should be added that the idea of participation may well be in conflict with the stress on efficiency in higher education. Democracy in governance inevitably means time-consuming committees and decisions made as the result of a political process rather than on purely academic or administrative grounds. In East Germany, participation in university governance and planning has been extended to community representatives in an effort to make universities 'relevant' to local needs.[475] Few systems have as yet reconciled the possible conflicts that may emerge in this area.

*The professoriate. Without question, the professoriate has been under attack in many nations. Trends toward democratization have weakened the traditional power of the faculty and accountability has eroded its autonomy. Rapid expansion increased the size of the faculty and at the same time has diminished its sense of cohesion and community. The faculty has lost some of its power over institutional governance. In few countries, however, has the status, working conditions or orientation of the faculty changed drastically. There have been some improvements of salary and status for the junior staff and a corresponding decline in the power of the senior professors.

*Miscellaneous innovations. A large number of unclassifiable reforms have occurred in universities in various countries. Such reforms have to some extent altered the nature of the academic enterprise. Rearranging the lock-step of academic degree programs has been attempted in many nations. 'Sandwich' courses which alternate academic work with on-the-job experience in Britain have proved successful. The Chinese practice of combining academic work with practical training is another trend in this direction.[476] In the United States, the Carnegie Commission has recommended that degree programs be shortened and that students be permitted to 'stop out' for varying periods of time.[477] New two-year degree programs in community colleges in the United States and short-cycle higher education in various European countries is another effort to provide post-secondary alternatives to traditional universities.[478]

These are some of the major trends in reform around the world. While this is by no means a complete listing of the reforms nor a full discussion of the motivating forces and means of implementation, it is possible to see that many of these innovations are the result of the pressures on higher education that have been discussed earlier in this essay. Some of these reforms have been more successful than others and some are still too recent to fully evaluate. Some nations have been virtually unaffected by academic change, while others have dramatically transformed their universities. The international trend, however, seems to be in the direction of at least some organizational and curricular change in higher education, although the pressure to change of the 1960s has abated in most countries.

Directions for Future Research

The national literatures on higher education, especially in the large industrialized nations, are by now quite substantial. International agencies such as UNESCO, O.E.C.D., the Organization of American States and others have sponsored cross-national studies and have collected valuable statistical information. A few scholars have engaged in comparative study, but the amount of effective comparative analysis is in general quite limited in quantity. The following listing of topics requiring further research and analysis is intended to provide broad guidelines for research priorities and to indicate key areas where further analysis, both on a national basis and in a comparative framework, may be useful.

*Additional statistical data. For many countries, accurate and up to date statistical information concerning higher education is unavailable or incomplete. This is particularly true for Third World nations. Accurate information concerning enrolments, numbers of institutions, the academic profession, financial affairs, and other elements of the operation of universities is needed. Additional data on drop-out rates, social mobility among students, the social class of the faculty, and other information would make the planning process easier and would permit more complete knowledge about the nature of the universities. To have such data available along common lines would be particularly valuable as comparative analysis would then be possible. At present, even where statistics are available, the kinds of questions asked are often sufficiently different as to make comparison difficult. And statistical data is often not generally available to researchers. Common statistical indices, functional data banks, and other means of retrieval would greatly assist the comparative use of statistical measures in research and analysis of higher education.

*University governance. In recent years, organizational theory has been applied to higher education so that there is now a basis for examining the nature of university governance in detail. The roles of administrative officers, faculty, and other segments of the academic community are quite important in understanding how the institution as a whole functions. The applications of the methodologies of organizational theory, political science and to some extent management studies to higher education have only recently begun. Studies of governance in individual nations are quite limited and they are glaringly absent in a comparative context.

*University management. Studies of efficient and effective means of administering institutions of higher education are needed. With increased demands for financial accountability, fiscal responsibility, and administrative efficiency, it is urgent that the most effective means of managing universites be found. The Program on Institutional Management in Higher Education of the O.E.C.D. has recently been established and reflects the growing concern in this field. The use of P.P.B.S. and other budgeting and administrative systems places a great premium of conducting relevant research in this area. The financial aspects of university management are also crucial. Such research should, of course, take into account the unique facets of the university as an institution, perhaps particularly the fact that productivity is often difficult to measure with regard to education at any level. There has been a tendency to simply equate universities with government bureaucracies or occasionally with business enterprises, with the result that the special characteristics of institutions of higher education are not considered and neither efficient management nor productive academic work is assisted. It is also true that few academic administrators have been trained in management, and the nature of this group needs to be considered in any research on the management of higher education.

*The university and society. The roles of government, politicians, and interest groups in the affairs of universities are crucial, especially in the current period. The impact of the university community and of intellectuals in general on society is also important. The politics of higher education and the ways in which universities and public policy interact should also receive additional analytic attention. Such research has direct implications for individual nations and would also be valuable in understanding in a comparative context how universities function in different societal settings.

*The academic profession. Few studies of the professoriate have been undertaken. Questions of social recruitment of academics, their status, problems and aspirations are all crucial to understanding the academic profession and the institutions in which they work. The opinions of faculty members on politics, university issues and other matters are also quite important. Since academic staff are the backbone of decision-making, of teaching, and in fact of the ethos of most universities, such studies are particularly important.

*University reform. There is still a need for studies of the process of change in higher education. Studies of the process of reform and of the factors that promote and inhibit it would be very useful. Research on reform may help in the planning of academic change, and it can also provide an increased understanding of the general issues related to university governance and politics. Comparative studies of academic reform would be particularly useful.

*Student problems and activism. Of all the areas related to comparative higher education, this one has probably received the most attention from researchers, particularly in those industrialized nations greatly affected by student activism. Further research, however, is needed and more comparative cross-cultural studies are particularly important. Attitude surveys, studies of the conditions of activism, and of the demands and concerns of student movements are needed. In addition, there is relatively little research available concerning the physical, psychological and academic problems of students, and such data would be useful not only in understanding the general conditions of students but in helping to find solutions to problems that exist.

*The university and the educational system. The inter-relationship between the university and other segments of the educational system is in need of systematic study. On the broadest scale, the articulation between higher education and secondary education is critically important and has not received much attention from researchers. The implications of policies such as the expansion of secondary education, changing examination policies, curriculum innovations or other alterations in policy can directly affect the universities. The incorporation of technological education into the universities and the raising of technical institutions to university status is an important international development and has had an impact on the traditional universities. The general impact of the university on primary and secondary education and vice versa is also important. Both national studies and comparative analysis are needed in these areas.

These are some of the important questions which require further attention from researchers. No doubt, there are many additional issues worthy of attention as well. One of the key needs is for more adequate means of obtaining data about these and other issues of concern. As indicated, this essay, and the bibliography reflect only a small proportion of the literature. Much material is very difficult to locate and even more difficult to obtain. There is a need for one or more data libraries which will make materials available to concerned professional audiences. There is a need for good bibliographical resources which will lead researchers and policy-makers to relevant materials. At present, despite the valuable work of the International Institute for Educational Planning and the recently terminated efforts of the International Council for Educational Development, there is virtually no agency which provides these services to an international community. Even the excellent E.R.I.C. (Educational Resources Information Center) data system in the United States has very little information in its large collections concerning other countries or in languages other than in English. Thus, not only additional research is needed but also the means of using the data and analysis which is generated.

Conclusion

This essay has illustrated some key areas of comparative higher education research and analysis. It has also indicated how some of this research can be relevant to thinking about national educational questions and seeking answers to complex policy questions. No nation has all the answers to the perplexing questions facing post-secondary education and consideration of the experience of other countries may illuminate national problems. It is hoped that this consideration will stimulate an international consciousness among educators and planners and that it will also indicate some of the avenues for future research. This essay has by no means considered all of the relevant issues or topics. The selection was made on the basis of what seemed to be important topics for current debate on higher education. In addition, the stress has been on reporting the English-language literature and on materials that will be available in a good research library. Thus, a large body of literature in other languages as well as a very substantial corpus of material issued by government ministries and other official or semi-official bodies has been excluded as this literature is not readily available. Much important research has been conducted in the form of doctoral dissertations. Theses and dissertations are also omitted from this essay and from the bibliography that follows because of the difficulty of gaining access to this material.[479]

This essay has also tried to help provide parameters for an emerging field of study. Because the field is in an early period of development and is also growing very rapidly, it is particularly difficult to define it adequately. Further, because comparative higher education is by its nature an interdisciplinary field, its practitioners come from a variety of disciplines, in many cases having little commitment to a long-term study of higher education. In addition, comparative higher education uses a range of methodologies and has not developed its own widely accepted methodology. Because the field has the world as its purview, it is divided by geographical distance, language differences, political and academic orientations, and other barriers. And because comparative study is by its nature fairly expensive, the field must depend on outside funding for its progress.

Despite these difficulties, the field of comparative higher education has grown in recent years. The establishment of journals like *Higher Education*, which has a clear international orientation, and the work of agencies like the O.E.C.D., UNESCO and the I.C.E.D. all indicate the emergence of a field of study and of academic concern. Clearly, the field is in its infancy, but the interest of the past decade indicates the emergence of an active and healthy field of inquiry. Models of higher education provided from abroad are not going to solve specific national problems in most cases. National circumstances—in terms of specific economic, sociological, political and educational realities—are just too great to permit simple transfer of institutions or even ideas. Yet, perspectives from other countries can at least suggest ways of approaching problems that might lead to solutions. For example, a careful study of Britain's Open University can have implications for adult and continuing education. The ways in which Japan or Britain dealt with student activism might be suggestive to other nations. The Indian examination system might well be seen as a practice to avoid. The ways in which Latin America, West Germany or France have involved students in academic governance may illustrate policies to consider—or to avoid. Comparative higher education can illuminate, can pose alternatives. This in itself is reason enough to give it serious attention.

Notes

1. Philip G. Altbach, *Comparative higher education*, (Washington, D.C.: American Association for Higher Education, 1973).

2. P. G. Altbach and David H. Kelly, *Higher education in developing nations: a select bibliography*, (New York: Praeger, 1975) and P. G. Altbach, ed., *Comparative higher education abroad: bibliography and analysis*, (New York: Praeger, 1976).

3. An example of a relatively successful and quite elaborate and expensive comparative empirical research project is the international study of educational achievement. See A. Harry Passow, Harold Noah, Max Eckstein and John Mallea, *The national case study: an empirical comparative study of twenty-one educational systems*, (New York: Wiley, 1976).

4. A listing of some of the journals devoted mainly to higher education with at least a partial emphasis on comparative analysis appears on pages 119 and 120.

5. Among the most prominent publishers of materials on comparative higher education are Elsevier (Netherlands), Jossey-Bass (United States), Praeger (United States), Luchterhand (West Germany) and others.

6. Barbara B. Burn, Philip G. Altbach, Clark Kerr and James Perkins, *Higher education in nine countries*, (New York: McGraw-Hill, 1971) and Joseph Ben-David, *Centers of learning: Britain, France, Germany, United States*, (New York: McGraw-Hill, 1977).

7. J. Ben-David, *American higher education*, (New York: McGraw-Hill, 1972); Michio Nagai, *An owl before dusk*, (New York: McGraw-Hill, 1975); Alain Touraine, *The academic system in American society*, (New York: McGraw-Hill, 1974); and Eric Ashby, *Any person, any study*, (New York: McGraw-Hill, 1971).

8. Committee on Higher Education, *Higher education: report of the Committee. Appendix 5: higher education in other countries*, (London: H.M.S.O., 1963).

9. The University of Tokyo Press has been most active in publishing materials on higher education in other countries.

10. One of the most extensive commission reports was made in India. See Ministry of Education, *Report of the Education Commission, 1964-66: education and national development*, (New Delhi: Ministry of Education, 1966).

11. The classic work concerning the transfer of academic models is E. Ashby, *Universities: British, Indian, African*, (Cambridge, Mass.: Harvard University Press, 1966).

12. See Paul Dressel and Lewis Mayhew, *Higher education as a field of study*, (San Francisco: Jossey-Bass, 1974) for survey of the growth of the field in the United States. The publications of the Association for the Study of Higher Education are also quite useful.

13. In the past decade, journals such as *Research in Higher Education, Change,* and the *Chronicle of Higher Education* have been established, and Jossey-Bass Publishers has started a quarterly 'sourcebook' series in three fields of higher education (institutional research, higher education, and community colleges).

14. India now has three journals focusing on higher education; the *Journal of Higher Education, New Frontiers in Education* and *University Administration*.

15. C. F. Thwing, *Universities of the World*, (London: Macmillan, 1911). See also C. F. Thwing, *The American and the German university*, (New York: Macmillan, 1928).

16. V. A. Huber, *The English universities*, 2 vols. (London: W. Pickering, 1843).

17. Contemporary accounts of the development of the American university in the nineteenth century include James C. Stone and Donald DeNevi, eds., *Portraits of the American university*, (San Francisco: Jossey-Bass, 1971) and Daniel Coit Gilman, *University problems in the United States*, (New York: Century, 1898).

18. Hastings Rashdall, *The universities of Europe in the Middle Ages*, (Oxford: Clarendon Press, 1936).

19. Robert S. Rait, *Life in the medieval university*, (Cambridge: Cambridge University Press, 1912).

20. John Tate Lanning, *Academic culture in the Spanish colonies*, (New York: Oxford University Press, 1940).

21. Abraham Flexner, *Universities: American, English, German*, (New York: Oxford University Press, 1930).

22. Edward Shils, *Max Weber on universities*, (Chicago: University of Chicago Press, 1973).

23. Walter Kotschnig, *Unemployment in the learned professions: an international study of occupational and educational planning*, (London: Oxford University Press, 1937) and W. Kotschnig, ed., *The university in a changing world*, (London: Oxford University Press, 1932).

24. Frederick Lilge, *The abuse of learning: the failure of the German university*, (New York: Macmillan, 1948). Other volumes also dealt with the Nazi period. See, for example, Helmut Kuhn, *et al.*, *Die deutsche Universität im Dritten Reich*, (Munich: Piper, 1966).

25. Bruce L. R. Smith and Joseph Karlesky, *The state of American science*, (New York: Change Magazine Press, 1977).

26. One of the best analyses of student activism in the United States, for example, is the result of a governmental inquiry. See *Report of the President's Commission on campus unrest*, (New York: Arno Press, 1970).

27. For a summary of the Carnegie Commission's work, see Lewis B. Mayhew, *The Carnegie Commission on Higher Education*, (San Francisco: Jossey-Bass, 1973). See also Carnegie Commission on Higher Education, *A digest of reports of the Carnegie Commission on Higher Education*, (New York: McGraw-Hill, 1974); Carnegie Commission on Higher Education, *Priorities for action: final report*, (New York: McGraw-Hill, 1973).

28. For example, such criticisms were raised concerning the work of the Carnegie Commission and its successor group, the Carnegie Council on Policy Studies in Higher Education in the United States. See Donald McDonald, 'A six million dollar misunderstanding', *Center Magazine*, 6 (September-October, 1973), 32-50. See also Frank Darknell, 'The Carnegie Council for Policy Studies in Higher Education: a new policy group for the ruling class', *Insurgent Sociologist*, 5 (Spring 1975), 106-14.

29. The International Council for Educational Development (I.C.E.D.) issued a number of Occasional Papers dealing with many aspects of comparative higher education. These papers are valuable resources, although a number of them are out of print. The Council also published other books and reports. For a listing of I.C.E.D. publications, write to the Council at 680 Fifth Avenue, New York, NY 10019.

30. Kenneth Thompson and Barbara Fogel, *Higher education and social change*, (New York: Praeger, 1976).

31. See, for example, F. C. Ward, ed., *Education and development reconsidered*. (New York: Praeger, 1974). This volume resulted from a Ford-Rockefeller-sponsored conference.

32. The International Association of Universities (I.A.U.), for example, has published a series of Occasional Papers on such issues as university administration, the social responsibilities of universities, and related questions. See *The social responsibility of universities in Asian Countries*, (Paris: I.A.U., 1973); *The administration of universities*, (Paris: I.A.U., 1967); and *University autonomy: its meaning today*, (Paris: I.A.U., 1965).

33. Among the nations covered in O.E.C.D. educational surveys are Austria, the Netherlands, the United States, France, Japan, West Germany, Canada and others.

34. Among O.E.C.D.'s publications which have a comparative dimension are the following: *Economic aspects of higher education*, (Paris: O.E.C.D., 1964); *The development of higher education, 1950-67: quantitative trends*, (Paris: O.E.C.D., 1969); *Development of higher education, 1950-67: analytical report*, (Paris: O.E.C.D., 1971; *Policies for higher education (general report)*, (Paris: O.E.C.D., 1974).

35. The International Institute for Educational Planning has a major publishing program. Among its recent publications is a four-volume study, Victor Onushkin, ed., *Planning the development of universities*, (Paris: Unesco Press, 1971-5).

36. The Council of Europe's Committee for Higher Education and Research regularly issues mimeographed reports on aspects of higher education in its member countries. These reports range from synopses of discussions to statistical surveys.

37. E. Shils, 'The academic ethos under strain,' *Minerva* 13 (Spring 1975), 1-37.

38. E. Shils, 'Sources of change in the character and functions of universities,' *Universities Quarterly* 28 (Summer 1974), 310-17; and A. H. Halsey, 'The changing functions of universities in advanced industrial societies,' *Harvard Educational Review* 30 (Spring 1960), 118-27.

39. See Joseph Schwab, *College curriculum and student protest*, (Chicago: University of Chicago Press, 1969).

40. Many conservative critics have argued that politicization of the academy has been due to the dramatic radicalism of the 1960s. See, for example, Paul Seabury, ed., *Universities in the western world*, (New York: Free Press, 1975). See also Alan Montefiore, ed., *Neutrality and impartiality: the university and political commitment*, (Cambridge: Cambridge University Press, 1975).

41. Immanuel Wallerstein and Paul Starr, eds., *The university crisis reader*, 2 vols. (New York: Random House, 1971). See also Ronnie Dugger, *Our invaded universities*, (New York: Norton, 1974).

42. David Martin, ed., *Anarchy and culture: the problem of the contemporary university*, (London: Routledge & Kegan Paul, 1969).

43. Amrik Singh and P. G. Altbach, eds., *The higher learning in India*, (New Delhi: Vikas, 1974) and J. Kaul, *Higher education in India: two decades of planned drift*, (Simla: Indian Institute of Advanced Study, 1974).

44. T. M. Yesufu, ed., *Creating the African university: emerging issues of the 1970s*, (Ibadan, Nigeria: Oxford University Press, 1973).

45. B. B. Burn *et al.*, *op. cit.*

46. Christopher Driver, *The exploding university*, (Indianapolis, Indiana: Bobbs-Merrill, 1972).

47. P. Seabury, ed., *op. cit.*

48. W. R. Niblett and R. F. Butts, eds., *Universities facing the future*, (San Francisco: Jossey-Bass, 1972) and W. R. Niblett, ed., *Higher education: demand and response*, (San Francisco: Jossey-Bass, 1970). See also W. R. Niblett, *Universities between two worlds*, (New York: Wiley, 1974).

49. Brian Holmes and David Scanlon, eds., *Higher education in a changing world*, (New York: Harcourt Brace Jovanovich, 1971).

50. Michael Stephens and Gordon Roderick, eds., *Universities for a changing world*, (New York: Wiley, 1975).

51. Margaret S. Archer, ed., *Students, university and society,* (London: Heinemann Educational, 1972).

52. E. Ashby, *Adapting universities to a technological society,* (San Francisco: Jossy-Bass, 1974).

53. Ladislav Cerych, *A global approach to higher education,* (New York: I.C.E.D., 1971).

54. Organization for Economic Cooperation and Development, *Development of higher education, 1950-67: statistical survey,* (Paris: O.E.C.D., 1970) and *Towards Mass higher education: trends issues and dilemmas,* (Paris: O.E.C.D., 1974).

55. George Z. F. Bereday, *Universities for all,* (San Francisco: Jossey-Bass, 1973).

56. Council for Cultural Cooperation, Council of Europe, *Reform and expansion of higher education in Europe: national reports,* (Strasbourg: Council of Europe, 1967).

57. M. J. Bowman and C. A. Anderson, *Mass higher education: some perspectives from experience in the United States,* (Paris: O.E.C.D., 1974).

58. Committee on Higher Education, *op. cit.*

59. For a useful historical discussion of the American situation, see David D. Henry, *Challenges past, challenges present,* (San Francisco: Jossey-Bass, 1975).

60. Carol Herrnstadt Shulman, *Enrollment trends in higher education,* (Washington, D.C.: American Association for Higher Education, 1976) and I. Hecquet *et al., Recent student flows in higher education,* (New York: I.C.E.D., 1976).

61. Carnegie Foundation for the Advancement of Teaching, *More than survival: prospects for higher education in a period of uncertainty,* (San Francisco: Jossey-Bass, 1975).

62. I. Hecquet *et al., op. cit.*

63. Jacques Waardenberg, *Les universités dans le monde arabe actuel,* 2 vols. (Paris: Mouton, 1966).

64. D. Crecelius, 'Al-Azhar in the revolution,' *Middle East Journal* 20 (Winter 1966), 31-49.

65. E. Ashby, *Universities: British, Indian, African.* See also E. Ashby, *African Universities and the western tradition,* (Cambridge, Mass.: Harvard University Press, 1964).

66. E. Shils, 'Change and reform' in P. G. Altbach, ed., *University reform,* (Cambridge, Mass.: Schenkman, 1974), pp. 15-27.

67. John Henry Newman, *The idea of a university,* (New York: Holt Rinehart & Winston, 1964), originally published in 1852.

68. José Ortega y Gasset, *The mission of the university,* (New York: Norton, 1944).

69. Karl Jaspers, *The idea of the university,* (Boston: Beacon, 1969).

70. Robert Hutchins, *The higher learning in America,* (New Haven: Yale University Press, 1936).

71. Robert Paul Wolff, *The ideal of the university,* (Boston: Beacon, 1969).

72. Sidney Hook, *Academic freedom and academic anarchy,* (New York: Cowles, 1969).

73. Clark Kerr, *The uses of the university,* (New York: Harper Torchbooks, 1966).

74. Robert Nisbet, *The degradation of the academic dogma,* (New York: Basic Books, 1971).

75. The classic study of the medieval university is H. Rashdall, *op. cit.* See also Charles H. Haskins, *The rise of universities,* (Ithaca, New York: Cornell University Press, 1965); Helene Wieruszowski, *The medieval university,* (Princeton, New Jersey: Van Nostrand, 1966); A. B. Cobban, *The medieval universities: their development and organization,* (London: Methuen, 1975); and Marjorie Reeves, 'The European university from medieval times' in W. R. Niblett, ed., *Higher education: demand and response,* pp. 61-84.

76. Nathan Schachner, *The medieval universities,* (New York: Barnes, 1962), pp. 147-85.

77. C. H. Haskins, *op. cit.*

78. J. K. Hyde, 'Commune, university and society in early medieval Bologna' in J. Baldwin and R. Goldthwaite, eds., *Universities in politics,* Baltimore: Johns Hopkins

University Press, 1972), pp. 17-46.

79. The history of British higher education has been well covered, For example, see Hugh Kearney, *Scholars and gentlemen: universities and society in pre-industrial Britain, 1500-1700,* (Ithaca, N.Y.: Cornell University Press, 1970); Lawrence Stone, ed., *The university in society, Vol. 1: Oxford and Cambridge from the 14th to the early 19th century,* (Princeton: Princeton University Press, 1974); and V. H. H. Green, *The universities* (Harmondworth: Penguin, 1969), pp. 13-74.

80. V. H. H. Green, *op. cit.,* pp. 75-97. See also Nicholas Philipson, 'Culture and society in the eighteenth century province: the case of Edinburgh and the Scottish Enlightenment' in L. Stone, ed., *The university in society, vol. 2,* pp. 407-48.

81. Howard Kaminsky, 'The University of Prague in the Hussite Revolution: the role of the masters' in J. Baldwin and R. Goldthwaite, eds., *op. cit.,* pp. 79-106.

82. Richard L. Kagan, *Students and society in early modern Spain,* (Baltimore: Johns Hopkins University Press, 1974).

83. John T. Lanning, *The eighteenth-century enlightenment in the University of San Carlos de Guatemala,* (Ithaca, N. Y.: Cornell University Press, 1956) and J. T. Lanning, *Academic culture in the Spanish colonies,* (New York: Oxford University Press, 1940).

84. J. Ben-David and A. Zloczower, 'Universities and academic systems in modern societies,' *European Journal of Sociology* 3 (1962), 45-84.

85. *Ibid.*

86. The classic study of university reform in Latin America is G. del Mazo, *La reforma universitaria* (Buenos Aires: C.M.S., 1927). See also Richard Walter, *Student politics in Argentina: the university reform and its effects, 1918-1964,* (New York: Basic Books, 1968).

87. The historical development of German higher education in the nineteenth century has been extensively analyzed. See Fritz Ringer, *The decline of the German mandarins: the German academic community, 1890-1933,* (Cambridge, Mass.: Harvard University Press, 1969); R. S. Turner, 'University reformers and professorial scholarship in Germany, 1760-1806' in L. Stone, ed., *op. cit.,* vol. 2, pp. 495-532; Charles E. McClelland, 'The aristocracy and university reform in eighteenth-century Germany' in L. Stone, ed., *Schooling and society,* (Baltimore: Johns Hopkins University Press, 1976), pp. 146-76; and Abraham Flexner, *op. cit.*

88. J. Ben-David, 'The universities and the growth of science in Germany and the United States,' *Minerva* 7 (Autumn-Winter 1968-9), 1-35. See also Frank Pfetsch, 'Scientific organization and science policy in Imperial Germany, 1871-1914: The foundation of the Imperial Institute of Physics and Technology,' *Minerva* 8 (October 1970), 557-80.

89. Fritz Ringer, *op. cit.*

90. See E. Shils, *Max Weber on universities.*

91. For a discussion of the conservative tendencies of the German universities during the Weimar Republic, see Walter Laqueur, *Weimar: a cultural history,* (New York: Putnam, 1974), pp. 183-233.

92. It has been said the last 'pure' Germanic universities exist at present in the socialist countries of Eastern Europe. The Germans themselves have broken with the old patterns.

93. Merle Curti and Vernon Carstenson, *The University of Winconsin: a history* (Madison: University of Winconsin Press, 1949).

94. Laurence Veysey, *The emergence of the American university,* (Chicago: University of Chicago Press, 1965). See also Richard J. Storr, *The beginning of the future: a historical approach to graduate education,* (New York: McGraw-Hill, 1973).

95. For a critique of American 'deviationism', see Abraham Flexner, *op. cit.*

96. See E. Ashby, *Universities: British, Indian, African.*

97. Aparna Basu, *The growth of education and political development in India, 1898-1920*, (Delhi: Oxford University Press, 1974).

98. B. S. Goel, 'Changing functional character and organization of the Indian university, 1905-1929', *Paedagogica Historica* 14 (No. 1, 1974), 34-63.

99. N. Okafor, *The development of universities in Nigeria*, (London: Longman, 1971).

100. Michio Nagai, *Higher education in Japan: its take-off and crash*, (Tokyo: University of Tokyo Press, 1971). See also Shigeru Nakayama, 'The role played by universities in scientific and technological development in Japan,' *Journal of World History* 9 (No. 2, 1965), 340-62.

101. Martin Trow, 'Problems in the transition from élite to mass higher education', (paper prepared for a conference on mass higher education held by the O.E.C.D., 1973) and M. Trow, 'The expansion and transformation of higher education', *International Review of Education* 18 (No. 1, 1972), 61-84. See also T. R. McConnell *et al., From élite to mass to universal higher education*, (Berkeley, Calif.: Center for Research and Development in Higher Education, 1973).

102. L. Cerych, *op. cit.*

103. For a perspective on foreign aid and education, see P. G. Altbach, 'Education and neocolonialism,' *Teachers College Record* 72 (May 1971), 543-58, Ali Mazrui, 'The African university as a multinational corporation,' *Harvard Educational Review* 45 (May 1975), 191-210. See also K. Thompson and B. Fogel, *op. cit.*

104. For a general discussion of the current status of the academic department in the United States, see Dean E. McHenry *et al., Academic departments*, (San Francisco: Jossey-Bass, 1977).

105. John W. Hanson, *Education, Nsukka* (East Lansing: Michigan State University, 1968). See also Harry Case and Robert Bunnell, *The University of the Philippines; external assistance and development*, (East Lansing: Michigan State University, 1970).

106. M. J. Bowman and C. A. Anderson, *op. cit.*

107. Seth Spaulding and Michael J. Flack, *The world's students in the United States* (New York: Praeger, 1976).

108. The American community college model has had less impact overseas, although it has been widely used in Japan. The 'land grant' research-oriented university has been the main American export model.

109. For perspectives on planning in American higher education, see the Jossey-Bass quarterly series, *New Directions in Institutional Research*.

110. V. Onushkin, ed., *op. cit.*

111. See, for example, A. Matejko, 'Planning and tradition in Polish higher education,' *Minerva* 7 (Summer 1969), 621-48.

112. Committee on Higher Education, *op. cit.*

113. India, Ministry of Education, *op. cit.*

114. *Report of the President's Commission on campus unrest.*

115. *The second Newman Report: national policy and higher education* (Cambridge, Mass.: M.I.T. Press, 1974).

116. James Duff and Robert Berdahl, *University government in Canada*, (Toronto: University of Toronto Press, 1966). See also René Hurtubise and Donald Rowat. *The university, society and government*, (Ottawa: University of Ottawa Press, 1970).

117. *The learning society: report of the Commission on post-secondary education in Ontario*, (Toronto: Ministry of Government Services, 1972).

118. T. H. B. Symons, *To know ourselves: the report of the Commission on Canadian studies*, 2 vols. (Ottawa: Association of Universities and Colleges of Canada, 1975).

119. See also Ludwig Raiser, 'A German view of the Robbins Committee's report,' *Minerva* 2 (Spring 1964), 336-42 and A. K. Das Gupta, 'Reflections on higher education in India in the light of the Robbins report,' *Minerva* 2 (Winter 1964), 160-8.

120. 'The James Report: radical reforms proposed for teacher education,' *Times*

Higher Education Supplement (28 January 1972), 1-12.

121. Richard Layard, John King and Claus Moser, *The impact of Robbins: expansion in higher education* (London: Penguin, 1969).

122. Tyrrell Burgess, ed., *Planning for higher education* (London: Cornmarket Press, 1972). See also T. R. McConnell and R. Berdahl, 'Planning mechanisms for British transition to mass higher education,' *Higher Education Review* 3 (Autumn 1971) 3-22; Harold Perkin, 'University planning in Britain in the 1960s,' *Higher Education* 1 (February 1972), 111-20; and H. Perkin, 'The new universities in Britain,' *Western European Education* 2 (Winter 1970-1), 290-313.

123. Gareth Williams, 'The events of 1973-4 in a long-range planning perspective,' *Higher Education Bulletin* 3 (Autumn 1974), 17-44 and G. Williams, 'Graduates and the labour market,' *Three Banks Review* (September 1973), 1-24.

124. Keith Lumsden, ed., *Efficiency in universities: the LaPaz Papers*, (Amsterdam: Elsevier, 1976).

125. Donald Verry and Bleddyn Davies, *University costs and outputs*, (Amsterdam: Elsevier, 1976).

126. Brian MacArthur, *Beyond 1980: the evolution of British higher education.* (New York: I.C.E.D., 1975).

127. Michael Beloff, *The plate-glass universities*, (London: Secker & Warburg, 1968).

128. David Daiches, ed., *The idea of a new university: an experiment at Sussex*, (Cambridge, Mass.: M.I.T. Press, 1964).

129. Douglas Windham, 'The economics of higher education' in P. G. Altbach, ed., *Comparative higher education abroad* (New York: Praeger, 1976), pp. 183-221.

130. Grant Harman and C. S. Smith, eds., *Australian higher education: problems of a developing system* (Sydney: Angus & Robertson, 1972). See also 'Tertiary education in Australia,' *Minerva* 4 (Summer 1966), 505-41.

131. E. Ashby, *Universities: British, Indian, African.*

132. For examples of academic planning in Africa, see *Report of the Commission on University Education (Ghana)*, (Accra: Ministry of Education, 1961); Gerald Rimmington, 'The development of universities in Africa,' *Comparative Education* 1 (March 1965), 105-12; and 'University development in Nigeria: report of the National Universities Commission,' *Minerva* 3 (Winter 1965), 210-28.

133. P. G. Altbach, 'Problems of university reform in India,' *Comparative Education Review* 16 (June 1972), 251-67; J. N. Kaul, *op. cit.;* and Amrik Singh, 'The Education Commission and after,' *Asian Survey* 9 (October 1969), 734-41.

134. India, Ministry of Education, *op. cit.* See also 'Indian university reform,' *Minerva* 5 (Autumn, Winter, Spring 1966-7), 47-81, 242-64, 391-412.

135. For an overview, see T. M. Yesufu, ed., *op. cit.*

136. A. B. Fafunwa and John Hanson, 'The post-independence Nigerian university' in P. G. Altbach, ed., *University reform*, (Cambridge, Mass.: Schenkman, 1974), pp. 95-113.

137. V. Onushkin, ed., *op. cit.*

138. Michio Nagai, *op. cit.*

139. John Blewett, ed., *Higher education in post-war Japan*, (Tokyo: Sophia University, 1965).

140. William Cummings, 'The conservatives reform higher education,' *Japan Interpreter* 8 (Winter 1974), 421-31.

141. William Cummings and Ikuo Amano, 'Japanese higher education' in P. G. Altbach, ed., *Comparative higher education abroad*, pp. 222-62.

142. Organization for Economic Cooperation and Development, *Review of national policies for education: Japan*, (Paris: O.E.C.D., 1971).

143. C. A. Anderson, 'University planning in an underdeveloped country: a

commentary on the University of East Africa plan,' *Minerva* 7 (Autumn-Winter 1968-9), 36-51.

144. Richard Pelczar, 'The Latin American professoriate: progress and prospects,' *Higher Education* 6 (May 1977), 235-54.

145. For pioneering American studies of work patterns of academic work, see Peter Blau, *The organization of academic work*, (New York: Wiley, 1973) and Charles Anderson and John Murray, eds., *The professors*, (Cambridge, Mass.: Schenkman, 1971).

146. P. G. Altbach, ed., *Comparative perspectives on the academic profession*, (New York: Praeger, 1978).

147. A. H. Halsey and M. Trow, *The British academics*, (Cambridge, Mass.: Harvard University Press, 1971).

148. See E. C. Ladd and S. M. Lipset, *The divided academy: professors and politics*, (New York: McGraw-Hill, 1975) and M. Trow, ed., *Teachers and students*, (New York: McGraw-Hill, 1975).

149. Walter Metzger, ed., *Reader on the sociology of the academic profession*, (New York: Arno Press, 1977).

150. H. Rashdall, *op. cit.*

151. C. H. Haskins, *op. cit.*

152. Howard Kaminsky, 'The university of Prague in the Hussite revolution; the role of the masters' in J. Baldwin and R. Goldthwaite, eds., *op. cit.*, pp. 79-106.

153. Arthur Engel, 'The emerging concept of the academic profession at Oxford' in L. Stone, ed., *op. cit.*, vol. 1, pp. 305-51.

154. Sheldon Rothblatt, *The revolution of the dons: Cambridge and society in Victorian England*, (London: Faber, 1968).

155. A. H. Halsey and M. Trow, *op. cit.*

156. Gareth Williams, Tessa Blackstone and David Metcalf, *The academic labor market: economic aspects of a profession*, (Amsterdam: Elsevier, 1974).

157. H. Perkin, *Key profession: the history of the Association of University Teachers*, (London: Routledge & Kegan Paul, 1969).

158. M. P. Hornsby-Smith, 'The working life of the university lecturer,' *Universities Quarterly* 28 (Spring 1974), 149-63.

159. See J. Ben-David and A. Zloczower, *op. cit.*, for a discussion of the German influence.

160. R. Steven Turner, 'University reformers and professorial scholarship in Germany, 1760-1806' in L. Stone, ed., *op. cit.*, vol. 2, pp. 495-532.

161. Alexander Busch, *Die Geschichte des Privatdozenten*, (New York: Arno Press, 1977).

162. F. Ringer, *op cit.*

163. E. Shils, ed., *Max Weber on universities*.

164. Hans Anger *et al.*, *Probleme der deutschen Universität*, (Tubingen: Mohr, 1960).

165. Helmuth Plessner, ed., *Unterschungen zur Lage der deutschen Hochschullehrer*, 3 vols., (Gottingen: Vandenhoeck & Ruprecht, 1956).

166. Alexander Busch, 'The vicissitudes of the privatdozent: breakdown and adaptation in the recruitment of the German university teacher,' *Mineva* 1 (Spring 1963), 319-41.

167. Guido Martinotti and Alberto Giasanti, 'The robed baron: the academic profession in the Italian university,' *Higher Education* 6 (May 1977), 189-208.

168. Burton Clark, *Academic power in Italy: bureaucracy and oligarchy in a national university system*, (Chicago: University of Chicago Press, 1977).

169. C. J. Lammers, 'Localism, cosmopolitanism and faculty response: case study of Leyden University,' *Sociology of Education* 48 (Winter 1974), 129-58.

170. Hana Daalder, 'The Dutch universities between the "new democracy" and the "new management",' *Minerva* 12 (April 1974), 221-57.

171. F. Gaussen, 'The human cost of French university expansion: academics without careers,' *Minerva* 11 (July 1973), 373-86.

172. Stephen Lofthouse, 'Thoughts on "publish or perish",' *Higher Education* 3 (February 1974), 59-80.

173. E. Ashby, 'The academic profession,' *Minerva* 8 (January 1970), 90-99.

174. C. Campos, 'Mobility of university staff in Europe,' *Universities Quarterly* 25 (Winter 1970) 28-48; Richard Shryock, ed., *The status of university teachers*, (Ghent: International Association of University Professors, 1961); and Council for Cultural Cooperation, Council of Europe, *Structure of university staff*, (Strasbourg: Council of Europe, 1966).

175. Organization for Economic Cooperation and Development, *Quantitative trends in teaching staff in higher education*, (Paris: O.E.C.D., 1971).

176. Michiya Shimbori, 'Comparative study of career patterns of college professors,' *International Review of Education* 10 (No. 3, 1964), 284-96. This article deals with several nations including Japan. See also M. Shimbori, 'The academic marketplace in Japan,' *The Developing Economies* 7 (December 1969), 617-39.

177. William Cummings and Ikuo Amano, 'The changing role of the Japanese professor,' *Higher Education* 6 (May 1977), 209-34. See also W. Cummings, 'Understanding behavior in Japan's academic marketplace,' *Journal of Asian Studies* 34 (February 1975), 313-40.

178. P. G. Altbach, 'In search of Saraswati: the ambivalence of the Indian academic,' *Higher Education* 6 (May 1977), 255-75.

179. Suma Chitnis, 'Teachers in higher education' in A. Singh and P. G. Altbach, eds., *The higher learning in India* (Delhi: Vikas, 1974), pp. 237-50.

180. Irene Gilbert, 'The Indian academic profession: the origins of a tradition of subordination,' *Minerva* 10 (July 1972), 384-411.

181. Thomas Eisemon, 'Institutional correlates of faculty outlooks and professional behaviors: a study of Indian engineering faculty,' *Higher Education* 3 (November 1974), 419-38.

182. E. Shils, 'The academic profession in India,' *Minerva*, 7 (Spring 1969), 345-72.

183. Pierre Van den Berghe, 'The first estate: senior staff' in P. L. Van den Berghe, *Power and Privilege at an African University* (London: Routledge & Kegan Paul, 1973), pp. 111-46.

184. R. Pelczar, 'The Latin American professoriate; progress and prospects,' *Higher Education* 6 (May 1977), 235-54.

185. D. J. Socolow, 'Argentine professoriate: occupational insecurity and political interference,' *Comparative Education Review* 17 (October 1973), 375-88.

186. Grant Harman, 'Academic staff and academic drift in Australian colleges of advanced education,' *Higher Education* 6 (August 1977), 313-36.

187. Carnegie Commission on Higher Education, *Reform on Campus: changing students, changing academic programs*, (New York: McGraw-Hill, 1972).

188. Talcott Parsons and Gerald Platt, *The American university*, (Cambridge, Mass.: Harvard University Press, 1973).

189. James Perkins, ed., *The university as an organization*, (New York: McGraw-Hill, 1973); see particularly the chapter by Barbara Burn, 'Comparisons of four foreign universities', pp. 79-106.

190. A. Touraine, *The academic system in American society*.

191. J. Perkins, ed., *Higher education: from autonomy to systems*, (New York: I.C.E.D., 1972).

192. J. V. Baldridge, *Power and conflict in the university*, (New York: Wiley, 1971).

193. J. V. Baldridge, ed., *Academic governance*, (Berkeley, Cal.: McCutcheon, 1971); and Gary Riley and J. V. Baldridge, eds., *Governing academic organizations*, (Berkeley, Cal.: McCutcheon, 1977).

194. Leon Epstein, *Governing the university*, (San Francisco: Jossey-Bass, 1974).

195. John J. Corson, *The governance of colleges and universites*, (New York: McGraw-Hill, 1975).

196. E. Ashby, *The structure of higher education: a world view* (New York: I.C.E.D., 1973).

197. B. B. Burn, 'Comparisons of four foreign universities'.

198. International Association of Universities, *The administration of universities* (Paris: I.A.U., 1967).

199. J. P. Clerk and C. Debbasch, 'Student participation in university governance,' *Western European Education* 3 (Winter 1971-2), 349-54.

200. Hugh Livingstone, *The university: an organizational analysis*, (Glasgow: Blackie, 1974).

201. Colin Flood Page and Mary Yates, eds., *Power and authority in higher education*, (Guildford, England: Society for Research into Higher Education, 1976).

202. Grame Moodie and Rowland Eustace, *Power and authority in British universities*, (Montreal: McGill-Queens University Press, 1974).

203. Janice Beyer and Thomas Lodahl, 'A comparative study of patterns of influence in the United States and English universities,' *Administrative Science Quarterly* 21 (March 1976), 104-29.

204. Bruce Williams, 'University values and university organization,' *Minerva* 10 (April 1972), 259-79.

205. J. Duff and R. Berdahl, *op. cit.*

206. Murray Ross, 'The dilution of academic power in Canada: the University of Toronto Act,' *Minerva* 10 (April 1972), 242-58.

207. Terence Halliday, 'The politics of "Universal Participatory Democracy": a Canadian case study,' *Minerva* 13 (Autumn 1975), 404-27.

208. S. C. Malik, ed., *Management and organization of Indian universities*, (Simla, India: Indian Institute of Advanced Study, 1971).

209. Susanne and Lloyd Rudolph, 'Parochialism and cosmopolitanism in university government: the environment of Baroda University' in S. and L. Rudolph, eds., *Education and politics in India*, (Cambridge, Mass.: Harvard University Press, 1972), pp. 207-72.

210. A. K. Rice, *The modern university: a model organization*, (London: Tavistock, 1970).

211. Murray Ross, *The university: anatomy of academe*, (New York: McGraw-Hill, 1976).

212. J. Baldwin and R. Goldthwaite, eds., *op. cit.*

213. See Robert Nisbet, *op. cit.*, for an effective critique of the American university for taking on too many diffuse and unrelated roles. At an earlier time, Abraham Flexner, *op. cit.* also criticized American higher education for taking on too much.

214. Kenneth P. Mortimer, *Accountability in higher education*, (Washington, D.C.: American Association for Higher Education, 1972). See also Dietrich Goldschmidt, 'Autonomy and accountability of higher education in the Federal Republic of Germany' in P. G. Altbach, ed., *The university's response to societal demands*, (New York: I.C.E.D., 1975), pp. 151-72.

215. *Higher education: Crisis and support*, (New York: I.C.E.D., 1974). For an excellent general analysis of the problems of American higher education, see Burton Clark and Ted I. K. Youn, *Academic power in the United States*, (Washington, D.C.: American Association for Higher Education, 1976).

216. See, for example, J. Ben-David, *Centers of learning*; R. Dugger, *op. cit.*, and M. Ross, *op. cit.*

217. L. Stone, ed., *op. cit.*

218. J. Baldwin and R. Goldthwaite, eds., *op. cit.*

219. International Association of Universities, *The university and the needs of contemporary society*, (Paris, I.A.U., 1970), and *University autonomy, its meaning today*, (Paris, I.A.U., 1965).

220. A. H. Halsey, 'Universities and the state,' *Universities Quarterly* 23 (Spring 1969), 123-48.

221. Sydney Caine, 'Universities and the state,' *Political Quarterly* 37 (July-September 1966), 237-54.

222. T. R. McConnell, *The university and the state: a comparative study*, (Berkeley, Calif.: Center for Research and Development in Higher Education, 1967).

223. See J. Ben-David and A. Zloczower, *op. cit.* and F. Ringer, *op. cit.*

224. Olga Narkiewicz, 'Polish universities: Polish or socialist?' *Universities Quarterly* 19 (September 1965), 345-60.

225. E. Ashby, *Universities, British, Indian, African*, pp. 47-146.

226. S. R. Dongerkery, *University autonomy in India*, (Bombay: Lalvani, 1967).

227. S. and L. Rudolph, eds. *op. cit.*

228. Eric Ashby and Mary Anderson, 'Autonomy and academic freedom in Britain and in English-speaking countries of tropical Africa,' *Minerva* 4 (Spring 1966), 317-64.

229. Dennis Austin, 'Et in arcadia ego: politics and learning in Ghana,' *Minerva* 13 (Summer 1975), 236-69.

230. 'Suspension of university autonomy in the Argentine,' *Minerva* 5 (Autumn 1966), 93-99. See also Luigi Einaudi, 'University autonomy and academic freedom in Latin America,' *Law and Contemporary Problems* 28 (Summer 1963), 636-46.

231. Eric Hutchinson, 'The origins of the University Grants Committee,' *Minerva* 13 (Winter 1975), 583-620.

232. Robert Berdahl, *British universities and the state*, (Berkeley, Calif.: University of California Press, 1959).

233. Edward Boyle, 'Parliament and university policy,' *Minerva* 5 (Autumn 1966), 3-19.

234. E. Ashby, 'Government, the University Grants Committee and the universities: hands off the universities,' *Minerva* 6 (Winter 1968), 244-56.

235. Samuel Mathai, 'The University Grants Commission' in A. Singh and P. G. Altbach, eds., *op. cit.*, pp. 25-37.

236. Amrik Singh, 'Universities and the government' in A. B. Shah, ed., *Higher education in India*, (Bombay: Lalvani, 1968), pp. 66-75.

237. P. Seabury, ed., *op. cit.*

238. E. Shils, 'The academic ethos under strain'.

239. Henry L. Mason, 'Reflections on the politicized university: the academic crisis in the Federal Republic of Germany,' *AAUP Bulletin* 60 (September 1974), 299-312; and Henry Mason, 'Reflections on the politicized university, II: Triparity and Tripolarity in the Netherlands,' *AAUP Bulletin* 60 (December 1974), 383-400.

240. Hans Daalder, 'The Dutch universities between the "new democracy" and the "new management",' *Minerva* 12 (April 1974), 221-57.

241. Henri Janne, 'The European university in society,' *Prospects* 3 (Winter 1973), 482-92.

242. Julius Gould, Politics and the academy,' *Government and Opposition* 3 (Winter 1968), 23-47.

243. 'University and society,' *Journal of Social and Political Ideas in Japan* 5 (December 1967), 117-345.

244. Lucian Pye and A. L. Singer, 'Higher education and politics in Singapore,' *Minerva* 3 (Spring 1965), 321-35; and Roland Puccetti, 'Authoritarian government and academic subservience: the University of Singapore,' *Minerva* 10 (April 1972), 223-41.

245. R. C. Pratt, 'University and state in independent tropical Africa,' *Universities Quarterly* 21 (December 1966), 91-100.

246. M. Crawford *et al.*, 'Government and universities in East Africa,' *Minerva* 5 (No. 3, 1967), 376-86.

247. Joseph Fischer, 'Universities and the political process in Southeast Asia,' *Pacific Affairs* 36 (Spring 1963), 3-15.

248. Amrik Signh and P. G. Altbach, eds., *op. cit.*

249. Michelle Patterson, 'Governmental policy and equality in higher education: the junior collegization of the French university,' *Social Problems* 24 (December 1976), 173-83.

250. André Philippart, 'The university in Belgian politics since the contestation of 1968,' *Government and Opposition* 7 (Autumn 1972), 450-63.

251. Richard Walter, *Student politics in Argentina: the university reform and its effects, 1918-1964,* (New York: Basic, 1968).

252. P. G. Altbach and David H. Kelly, *American students: a selected bibliography on student activism and related topics,* (Lexington, Mass.: Lexington, 1973); P. G. Altbach, *A select bibliography on students, politics and higher education,* (Cambridge, Mass.: Harvard Center for International Affairs, 1970). See also Kokusai Bunka Shinkokai, *Higher Education and the student problem in Japan,* (Tokyo: K.B.S., 1972).

253. For a comprehensive bibliography and analysis of the effects of the collegiate experience on students, see Kenneth Feldman and Theodore Newcomb, *The impact of college on students,* 2 vols., (San Francisco: Jossey-Bass, 1969).

254. Perhaps the most comprehensive student-devised plan for university reform was done in West Germany. See Wolfgang Nitsch *et al.*, *Hochschule in der Demokratie,* (New York: Arno Press, 1977).

255. Lewis S. Feuer, *The conflict of generations: the character and significance of student movements,* (New York: Basic Books, 1969).

256. See M. S. Steinberg, *Sabers and brown shirts: the German Students' path to National Socialism,* (Chicago: University of Chicago Press, 1977) for an analysis of the rightist trend in Germany.

257. S. M. Lipset, ed., *Student politics,* (New York: Basic Books, 1967).

258. S. M. Lipset and P. G. Altbach, eds., *Students in revolt,* (Boston: Houghton Mifflin, 1969).

259. M. S. Archer, ed., *op. cit.*

260. Alexander Cockburn and Robin Blackburn, eds., *Student power: problems, diagnosis, action,* (Baltimore: Penguin, 1969).

261. Julian Nagel, ed., *Student power,* (London: Merlin Press, 1969).

262. Gerald McGuigan, ed., *Student protest,* (Toronto: Methuen, 1969).

263. Donald Emmerson, ed., *Students and politics in developing nations,* (New York: Praeger, 1968).

264. W. J. and J. L. Hanna, eds., *University students and African politics,* (New York: Africana, 1975).

265. L. S. Feuer, *op. cit.*

266. Kenneth Keniston, *Youth and dissent,* (New York: Harcourt Brace Jovanovich, 1972).

267. Michael Miles, *The radical probe: the logic of student rebellion,* (New York: Atheneum 1971).

268. Daniel and Gabriel Cohn-Bendit, *Obsolete communism: the left-wing alternative* (London: André Deutsch, 1968).

269. Alain Touraine, *The May Movement: reform and revolt* (New York: Random House, 1971).

270. S. M. Lipset, 'University students and politics in underdeveloped countries,' *Minerva* 3 (Autumn 1964), 15-56.

271. P. G. Altbach, 'Students and politics,' *Comparative Education Review* 10 (June 1966), 175-87.

272. Frank Pinner, 'Transition and transgression; some characteristics of student movements in Western Europe,' *Daedalus* 97 (Winter 1968), 137-55, and F Pinner, 'Student trade unionism in France, Belgium and Holland,' *Sociology of Education* 37 (Spring 1964), 1-23.

273. Ian Weinberg and Kenneth Walker, 'Student politics and political systems,' *American Journal of Sociology* 75 (July 1969), 77-96.

274. P. G. Altbach, 'Student movements in historical perspective: the Asian case,' *Youth and Society* 1 (March 1970) 333-57.

275. G. A. D. Soares, 'The active few: student ideology and participation in developing countries' in S. M. Lipset, ed., *Student Politics*, pp. 127-47.

276. E. W. and M. S. Bakke, *Campus challenge; student activism in perspective*, (Hamden, Ct.: Archon Books, 1971).

277. P. G. Altbach and D. H. Kelly, *op. cit.*

278. P. G. Altbach, *Student politics in America* (New York: McGraw-Hill, 1974).

279. S. M. Lipset, *Rebellion in the University* (Chicago: University of Chicago Press, 1977).

280. Steven J. Novak, *The rights of youth: American colleges and student revolt, 1798-1815* (Cambridge, Mass.: Harvard University Press, 1977).

281. Richard Flacks, *Youth and Social Change*, (Chicago: Markham, 1971).

282. I. Wallerstein and P. Starr, eds., *op. cit.*

283. Kirkpatrick Sale, *SDS*, (New York: Random House, 1973).

284. James L. Wood, *The sources of American student activism*, (Lexington, Mass: Lexington, 1974).

285. Edward Sampson and Harold Korn, eds., *Student activism and protest*, (San Francisco: Jossey-Bass, 1970).

286. Alain Schnapp and Pierre Vidal-Nacquet, eds., *The French student uprising, November, 1967-June, 1968: an analytical documentary*, (Boston: Beacon, 1971).

287. A. Touraine, *The May movement*.

288. John and Barbara Ehrenreich, *Long march, short spring*, (New York: Monthly Review Press, 1969).

289. 'Mai, 1968,' *Esprit* 36 (June-July 1968), 961-1080.

290. 'Prelude to disorder: late opening and overcrowding in French universities,' *Minerva* 6 (Spring 1968), 441-47; 'A phantasm of revolution and the possibility of reform in French universities,' *Minerva* 6 (Summer 1968), 630-89.

291. Richard Merritt, 'The student protest movement in West Berlin' *Comparative Politics* 1 (July 1969), 516-32.

292. Jurgen Habermas, *Protestbewegung und Hochschulreform*, (Frankfurt: Suhrkamp, 1969).

293. Ludwig von Friedeberg *et al.*, *Freie universität und politisches potential der studenten*, (Neuweid: Luchterland, 1968). See also Ludwig von Friedeberg, 'Youth and politics in the Federal Republic of Germany,' *Youth and Society* 1 (September 1969), 91-109.

294. 'A steady state of disorder: the SDS at work,' *Minerva* 7 (Spring 1969), 533-44, and 'Students as an anti-parliamentary opposition in West Germany,' *Minerva* 6 (Spring 1968), 448-56.

295. Uwe Bergmann, R. Deutschke, W. Lefevre and B. Rabehl, *Rebellion der Studenten oder die neue Opposition*, (Reinbeck: Rowohlt, 1968).

296. A. H. Halsey and S. Marks, 'British student politics' in S. M. Lipset and P. G. Altbach, eds., *Students in revolt*, pp. 35-59.

297. T. Blackstone and R. Hadley, 'Student protest in a British university; some comparisons with American research,' *Comparative Education Review* 15 (February 1971), 1-19.

298. Guido Martinotti, *Studenti universitari: profilo sociologico* (Padua: Marsilio,

1968); and G. Martinotti, 'The positive marginality: notes on Italian students in periods of political mobilization' in S. M. Lipset and P. G. Altbach, eds., *Students in revolt*, pp. 167-201. See also Burton Clark, *op. cit.*

299. Frederico Mancini, 'The Italian student movement,' *AAUP Bulletin* 54 (December 1968), 427-44.

300. E. T. Galvin, 'Student opposition in Spain,' *Government and Opposition* 1 (May-August 1966), 467-86.

301. Richard Cornell, 'Students and politics in the communist countries of Eastern Europe,' *Daedalus* 97 (Winter 1968) 166-83.

302. David Burg, 'Observations on Soviet university students,' *Daedalus* 89 (Summer 1960), 520-40.

303. Aleksander Gella, 'Student youth in Poland: four generations, 1945-1970,' *Youth and Society* 6 (March 1975), 309-43.

304. Gianni Statera, *Death of a utopia: the development and decline of student movements in Europe*, (New York: Oxford University Press, 1975).

305. See Kokusai Bunka Shinkokai, *op. cit.*

306. Stewart Dowsey, ed., *Zengakuren: Japan's revolutionary students*, (Berkeley, Calif.: Ishii Press, 1970).

307. Ellis Krauss, *Japanese radicals revisited: student protest in postwar Japan*, (Berkeley, Calif.: University of California Press, 1974).

308. Michiya Shimbori, 'Comparisons between pre- and post-war student movements in Japan,' *Sociology of Education* 37 (Fall 1963), 59-70, M. Shimbori, 'Zengakuren: a Japanese case study of a student political movement,' *Sociology of Education* 37 (Spring 1964), 229-53, and M. Shimbori, 'Sociology of a student movement—a Japanese case study,' *Daedalus* 97 (Winter 1968), 204-28.

309. Kazuko Tsurumi, 'The Japanese student movement; group portraits,' *Japan Quarterly* 16 (January-March 1969), 25-44; and K. Tsurumi, 'Some comments on the Japanese student movement in the 1960s,' *Journal of Contemporary History* 5 (No. 1, 1970), 104-12.

310. P. G. Altbach, 'Student movements in historical perspective: the Asian case'.

311. John Israel, *Student nationalism in China: 1927-1937* (Stanford: Stanford University Press, 1966); J. Israel, 'The Red Guards in historical perspective,' *China Quarterly* No. 30 (April-June 1967), 1-32; and J. Israel, 'Reflections on the modern Chinese student movement,' *Daedalus* 97 (Winter 1968), 229-53.

312. Victor Nee, 'The cultural revolution at Peking University,' *Monthly Review* 21 (July-August 1969), 11-91.

313. Bruce Larkin, 'China' in D. Emmerson, ed., *op. cit.*, pp. 146-79.

314. Tse-tung Chow, *The May Fourth movement*, (Cambridge, Mass.: Harvard University Press, 1960).

315. P. G. Altbach, ed., *Turmoil and transition: higher education and student politics in India*, (New York: Basic Books, 1970).

316. Dawn and Rodney Jones, 'The scholars' rebellion: educational interests and agitational politics in Gujarat,' *Journal of Asian Studies* 36 (May 1977), 457-76.

317. Aileen Ross, *Student unrest in India*, (Montreal: Queens-McGill University Press, 1970).

318. Harsja Bachtiar, 'Indonesia,' in D. Emmerson, ed., *op. cit.*, pp. 180-214; Stephen A. Douglas, *Political socialization and student activism in Indonesia*, (Urbana, Ill.: University of Illinois Press, 1970); and 'Continuing student agitation in Indonesia,' *Minerva* 5 (Autumn 1966), 116-22.

319. Robert F. Zimmerman, 'Student "revolution" in Thailand: the end of the Thai bureaucratic polity?' *Asian Survey* 14 (June 1974), 509-29.

320. Ruth-Inge Heinze, 'Ten days in October—students *vs.* the military: an account of the student uprising in Thailand,' *Asian Survey* 14 (June 1974), 491-508.

321. William Douglas, 'Korean students and politics,' *Asian Survey* 3 (December 1963), 584-95.

322. Princeton Lyman, 'Students and politics in Indonesia and Korea,' *Pacific Affairs* 38 (Fall-Winter 1965-6), 582-93.

323. W. and J. Hanna, eds., *op. cit.*

324. Dwaine Marvick, 'African university students: a presumptive élite,' in J. S. Coleman, ed., *Education and political development* (Princeton: Princeton University Press, 1965), pp. 463-98.

325. Joel Barkan, *An African dilemma: university students, politics, and development in Ghana, Tanzania and Uganda*, (Nairobi: Oxford University Press, 1975).

326. D. Emmerson, ed., *op. cit.*

327. See also David Finlay, 'Students and politics in Ghana,' *Daedalus* 97 (Winter 1968), 51-69.

328. R. Walter, *op. cit.*

329. Jaime Suchlicki, *University students and revolution in Cuba 1920-1968*, (Coral Gables, Fla.: University of Miami Press, 1969).

330. Frank Bonilla and Myron Glazer, *Student politics in Chile*, (New York: Basic Books, 1970).

331. Arthur Liebman, Kenneth Walker and Myron Glazer, *Latin American university students: a six-nation study*, (Cambridge, Mass.: Harvard University Press, 1972).

332. David H. Smith, *Latin American student activism*, (Lexington, Mass.: Heath-Lexington, 1973).

333. Orlando Albornoz, 'Academic freedom and higher education in Latin America' in S. M. Lipset, ed., *Student politics*, pp. 283-92; and Orlando Albornoz, 'Student opposition in Latin America,' *Government and Opposition* 2 (October 1966-January 1967), 105-18.

334. Kenneth Walker, 'Comparison of the university reform movements in Argentina and Columbia,' *Comparative Education Review* 10 (June 1966), 257-72.

335. Alastair Hennessy, 'University students in national politics' in C. Veliz, ed., *The politics of conformity in Latin America*, (New York: Oxford University Press, 1967), pp. 119-57.

336. Kalman Silvert, 'The university student,' in John Johnson, ed., *Continuity and change in Latin America*, (Stanford, Cal.: Stanford University Press, 1964), pp. 206-26.

337. Dani Thompson and R. B. Craig, 'Student dissent in Latin America: a comparative analysis,' *Latin American Research Review* 8 (Spring 1973), 71-96.

338. John Peterson, 'Recent research on Latin American students,' *Latin American Research Review* 5 (Spring 1969), 37-58.

339. For a more complete discussion of dependency as it applies to higher education, see P. G. Altbach, 'Servitude of the mind?: education, dependency and neo-colonialism,' *Teachers College Record* 79 (December 1977), 188-204. See also Johann Galtung, 'A structural theory of imperialism,' *African Review* 1 (1972), 93-138.

340. P. G. Altbach, 'Education and neo-colonialism,' *Teachers College Record* 72 (May 1971), 543-58.

341. For further discussion of the roles of Third World and industrialized nations, see Luis Scherz-Garcia, 'Some disfunctional aspects of inernational assistance and the role of the university in social change,' *International Social Science Journal* 19 (No. 3, 1967), 387-403 and Ali Mazrui, 'The African university as a multinational corporation: problems of penetration and dependency,' *Harvard Educational Review* 45 (May 1975), 191-210.

342. John Tate Lanning, *Academic culture in the Spanish colonies*, (New York: Oxford University Press, 1940).

343. For a discussion of Anglophone Africa and Asia, see E. Ashby, *Universities:*

British, Indian, African, and E. Ashby, *African universities and the western tradition.*

344. Robert Koehl, 'The uses of the university: past and present in Nigerian educational culture,' *Comparative Education Review* 15 (June and October 1971), 116-32 and 367-77.

345. A. B. Fafunwa, *A history of Nigerian higher education,* (Lagos: Macmillan, 1971).

346. Aparna Basu, *op. cit.*

347. B. S. Goel, *op. cit.*

348. Audrey Richards, 'The adaptation of universities to the African situation: review article,' *Minerva* 3 (Spring 1965), 336-42.

349. J. Lockwood, 'The transplantation of the university: the case of Africa' in W. Hamilton *et al.,* eds., *A decade of the Commonwealth: 1955-64,* (Durham, N.C.: Duke University Press, 1966), pp. 259-73.

350. Eugene Lubot, 'Peking University fifty-five years ago: perspectives on higher education in China today,' *Comparative Education Review* 17 (February 1973), 44-57.

351. David Wyatt, *The politics of reform in Thailand: education in the reign of King Chulalongkorn,* (New Haven: Yale University Press, 1969).

352. Michio Nagai, *Higher Education in Japan.*

353. P. van den Berghe, *op. cit.*

354. T. M. Yesufu, ed. *op. cit.* For a critique of this volume see Philip Foster, 'False and real problems of African universities,' *Minerva* 13 (Autumn 1975), 466-78.

355. Robert Arnove, 'A survey of literature and research on Latin American universities,' *Latin American Research Review* 3 (Fall 1967), 45-62.

356. Darcy Riberio, 'Rethinking the university in Latin America,' *Prospects* 4 (Autumn 1974), 315-30.

357. Robert L. Gaudino, *The Indian university,* (Bombay: Popular Prakashan, 1965).

358. S. R. Dongerkery, *University education in India,* (Bombay: Manaktakas, 1967).

359. Amrik Singh and P. G. Altbach, eds., *op. cit.*

360. P. G. Altbach, 'Higher education in India' in B. B. Burn, *op. cit.,* pp. 317-44; and P. G. Altbach, *The university in transition: an Indian case study,* (Cambridge, Mass.: Schenkman, 1972).

361. Joseph DiBona, *Change and conflict in the Indian university,* (Bombay: Lalvani, 1972).

362. For example, see 'A miscellany of tribulations in India,' *Minerva* 7 (Autumn-Winter 1964), 256-67.

363. For a bibliography on Indian higher education, see P. G. Altbach, 'Bibliography on higher education in India,' *New Frontiers in Education* (Delhi) 4 (October 1974), 85-196 and 5 (January 1975), 75-101.

364. Theodore Chen, *The Maoist educational revolution,* (New York: Praeger, 1974).

365. R. C. Hunt, 'Change in higher education in the People's Republic of China,' *Higher Education* 4 (February 1975), 45-60.

366. Joseph Fischer, *Universities in Southeast Asia,* (Columbus, Ohio: Ohio State University Press, 1964).

367. T. H. Silcock, *Southeast Asian University: a comparative account of some development problems,* (Durham, N.C.: Duke University Press, 1964).

368. J. J. Waardenburg, *op. cit.*

369. Kenneth Thompson, *el al., op. cit.*

370. F. C. Ward, ed., *op. cit.*

371. Bikas Sanyal and E. S. A. Yacoub, *Higher education and employment in the Sudan,* (Paris: International Institute for Educational Planning, 1975); Bikas Sanyal *et al., Higher education and the labor market in Zambia,* (Paris: Unesco Press, 1976); and Bikas Sanyal and J. Versluis, *Higher education, human capital and labor market segmentation in the Sudan,* (Paris: International Institute for Educational Planning, 1976).

372. Amnuay Tapingkae, ed., *Higher education and economic growth in Southeast Asia.*

(Singapore: Regional Institute for Higher Education and Development, 1976).

373. India, Ministry of Education, *op. cit.*

374. David Lim, 'The role of the university in development planning in Malaysia,' *Minerva* 12 (January 1974), 18-31.

375. J. N. Kaul, ed., *Higher education, social change and national development* (Simla, India: Indian Institute of Advanced Study, 1975).

376. *Higher education and development in South-east Asia*, (Paris: UNESCO and I.A.U., 1965).

377. Immanuel Hsu, 'The impact of industrialization on higher education in Communist China' in F. Harbison and C. Myers, eds., *Manpower and education*, (New York: McGraw-Hill, 1965), pp. 202-31.

378. F. X. Sutton, 'African universities in the process of change in Middle Africa' in S. Kertesz, ed., *The task of universities in a changing world*, (South Bend, Indiana: Notre Dame University Press, 1971), pp. 383-404.

379. Darcy Riberio, 'Universities and social development' in S. M. Lipset and A. Solari, eds., *Elites in Latin America*, (New York: Oxford University Press, 1967), pp. 343-82.

380. V. Onushkin, *op. cit.*

381. Daniel Rogers, 'Financing higher education in less developed countries,' *Comparative Education Review* 15 (February 1971), 20-27.

382. J. W. Hanson, *op. cit.*

383. E. M. Godfrey, 'The economics of an African university,' *Journal of Modern African Studies* 4 (December 1966), 435-55.

384. J. L. Azad, *Financing of higher education in India*, (New Delhi: Sterling, 1975), and J. L. Azad, 'Financing institutions of higher education in India,' *Higher Education* 5 (February, 1975), 1-8.

385. Amnuay Tapingkae, *The growth of Southeast Asian universities: expansion versus consolidation*, (Singapore: Regional Institute for Higher Education and Development, 1974).

386. Richard D. King, *The provincial universities of Mexico: an analysis of growth and development*, (New York: Praeger, 1971).

387. Jerry Haar, *Higher education and politics in Brazil*, (New York: Praeger, 1977).

388. John P. Harrison, 'Learning and politics in Latin American universities,' *Proceedings of the Academy of Political Science* 27 (May 1964), 331-42.

389. Margaret Goodman, 'The political role of the university in Latin America,' *Comparative Politics* 5 (January 1973), 279-92.

390. Davidson Nichol, 'Politics, nationalism and universities in Africa,' *African Affairs* 62 (January 1963), 20-28.

391. A. A. Mazrui and Y. Tandon, 'The University of East Africa as a political institution,' *Minerva* 5 (Spring 1967), 381-86.

392. S. and L. Rudolph, eds., *op. cit.*

393. G. E. von Grunebaun, 'The political role of the university in the Near East as illustrated by Egypt' in G. E. von Grunebaum, ed., *Modern Islam*, (Berkeley, Calif.: University of California Press, 1962), 258-75.

394. For a general discussion of university reform, see P. G. Altbach, 'University reform' in Asa Knowles, ed., *International encyclopedia of higher education*, vol. 9, (San Francisco: Jossey-Bass, 1977), 4263-4274. See also, P. G. Altbach, ed., *University reform: comparative perspectives for the seventies*, (Cambridge, Mass.: Schenkman, 1974).

395. L. Veysey, *op. cit.*

396. See W. Nitsch *et al.*, *op. cit.*

397. K. Kitamura and W. Cummings, 'The "big bang" theory and Japanese university reform,' *Comparative Education Review* 16 (June 1972), 303-24.

398. H. Perkin, *Innovations in higher education: new universities in the United Kingdom*, (Paris: O.E.C.D., 1969).

399. C. Grignon and J. C. Passeron, *Innovations in higher education: French experiences before 1968*, (Paris: O.E.C.D., 1970).

400. E. Boning and K. Roeloffs, *Innovation in higher education: three German universities: Aachen, Bochum, Konstanz* (Paris: O.E.C.D., 1970).

401. E. Shils, 'The academic ethos under strain,' *op. cit.*; and E. Shils, 'Change and reform' in P. G. Altbach, ed., *University Reform*, pp. 15-27

402. Robert Nisbet, *The degradation of the academic dogma*, (New York: Basic Books, 1971).

403. P. Seabury, ed., *op. cit.*

404. J. Perkins, *Reform of higher education: mission impossible?* (New York: I.C.E.D., 1971).

405. Organization for Economic Cooperation and Development, *Towards new structures of post-secondary education: a preliminary statement of issues*, (Paris: O.E.C.D., 1971).

406. Jack Embling, *A fresh look at education: European implications of the Carnegie Commission reports*, (Amsterdam: Elsevier, 1974).

407. Eric Bockstael and Otto Feinstein, *Higher education in the European Community: reform and economics*, (Lexington, Mass.: Lexington, 1970).

408. David Riesman, 'Notes on educational reform,' *Journal of General Education* 23 (No. 2, 1971), 81-110 and D. Riesman, 'Notes on new universities: British and American,' *Universities Quarterly* 20 (March 1966), 128-46.

409. L. Cerych, 'Academic reforms of higher education in Europe: overview of major trends and innovations' in Carnegie Commission on Higher Education, *Reform on campus* (New York: McGraw-Hill, 1972), pp. 105-19.

410. Noel Annan, 'The reform of higher education', *Political Quarterly* 38 (July-September 1967), 234-52.

411. R. W. Connell, 'Anti-Pygmalion: reflections on some experiments in reforming universities,' *International Social Science Journal* (No. 3, 1974), 483-97.

412. L. Cerych, 'On the threshold of mass higher education' in W. R. Niblett and R. F. Butts, eds., *op. cit.*

413. I. Hecquet, 'Demographic change as a factor influencing the development of higher education' in B. Holmes and D. Scanlon, eds., *op. cit.*, pp. 149-60.

414. Council for Cultural Cooperation, Council of Europe, *Reform and expansion of higher education in Europe: national reports*, (Strasbourg: Council of Europe, 1967).

415. UNESCO, *Reform and development of higher education in Europe: France, the Netherlands and Poland*, (Paris: Unesco, 1964).

416. Terry N. Clark, 'Institutionalization of innovations in higher education: four models,' *Administrative Science Quarterly* 13 (June 1968), 1-25.

417. Ralf Dahrendorf, 'Starre und Offenheit der deutschen Universität: die Chancen der Reform,' *European Journal of Sociology* 3 (1962), 263-93.

418. Erich Jantsch, 'Inter- and trans-disciplinary university: a systems approach to education and innovation,' *Higher Education* 1 (February 1972) 7-38.

419. K. Kitamura and R. Cummings, *op. cit.*

420. For a summary of the Carnegie Commission's work, see L. Mayhew, *op. cit.* and Carnegie Commission on Higher Education, *A digest of reports*.

421. Carnegie Commission on Higher Education, *Reform on campus*.

422. *The second Newman Report: national policy and higher education*, (Cambridge, Mass.: M.I.T. Press, 1974).

423. 'University reform in Japan,' *Minerva* 8 (October 1970) 581-93; and 'The reform of Japanese higher education: report of the Central Council for Education in Japan,' *Minerva* 11 (July 1973), 387-414.

424. William Cummings, 'The Conservatives reform higher education,' *Japan*

Interpreter 8 (Winter 1974), 421-31.

425. *Higher education: proposals by the Swedish 1968 Educational Commission*, (Stockholm: Allmanna, 1973). See also 'The reorganization of higher education in Sweden,' *Minerva* 12 (January 1974), 83-114.

426. C. A. Anderson, 'Sweden re-examines higher education: a critique of the U-68 report,' *Comparative Education* 10 (October 1974), 167-80; Gunnar Bergendal, 'U-68—a reform proposal for Swedish higher education,' *Higher Education* 3 (August 1974), 353-64; and Torsten Husen, 'Swedish university research at the crossroads,' *Minerva* 14 (Winter 1976-77), 419-46.

427. V. Nee, *op. cit.*

428. Marianne Bastid, 'Economic necessity and political ideals in educational reform during the Cultural Revolution,' *China Quarterly* 42 (April-June 1970), 16-45.

429. Chin Wang, 'Current trends in the reform of higher education in Communist China,' *Chinese Education* 2 (Winter 1969-70), 27-52.

430. Julie W. Munro, 'A major turnaround in China,' *Chronicle of Higher Education* 15 (7 November 1977), 1, 10.

431. For material on French university reform prior to 1968, see 'Faire l'université', *Esprit* 32 (May-June 1964) 705-1214; Ann Williamson, 'Innovation in higher education: French experience before 1968' in B. Holmes and D. Scanlon, eds., *op. cit.*, 251-64; Gerald Antoine and Jean-Claude Passeron, *La réforme de l'université* (Paris: Calmann-Levy, 1966); and Stuart Walters, 'University reform: a case study from France,' *Universities Quarterly* 18 (March 1964), 169-79.

432. Edgar Faure, *Philosophie d'une réforme,* (Paris: Plon, 1969).

433. 'A phantasm of revolution and the possibility of reform in French universities,' *Minerva* 6 (Summer 1968) 630-89; 'University reform in France,' *Minerva* 7 (Summer 1969); Michelle Patterson, 'French university reform: renaissance or restoration, *Comparative Education Review* 16 (June 1972), 281-302; Jacques Fomerand, 'The French university: what happened after the revolution?' *Higher Education* 6 (February 1977), 93-116.

434. E. Boning and K. Roeloffs, *op. cit.* See also Walter Hahn, 'Higher education in West Germany: reform movements and trends,' *Comparative Education Review* 7 (June 1963), 51-60.

435. International Association of Universities, *Problems of integrated higher education: an international case study of the Gesamthochschule,* (Paris: I.A.U., 1972).

436. Ulrich Teichler, 'University reform and skeleton legislation in the Federal Republic of Germany,' *Western European Education* 5 (Winter 1973-4), 34-55.

437. M. Krueger and B. Wallisch-Prinz, 'University reform in West Germany,' *Comparative Education Review* 16 (June 1972), 340-51.

438. I. N. Sommerkorn, 'The Free University of Berlin: case study of an experimental seminar' in W. R. Niblett and R. F. Butts, eds., *op. cit.*, pp. 336-46; H. Schelsky, *Einsamkeit und Freiheit: zur Idee und Gestalt der deutschen Universität und ihrer Reformen* (Reinbeck: Rowohlt, 1963); and 'University reform in Germany,' *Minerva* 8 (April 1970), 242-67.

439. 'Irreconcilables and fumbling reformers in West Germany,' *Minerva* 7 (Autumn-Winter 1968-9), 153-77.

440. G. Kloss, 'University reform in West Germany: the burden of tradition,' *Minerva* 6 (Spring 1968), 323-52.

441. Wolfgang Nitsch, 'Zur Struktur der Bremer "Reformsuniversität",' *Zeitschrift der Technischen Universität Berlin* No. 1, (1972), 1-36. See also E. B. Berndt *et al.*, *Erziehung der erzieher: das Bremer Reformmodell* (Reinbeck: Rowohlt, 1972).

442. For a critical examination of the German situation, see International Council on the Future of the University, *Report on the German universities* (New York: International Council on the Future of the University, 1977).

443. Committee on Higher Education, *op. cit.*

444. R. Layard, J. King, and C. Moser, *op. cit.*

445. Sir Charles Morris, 'Second thoughts on Robbins: university commentary,' *Universities Quarterly* 18 (March 1964), 119-28.

446. David Daiches, ed., *The idea of a new university: an experiment in Sussex*, (Cambridge, Mass.: M.I.T. Press, 1974).

447. M. Beloff, *The plateglass universities*.

448. H. Perkin, 'A British university designed for the future; Lancaster' in W. R. Niblett and R. E. Butts, eds., *op. cit.*, pp. 183-194. See also H. Perkin, *Innovations in higher education: new universities in the United Kingdom*.

449. Rodney Hartnett, *The British Open University in the United States: adaptation and use at three universities*, (Princeton: Educational Testing Service, 1974).

450. Jeremy Tunstall, ed., *The Open University opens*, (Amherst, Mass.: University of Massachusetts Press, 1974).

451. Naomi E. McIntosh *et al.*, *A degree of difference: the Open University of the United Kingdom*, (New York: Praeger, 1977).

452. John Ferguson, *The Open University from within*, (London: Hodder & Stoughton, 1975).

453. S. B. Crooks, *The Open University in the United Kingdom*, (Paris: International Institute for Educational Planning, 1976).

454. Jacques Fomerand, 'The politics of innovation in Great Britain: The Open University,' *Western European Education* 8 (No. 1-2, 1976), 121-50.

455. Christopher Driver, 'Higher education in Britain: the cow ruminant,' *Comparative Education Review* 16 (June 1972), 325-39.

456. 'The James Report: radical reforms proposed for teacher education,' *Times Higher Education Supplement* (January 28 1972), 1-12.

457. P. G. Altbach, 'Problems of university reform in India,' *Comparative Education Review* 16 (June, 1972), 251-66.

458. Glynn Wood, 'Planning university reform: an Indian case study,' *Comparative Education Review* 16 (June 1972), 267-80.

459. T. M. Yesufu, ed., *op. cit.*

460. Don Adams, *Higher education reforms in the Republic of Korea*, (Washington, D.C.: U.S. Office of Education, 1965).

461. L. S. Atanassian, *The reform of higher education, Iran*, (Paris: Unesco, 1960).

462. 'Report on the development of a university in Northern Rhodesia (Zambia),' *Minerva* 3 (Winter 1965), 245-61.

463. Kenneth Mellanby, 'Establishing a new university in Africa,' *Minerva* 1 (Winter 1962), 149-58.

464. Gabriel del Mazo, *La reforma universitaria* (6 vols.), (Buenos Aires: Publicaciones del Circulo Medico Argentino, 1927). See also Gabriel del Mazo, *Reforma universitaria y cultura nacional*, (Buenos Aires: Editorial Raigal, 1955).

465. 'The anniversary of the Cordoba Declaration and its ramifications in the Argentine,' *Minerva* 7 (Autumn-Winter 1968-69), 95-112; and R. Pelczar, 'University reform in Latin America: the case of Colombia,' *Comparative Education Review* 16 (June 1972), 230-50.

466. C. O'Neil, 'Problems of innovation in higher education: the University of Brasilia, 1961-4,' *Journal of Inter-American Studies* 15 (November 1963), 415-31.

467. David Carneiro, jr., 'The university in Brazil: expansion and the problem of modernization' in W. R. Niblett and R. F. Butts, eds., *op. cit.*

468. H. Draheim, 'The gesamthochschule: a model of mobility,' *Prospects* 3 (Winter 1973) 505-14.

469. G. Fowler, 'The binary policy in England and Wales' in W. R. Niblett and R. F. Butts, eds., *op. cit.*, pp. 268-80.

470. For a recent discussion of the debate about the role of academic departments in the United States, see Dean McHenry, ed., *Academic departments*, (San Francisco: Jossey-Bass, 1977).

471. M. Krueger and B. Wallisch Prinz, *op. cit.*

472. M. Patterson, 'French university reform'.

473. K. G. Lumsden, ed., *op. cit.*

474. D. Goldschmidt, 'West Germany,' in M. S. Archer, ed., *Students, university and society*, pp. 154-66.

475. See G. J. Giles, 'The structure of higher education in the German Democratic Republic,' (New Haven, Conn.: Yale University Higher Education Program Working Paper, 1976).

476. C. T. Hu, 'The Chinese people's university: bastion of Marxism-Leninism' in W. R. Niblett and R. F. Butts, eds., *op. cit.*, pp. 63-74.

477. Carnegie Commission on Higher Education, *Less time, more options: education beyond the high school*, (New York: McGraw-Hill, 1971); and Ann Heiss, *An inventory of academic innovation and reform*, (New York: McGraw-Hill, 1973).

478. Organization for Economic Cooperation and Development, *Short-cycle higher education: a search for identity*, (Paris: O.E.C.D., 1973).

479. A number of industrialized nations now offer excellent bibliographies for retrieving dissertations. See, for example, *Dissertation Abstracts International*, a multi-volume research enterprise which lists by subject doctoral theses written in the United States.

THE BIBLIOGRAPHY

The Bibliography

This bibliography has a simple purpose: to present some of the best literature currently available on higher education in a comparative perspective and to provide some key references on higher education in many individual nations. The bibliography is far from complete. An effort has been made to list only materials of some lasting interest and analytical value. Much valuable material has been omitted because it is purely descriptive or of limited relevance. Listings on nations, such as most Third World countries, which have a very limited literature tend to be less selective than those for nations with a large body of available data. Most of the material cited in the bibliography is in English, thereby omitting much discussion in other languages. Materials which are likely to be found in a good research library or are in fairly standard journals have been included in the bibliography — other valuable items, such as doctoral dissertations, government documents and other more ephemeral writing have been excluded. Finally, the United States is not included to any significant degree. The American literature is very substantial and is, in any case, fairly adequately referenced through such services as the Educational Resources Information Center (E.R.I.C.). This bibliography should be used as a *beginning* point of reference rather than as a definitive guide to the literature. It will provide an overview to a field rather than a comprehensive listing of all materials.

ARRANGEMENT

The bibliography is divided by country and region, and within each section books are listed first, followed by articles in books and journals. Each sequence is arranged alphabetically by author.

There are three indexes to facilitate alternative approaches to this listing:

1. A topic cross-reference index, where the item numbers under each heading refer to the specific references in the country-region section. The topics have been chosen for simplicity rather than for taxonomic elegance.

2. A country and region index, which lists alphabetically by page number all the countries and regions appearing in the bibliography.

3. An author index which lists by item number all the authors of books and articles, both personal and institutional, that appear in the bibliography.

LIST OF JOURNALS

This listing of journals reflects periodicals that deal, on a regular basis, with post-secondary education and which were found to be especially useful in preparing this bibliography. It is not a comprehensive listing. A fuller listing may be found in the biennial *Ulrich's International Periodicals Directory: a Classified Guide to Current Periodicals, Foreign and Domestic* (New York, Bowker).

Adult Education (Great Britain)
Australian Journal of Higher Education
Australian University
Bildung und Erziehung (Germany, Federal Republic)
Bildung und Wissenschaft (Germany, Federal Republic)
Bulletin of the American Association of University Professors
Bulletin of the International Association of Universities (France)
Canadian and International Education
Canadian Journal of Higher Education
Change (U.S.A.)
Chinese Education (U.S.A.)
College and University (U.S.A.)
Comparative Education (Great Britain)
Comparative Education Review (U.S.A.)
Compare (Great Britain)
Convergence (Canada)
Democratic Education (Czechoslovakia)
Deutsche Universitätszeitung (Germany, Federal Republic)
Educación (Organization of American States)
Educational Record (U.S.A.)
Exchange (U.S. Department of State)
Higher Education (Netherlands)
Higher Education Bulletin (Great Britain)
Higher Education and Research in the Netherlands
Higher Education Review (Great Britain)
Hochschulwesen (Germany, Democratic Republic)
Intellect (formerly *School and Society*) (U.S.A.)
Interchange (Canada)
International Review of Education (UNESCO, Hamburg, Federal Republic of Germany)

*International Journal of Institutional Management in Higher
Education* (O.E.C.D., Paris, France)
Journal of General Education (U.S.A.)
Journal of Higher Education (India)
Journal of Higher Education (U.S.A.)
Konstanzer Blätter für Hochschulfragen (Germany, Federal Republic)
Liberal Education (U.S.A.)
Minerva (Great Britain)
Mundo Universitario (Colombia)
New Frontiers in Education (India)
*New Universities Quarterly (*formerly *Universities Quarterly)* (Great
Britain)
Prospects (UNESCO, Paris, France)
Research in Higher Education (U.S.A.)
Revista del Centro de Estudios Educativos (Mexico)
Revista de la Educación Superior (Mexico)
Scholarly Publishing (Canada)
Soviet Education (U.S.A.)
Studies in Higher Education (Great Britain)
Times Higher Education Supplement (Great Britain)
Universidades (Mexico)
University Administration (India)
Vergleichende Pädagogik (Germany, Democratic Republic)
Vestes (Australia)
West African Journal of Education (Nigeria)
Western European Education (U.S.A.)
Youth and Society (U.S.A.)

GENERAL

Books
1. Altbach, Philip G., ed. *Comparative Higher Education Abroad:
Bibliography and Analysis.* New York: Praeger, 1976
3. — — —. *Comparative Perspectives on the Academic Profession.*
New York: Praeger, 1977.
4. Altbach, Philip G. *A Select Bibliography on Students, Politics,
and Higher Education.* Revised edition. Cambridge, Mass.: Harvard
Center for International Affairs, 1970.
5. — — —., ed. *University Reform: Comparative Perspectives for
the Seventies.* Cambridge, Mass.: Schenkman, 1974.

6. Altbach, Philip G. ed. *The University's Response to Societal Demands: An International Perspective.* New York: I.C.E.D. 1975.

7. Archer, Margaret Scotford, ed. *Students, University, and Society.* London: Heinemann Educational Books, 1972.

8. Ashby, Eric. *Adapting Universities to a Technological Society.* San Francisco: Jossey-Bass, 1974.

9. — — —. *Community of Universities: An Informal Portrait of the Association of Universities of the British Commonwealth. 1913–1963.* Cambridge: Cambridge University Press, 1963.

10. — — —. *The Structure of Higher Education: A World View.* New York: I.C.E.D., 1973

11. — — —. *Technology and the Academics: An Essay on Universities, and the Scientific Revolution.* London: Macmillan, 1958.

12. Association of Commonwealth Universities. *Commonwealth Universities and Society.* London: Association of Commonwealth Universities, 1974.

13. Association des Universités Partiellement ou Entièrement de Langue Française. *L'Université et la Pluralité des Cultures.* Montreal: A.U.P.E.L.F., 1974.

13a. Bailey, Stephen, ed. *Higher Education in the World Community.* Washington, D.C.: American Council on Education, 1977.

14. Ben-David, Joseph. *Centers of Learning: Britain, France, Germany, United States.* New York: McGraw-Hill, 1977.

15. — — —. *Fundamental Research and the Universities: Some Comments on International Differences.* Paris: O.E.C.D., 1968.

16. Bereday, George Z. F. *Universities for All.* San Francisco: Jossey-Bass, 1973.

17. Bereday, George Z. F. and Joseph Lauwerys, eds. *The Yearbook of Education 1959: Higher Education.* London: Evans, 1959.

18. Bowles, Frank. *Access to Higher Education.* New York: Columbia University Press, 1963.

19. Bradley, E., ed. *The University Outside Europe: Essays in the Development of University Institutions in Fourteen Countries.* London: Oxford University Press, 1939.

20. Burn, Barbara B., Philip G. Altbach, Clark Kerr and James Perkins. *Higher Education in Nine Countries.* New York: McGraw-Hill, 1971.

21. Cerych, Ladislav. *A Global Approach to Higher Education.* New York: I.C.E.D., (Occasional Paper No. 3), 1972.

22. Clapp, Margaret, ed. *The Modern University.* Ithaca, N.Y.: Cornell University Press, 1950.

23. Clark, M. L. *Higher Education in the Ancient World.* London: Routledge and Kegan Paul, 1970.

24. Cohn-Bendit, Daniel and Gabriel. *Obsolete Communism: The Left Wing Alternative.* London: André Deutsch, 1968.

25. Committee on Higher Education (Robbins Committee). *Higher Education in Other Countries.* London: H.M.S.O., 1963.

26. Crawford, Elisabeth and Stein Rokkan, eds. *Sociological Praxis: Current Roles and Settings.* Beverly Hills, Calif.: Sage Publications, 1976.

27. Driver, Christopher. *The Exploding University.* Indianapolis, Ind.: Bobbs-Merrill, 1972.

28. Feuer, Lewis. *The Conflict of Generations: The Character and Significance of Student Movements.* New York: Basic Books, 1969.

29. Fielden, John and Geoffrey Lockwood. *Planning and Management in Universities.* London: Chatto and Windus, 1978.

30. Fletcher, Basil. *Universities in the Modern World.* Oxford: Pergamon Press, 1968.

31. Flexner, Abraham. *Universities: American, English, German.* New York: Oxford University Press, 1930.

32. Hacquaert, Armand. *The Recruitment and Training of University Teachers.* Ghent: International Association of University Professors and Lecturers, 1967.

33. Harris, Seymour, ed. *Economic Aspects of Higher Education.* Paris: O.E.C.D., 1964.

34. *Higher Education, Crisis and Support.* New York: I.C.E.D., 1974.

35. Holmes, Brian and David S. Scanlon, eds. *Higher Education in a Changing World: World Yearbook of Education, 1971–72.* New York: Harcourt Brace Jovanovich, 1971.

36. Hussain, K. M. *Institutional Resource Allocation Models in Higher Education.* Paris: O.E.C.D., 1976.

37. International Association of Universities. *The Administration of Universities.* Paris: I.A.U., 1967.

38. — — —. *The Expansion of Higher Education.* Paris: I.A.U., 1960.

39. — — —. *International University Cooperation.* Paris: I.A.U., 1969.

40. — — —. *University Autonomy: Its Meaning Today.* Paris: I.A.U., 1965.

41. — — —. *The University and the Needs of Contemporary Society.* Paris: I.A.U., 1970.

42. Jaspers, Karl. *The Idea of the University.* Boston, Mass: Beacon, 1969.

43. Kertesz, Stephen D., ed. *The Task of Universities in a Changing World.* South Bend, Ind.: Notre Dame University Press, 1971.

44. Knowles, Asa, ed. *International Encyclopedia of Higher Education*. San Francisco: Jossey-Bass, 1977.

45. Kotschnig, Walter M. *Unemployment in the Learned Professions: An International Study of Occupational and Educational Planning*. London: Oxford University Press, 1937.

46. — — —, ed. *The University in a Changing World: A Symposium*. London: Oxford University Press, 1932.

47. LeGall, A. *et al. Present Problems in the Democratization of Secondary and Higher Education*. Paris: UNESCO, 1973.

48. Lipset, S. M., ed. *Student Politics*. New York: Basic Books, 1967.

49. Lipset, S. M. and Philip G. Altbach, eds. *Students in Revolt*. Boston, Mass.: Houghton Mifflin, 1969.

50. Lumsden, Keith, ed. *Efficiency in Universities: The LaPaz Papers*. Amsterdam: Elsevier, 1974.

51. Martin, David, ed. *Anarchy and Culture: The Problem of the Contemporary University*. London: Routledge and Kegan Paul, 1969.

52. McConnell, T. R. *The University and the State: A Comparative Study*. Berkeley, Calif.: Center for Research and Development in Higher Education, 1967 (Reprint series).

53. McConnell, T. R., R. Berdahl and M. Fay. *From Elite to Mass to Universal Higher Education*. Berkeley, Calif.: Center for Research and Development in Higher Education, University of California, 1973.

54. Medsker, Leland L. *The Global Quest for Educational Opportunity*. Berkeley, Calif.: Center for Research and Development in Higher Education, University of California, 1972.

55. Montefiore, Alan, ed. *Neutrality and Impartiality: The University and Political Commitment*. Cambridge: Cambridge University Press, 1975.

56. Neumann, Frantz *et al. The Cultural Migration: The European Scholar in America*. New York: Arno Press, 1977.

57. Newman, John Henry. *The Idea of a University*. New York: Holt, Rinehart and Winston, 1964.

58. Niblett, W. Roy, ed. *Higher Education: Demand and Response*. San Francisco: Jossey-Bass, 1970.

59. — — —. *Universities Between Two Worlds*. London: University of London Press, 1974.

60. Niblett, W. R. and R. F. Butts, eds. *Universities Facing the Future*. San Francisco: Jossey-Bass, 1972.

61. Nitsch, Wolfgang and Walter Weller, eds. *Social Science Research on Higher Education: An Annotated Bibliography*. The Hague, Netherlands: Mouton, 1970.

62. Onushkin, Victor, ed. *Planning the Development of Universities*. 4 vols. Paris: Unesco Press, 1971–5.

63. Ortega y Gasset, José. *The Mission of the University*. New York: Norton, 1944.

64. Perkins, James, ed. *Higher Education: From Autonomy to Systems*. New York: I.C.E.D., 1972.

65. Perkins, James A. *Is the University an Agent for Social Reform?* New York: I.C.E.D., 1973.

66. — — —. *Reform of Higher Education: Mission Impossible?* New York: I.C.E.D., 1971.

67. Psacharopoulos, George. *Returns to Education: An International Comparison*. San Francisco: Jossey-Bass, 1973.

68. Rice, A. K. *The Modern University: A Model Organization*. London: Tavistock, 1970.

69. Robbins, Lord. *The University in the Modern World*. London: Macmillan, 1966.

70. Ross, Murray G., ed. *New Universities in the Modern World*. New York: St. Martin's, 1966.

71. Ross, Murray. *The University: The Anatomy of Academe*. New York: McGraw-Hill, 1976.

72. Schwarz, Richard, ed. *Universität und moderne Welt, ein internationales Symposium*. Berlin: De Gruyter, 1962.

73. Scott, Peter. *Strategies for Post-Secondary Education*. London: Croom Helm, 1975.

74. Seabury, Paul, ed. *Universities in the Western World*. New York: Free Press, 1975.

75. Stephens, Michael D. and Gordon W. Roderick, eds. *Universities for a Changing World: The Role of the University in the Late Twentieth Century*. New York: Wiley, 1975.

76. Thwing, C. F. *The American and the German University*. New York: Macmillan, 1928.

77. — — —. *Universities of the World*. London: Macmillan, 1911.

79. Weidner, Edward. *The World Role of Universities*. New York: McGraw-Hill, 1962.

80. *World Survey of Education*. Vol. 4. *Higher Education*. Paris: UNESCO, 1966.

81. Zweig, Michael. *The Idea of the World University*. Carbondale, Ill.: Southern Illinois University Press, 1967.

Articles

81*a*. 'Aid to Other Nations' in A. Knowles, ed., *International Encyclopedia of Higher Education*. San Francisco: Jossey-Bass, 1977, pp. 269–306.

82. Altbach, Philip G. 'Comparative University Reform' in P. G. Altbach, ed., *University Reform*. Cambridge, Mass.: Schenkman, 1974, pp. 1–14.

83. Altbach, Philip G. 'Higher Education without Boundaries,' *Chronicle of Higher Education* 14 (18 April 1977), 40.

84. — — —. 'Students and Politics,' *Comparative Education Review* 10 (June 1966), 175–87.

85. — — —. 'University Reform' in A. Knowles, ed. *International Encyclopedia of Higher Education.* San Francisco: Jossey-Bass, 1977, pp. 175–87.

86. Anderson, C. A. 'Access to Higher Education and Economic Development' in A. H. Halsey, J. Floud and C. A. Anderson, eds., *Education, Economy and Society.* New York: Free Press, 1962, pp. 252–68.

87. — — —. 'Emerging Common Problems in the World of Universities,' *International Review of Education* 11 (No. 1, 1965), 3–19.

88. — — —. 'Expanding Educational Opportunities: Conceptualization and Measurement,' *Higher Education* 4 (November 1975), 393–408.

89. Annan, Noel. 'The Reform of Higher Education,' *Political Quarterly* 38 (July–September 1967), 234–52.

90. Antoine, Gerald. 'Continuing Education for University Teachers,' *Prospects* 4 (Summer 1974), 173–80.

91. Ashby, Eric. 'The Academic Profession,' *Minerva* 8 (January 1970), 90–9.

92. — — —. 'The Future of the Nineteenth Century of a University,' *Minerva* 6 (Autumn 1967), 3–17.

93. — — —. 'Reconciliation of Tradition and Modernity in Universities' in S. McMurrin, ed., *On the Meaning of the University.* Salt Lake City: University of Utah Press, 1976, pp. 13–28.

94. — — —. 'Universities Under Siege,' *Minerva* 1 (Autumn 1962), 18–29.

95. Ben-David, Joseph. 'Science and the University System,' *International Review of Education* 18 (No. 1, 1972), 44–60.

96. — — —. 'The Profession of Science and Its Powers,' *Minerva* 10 (July 1972), 362–83.

97. — — —. 'Universities' in *International Encyclopedia of Social Sciences.* New York: Free Press, 1968, pp. 191–9.

98. Ben-David, Joseph and Randall Collins. 'A Comparative Study of Academic Freedom and Student Politics' in S. M. Lipset, ed. *Student Politics.* New York: Basic Books, 1967, pp. 148–95.

99. Ben-David, Joseph and Abraham Zloczower. 'Universities and Academic Systems in Modern Societies,' *European Journal of Sociology* 3 (1962), 45–84.

100. Bereday, George Z. F. 'Higher Education in Comparative Perspective,' *Annals of the American Academy of Political and Social*

Science 404 (November 1972), 21–30.

101. Bertram, Vivian B. B. 'The Place of Universities in Modern Society,' *Comparative Education* 1 (March 1965), 45–62.

102. Blaug, Mark. 'The Productivity of Universities,' *Minerva* 6 (Spring 1968), 398–408.

103. Bowden, Lord. 'The Place of Universities in Modern Society,' *Comparative Education* 2 (March 1965).

103a. Burn, Barbara. 'Comparative Higher Education' in A. Knowles, ed., *International Encyclopedia of Higher Education*. San Francisco: Jossey-Bass, 1977, pp. 969–77.

104. ———. 'Comparisons of Four Foreign Universities' in James Perkins, ed., *The University as an Organization*. New York: McGraw-Hill, 1973, pp. 79–106.

105. Cerych, Ladislav, and D. Furth. 'The Search for a Global System: Unity and Disparity of Post-Secondary Education' in B. Holmes and D. Scanlon, eds., *Higher Education in a Changing World*. New York: Harcourt Brace Jovanovich, 1971, pp. 108–19.

106. Clark, Burton. 'Development of the Sociology of Higher Education,' *Sociology of Education* 46 (Winter 1973), 2–14.

107. ———. 'Suggested Future Approaches to Research on Higher Education' in *Higher Education: Crisis and Support*. New York: I.C.E.D., 1974, pp. 117–32.

108. Clark, Terry N. 'Institutionalization of Innovations in Higher Education: Four Models,' *Administrative Science Quarterly* 13 (June 1968), 1–25.

109. Connell, R. W. 'Anti-Pygmalion: Reflections on Some Experiments in Reforming Universities,' *International Social Science Journal* 26 (No. 3, 1974), 483–97.

109a. Corcoran, Mary. 'Access to Higher Education' in A. Knowles, ed., *International Encyclopedia of Higher Education*. San Francisco: Jossey-Bass, 1977, pp. 83–90.

110. Crossland, Fred E. 'The Equilibrist's Query: Equality, Equity, or Equilibrium? Thoughts on Politics of Access to Higher Education,' *Prospects* 6 (No. 4, 1976), 526–39.

110a. Domonkos, L. 'History of Higher Education' in A. Knowles, ed., *International Encyclopedia of Higher Education*. San Francisco: Jossey-Bass, 1977, pp. 2017–40.

111. Duff, James 'The Ecology of Higher Education,' *Minerva* 5 (Autumn 1966), 39–46.

112. Durkheim, Emile. 'The Role of the Universities in the Social Education of the Country,' *Minerva* 14 (Autumn 1976), 377–88.

113. Eraut, Michael. 'Promoting Innovation in Teaching and Learning: Problems, Processes, and Institutional Mechanisms,' *Higher Education* 4 (February 1975), 12–26.

114. Froese, Leonhard. 'University Reform: a Comparative Analysis of the American, Russian, and German Universities' in D. Holmes and D. Scanlon, eds., *Higher Education in a Changing World.* New York: Harcourt Brace Jovanovich, 1971, pp. 135–46.

115. Gillispie, Charles C. 'English Ideas of the University in the Nineteenth Century' in M. Clapp, ed., *The Modern University.* Ithaca, N.Y.: Cornell University Press, 1950, pp. 27–58.

115*a*. Glaser, William A. 'Migration of Talent' in A. Knowles, ed., *International Encyclopedia of Higher Education.* San Francisco: Jossey-Bass, 1977, pp. 2731–41.

116. Goldschmid, Barbara and Marcel. 'Individualizing Instruction in Higher Education: A Review,' *Higher Education* 3 (February 1974), 1–24.

117. Halsey, A. H. 'The Changing Functions of Universities in Advanced Industrial Societies,' *Harvard Educational Review* 30 (Spring 1960), 118–27.

118. Hecquet, I. 'Demographic Change as a Factor Influencing the Development of Higher Education' in B. Holmes and D. Scanlon, eds., *Higher Education in a Changing World.* New York: Harcourt Brace Jovanovich, 1971, pp. 149–60.

119. Hoenack, Stephen *et al.* 'University Planning, Decentralization, and Research Allocation,' *Socio Economic Planning Sciences* 8 (October 1974), 257–72.

120. Holmes, B. 'The Development of Higher Education: A Comparative Survey,' *Paedagogica Europaea* 7 (1972), 17–25.

121. 'The Implications of Mass Higher Education,' *Higher Education* 2 (May 1973), 133–274.

122. Jantsch, Erich. 'Inter-and Transdiciplinary University: A Systems Approach to Education and Innovation,' *Higher Education* 1 (February 1972), 7–38.

122*a*. Kaplowitz, Richard A. 'Recruitment, Appointment, Promotion and Termination of Academic Personnel' in A. Knowles, ed., *International Encyclopedia of Higher Education.* San Francisco: Jossey-Bass, 1977, pp. 3457–71.

122*b*. Knowles, Asa. 'Governance and Administration' in A. Knowles, ed., *International Encyclopedia of Higher Education.* San Francisco: Jossey-Bass, 1977, pp. 1880–1901.

123. Legg, Keith. 'Economic Student Group Populations in Universities,' *Higher Education* 2 (November 1973), 423–38.

124. Lockwood, Geoffrey. 'Planning a University', *Higher Education* 1 (November 1972), 409–34.

125. Lofthouse, Stephen. 'Thoughts on "Publish or Perish",' *Higher Education* 3 (February 1974), 59–80.

126. Montague, H. Patrick. 'The Historic Function of the

University' in B. Holmes and D. Scanlon, eds., *Higher Education in a Changing World*. New York: Harcourt Brace Jovanovich, 1971, pp. 15–26.

127. Perkins, James. 'Organization and Functions of the University,' *Journal of Higher Education* 43 (December 1972), 679–91.

127*a*. 'Planning, Development and Coordination' in A. Knowles, ed., *International Encyclopedia of Higher Education*. San Francisco: Jossey-Bass, 1977, pp. 3259–303.

128. Psacharopoulos, George. 'The Economic Returns to Higher Education in Twenty-five Countries,' *Higher Education* 1 (May 1972), 141–58.

128*a*. 'Research' in A. Knowles, ed., *International Encyclopedia of Higher Education*. San Francisco: Jossey-Bass, 1977, pp. 3585–635.

129. Reynolds, Philip A. 'The University in the 1980's: An Anachronism', *Higher Education* 6 (November 1977), 403–16.

130. Riesman, David. 'Notes on Educational Reform,' *Journal of General Education* 23 (No. 2 1971), 81–110.

131. Ringer, Fritz K. 'Problems in the History of Higher Education,' *Comparative Studies in Society and History* 19 (April 1977), 239–54.

132. Robbins, Lord. 'Of Academic Freedom,' *Universities Quarterly* 20 (September 1966), 420–35.

133. Rosselli, John. 'Studying Higher Education in Britain and America,' *Universities Quarterly* 17 (March 1963), 126–48.

133*a*. 'Science Policies' in A. Knowles, ed., *International Encyclopedia of Higher Education*. San Francisco: Jossey-Bass, 1977, pp. 3685–792.

134. Shils, Edward. 'The Academic Ethos under Strain,' *Minerva* 13 (Spring 1975), 1–37.

135. – – –. 'Change and Reform' in P. G. Altbach, ed., *University Reform*. Cambridge, Mass.: Schenkman, 1974, pp. 15–27.

136. – – –. 'Dreams of Plentitude, Nightmares of Scarcity' in S. M. Lipset and P. G. Altbach, eds., *Students in Revolt*. Boston, Mass.: Houghton Mifflin, 1969, pp. 1–34.

137. – – –. 'The Enemies of Academic Freedom,' *Minerva* 12 (October 1974), 405–15.

138. – – –. 'Sources of Change in the Character and Functions of Universities,' *Universities Quarterly* 28 (Summer 1974), 310–17.

139. Sibley, W. M. 'Planning for Universities: The Contemporary Predicament,' *International Journal of Institutional Management in Higher Education* 1 (October 1977), 85–96.

139*a*. Smyth, D. McCormack. 'Academic Decision Making' in A. Knowles, ed., *International Encyclopedia of Higher Education*. San

Francisco: Jossey-Bass, 1977, pp. 1856–76.

140. Springer, George. 'Universities in Flux,' *Comparative Education Review* 12 (February 1968), 28–38.

140*a*. Stewart, C. T. and C. C. Gannon, 'Trends in Higher Education' in A. Knowles, ed., *International Encyclopedia of Higher Education*. San Francisco: Jossey-Bass, 1977, pp. 4138–52.

141. Suchodolski, Bogdan. 'The Future of Higher Education,' *Higher Education* 3 (August 1974), 331–40.

142. Sutherland, Gordon. 'Is There an Optimum Size for a University?' *Minerva* 11 (January 1973), 53–78.

143. Touraine, Alain. 'Death or Change of the Universities?' *Prospects* 3 (Winter 1973), 469–81.

144. Trow, Martin. 'The Expansion and Transformation of Higher Education,' *International Review of Education* 18 (No. 1, 1972), 61–84.

145. – – – . 'The Idea of a New University,' *Universities Quarterly* 19 (March, 1955), 162–72.

146. – – – . 'The Implications of Low Growth Rates for Higher Education,' *Higher Education* 5 (November 1976), 377–96.

147. Van de Graaff, John. 'Evolution in Higher and Professional Education: Questions of Authority' in E. J. King, ed., *Reorganizing Education: Management and Participation for Change*. Beverly Hills, Calif.: Sage Publications, 1977, pp. 187–206.

148. Von Weizsacker, Carl C. 'Problems in the Planning of Higher Education,' *Higher Education* 1 (November 1972), 391–408.

148*a*. Wasser, Henry. 'Structural Response to Mass Higher Education: Some Consideration of the Quality-Equality Debate,' *Paedagogica Europaea* 12 (No. 1, 1977), 93–100.

149. Windham, Douglas. 'The Economics of Higher Education' in P. G. Altbach, ed., *Comparative Higher Education Abroad: Bibliography and Analysis*. New York: Praeger, 1976, pp. 183–221.

150. – – – . 'Social Benefits and the Subsidization of Higher Education,' *Higher Education* 5 (August 1976), 237–62.

THIRD WORLD

Books

151. Altbach, Philip G. *Higher Education in Developing Countries: A Select Bibliography*. Cambridge, Mass.: Harvard Center for International Affairs, 1970.

152. Altbach, Philip G. and David H. Kelly. *Higher Education in Developing Nations: A Select Bibliography, 1969–1974*. New York: Praeger, 1975.

153. Ashby, Eric. *Universities: British, Indian, African.* Cambridge, Mass.: Harvard University Press, 1966.

154. Coleman, James S., ed. *Education and Political Development.* Princeton, N.J.: Princeton University Press, 1965.

155. Emmerson, Donald, ed. *Students and Politics in Developing Nations.* New York: Praeger, 1968.

156. Myers, Robert G. *Education and Emigration: Study Abroad and the Migration of Human Resources.* New York: McKay, 1972.

157. Shah, A. B., ed. *Education, Scientific Policy, and Developing Countries.* Bombay: Manaktalas, 1967.

158. Spaulding, Seth and Michael J. Flack. *The World's Students in the United States: A Review and Evaluation of Research on Foreign Students.* New York: Praeger, 1976.

159. Thompson, Kenneth *et al. Higher Education and Social Change.* 2 vols. New York: Praeger, 1976.

160. Ward, F. Champion, ed. *Education and Development Reconsidered: The Bellagio Conference Papers.* New York: Praeger, 1974.

Articles
161. Altbach, Philip G. 'Education and Neocolonialism,' *Teachers College Record* 72 (May 1971), 543–58.

162. — — —. 'Servitude of the Mind?: Education, Dependency and Neocolonialism,' *Teachers College Record* 79 (December 1977), 187–204.

163. Ashby, Eric. 'Some Problems of Universities in New Countries of the British Commonwealth,' *Comparative Education* 2 (November 1965), 1–10.

164. Dedijer, Stevan. 'Underdeveloped Science in Underdeveloped Countries,' *Minerva* 2 (Autumn 1963), 61–81.

165. Harbison, Frederick. 'Problems of Higher Education in the Newly Developing Countries,' *Educational Record* 46 (Spring 1965), 132–42.

166. Lipset, Seymour Martin. 'University Students and Politics in Underdeveloped Countries,' *Minerva* 3 (Autumn 1964), 15–56.

167. Grubel, Herbert G. 'Reflections on the Present State of the Brain Drain and a Suggested Remedy,' *Minerva* 14 (Summer 1976), 209–24.

168. Morison, Robert G. 'The University and Technical Assistance,' *Daedalus* 91 (Spring 1962), 319–40.

169. Rogers, Daniel. 'Financing Higher Education in Less Developed Countries,' *Comparative Education Review* 15 (February 1971), 20–27.

170. Shils, Edward. 'The Implantation of Universities: Reflections

on a Theme of Ashby,' *Universities Quarterly* 22 (March 1968), 142–66.

171. Shils, Edward. 'Modernization and Higher Education' in Myron Weiner, ed., *Modernization*. New York: Basic Books, 1966, pp. 81–97.

172. Todaro, Michael P. *et al.* 'Education for National Development: The University' in F. C. Ward, ed., *Education and Development Reconsidered*. New York: Praeger, 1974, pp. 204–13.

173. 'Universities in Rapidly Developing Countries' in W. R. Niblett and R. F. Butts, eds., *Universities Facing the Future*. San Francisco: Jossey-Bass, 1972, pp. 61–180.

174. Ward, F. Champion. 'University Initiative in Response to Change' in W. R. Niblett, ed., *Higher Education: Demand and Response*. San Francisco: Jossey-Bass, 1970, pp. 159–71.

175. Wilson, James A. and Jerry Gaston. 'Reflux from the "Brain Drain",' *Minerva* 12 (October 1974), 459–68.

AFRICA

General

Books

176. Ashby, Eric. *African Universities and Western Tradition*. Cambridge, Mass.: Harvard University Press, 1964.

177. Barkan, Joel. *An African Dilemma; University Students, Politics, and Development in Ghana, Tanzania and Uganda*. Nairobi: Oxford University Press, 1975.

178. *The Financing of Higher Education in Africa*. Paris: UNESCO, 1962.

179. Hanna, W. J. and J. L. Hanna, eds. *University Students and African Politics*. New York: Africana, 1975.

180. *Higher Education in East Africa*. Entebbe: Government Printer, 1958.

181. Ike, Vincent C. *University Development in Africa*. Nairobi: Oxford University Press, 1976.

182. Welsh, D., ed. *The Role of Universities in Southern Africa*. Capetown: David Philip, 1976.

183. Yesufu, T. M., ed. *Creating the African University: Emerging Issues of the 1970's*. Ibadan: Oxford University Press, 1973.

Articles

184. Adams, Walter. 'Colonial University Education,' *Universities Quarterly* 4 (May 1950), 283–92.

185. Anderson, C. A. 'University Planning in the Underdeveloped Country: A Commentary on the University of East Africa Plan 1967–1970,' *Minerva* 7 (No. 1 and 2, 1968–9), 36–51.

186. Ashby, Eric and Mary Anderson. 'Autonomy and Academic Freedom in Britain and in English-speaking Countries of Tropical Africa,' *Minerva* 4 (Spring 1966), 317–64.

187. Ashby, Sir Eric. 'A Contribution to the Dialogue on African Universities,' *Universities Quarterly* 20 (December 1965), 70–89.

188. Carr-Saunders, A. M. 'Britain and Universities in Africa; Results of the Report of the Asquith Commission,' *Universities Quarterly* 19 (June 1965), 227–39.

189. Chaglla, W. K. 'The East African Academy: Academic Freedom in the Economic, Social, and Political Context of East Africa,' *Minerva* 6 (Spring 1968), 408–18.

190. Court, David. 'East African Higher Education from the Community Standpoint,' *Higher Education* 6 (February 1977), 45–66.

191. Crawford, Malcolm. 'On Academic Freedom in Africa,' *Minerva* 5 (Spring 1967), 376–80.

192. Crawford, M., A. A. Mazrui and Y. Tandon. 'Government and Universities in East Africa,' *Minerva* 5 (Spring, 1967), 376–86.

193. Foster, Philip. 'False and Real Problems of African Universities,' *Minerva* 13 (Autumn 1975), 466–78.

194. Godfrey, E. M. 'The Economics of an African University,' *Journal of Modern African Studies* 4 (December 1966), 435–55.

195. Hyslop, J. M. 'The University of East Africa,' *Minerva* (Spring 1964), 286–302.

196. Kilson, Martin. 'Trends in Higher Education' in Helen Kitchen, ed., *Africa and the United States: Images and Realities.* Boston, Mass.: U.S. National Commission for UNESCO, 1961, pp. 61–80.

197. Marvick, Dwaine. 'African University Students: Presumptive Elite' in James S. Coleman, ed., *Education and Political Development.* Princeton, N.J.: Princeton University Press, 1965, pp. 463–98.

198. Mazrui, Ali. 'The African University as a Multinational Corporation: Problems of Penetration and Dependency,' *Harvard Educational Review* 45 (May 1975), 191–210.

199. – – –. 'The English Language and Political Consciousness in British Colonial Africa,' *Journal of Modern African Studies* 4 (November 1966), 295–311.

200. Mazrui, Ali A. and Yash Tandon. 'The University of East Africa as a Political Institution,' *Minerva* 5 (Spring 1967), 381–6.

201. Mellanby, Kenneth. 'Establishing a New University in Africa,' *Minerva* 1 (Winter 1962), 149–58.

202. Moore, Clement and Arlie Hochschild. 'Student Unions in North African Politics,' *Daedalus* 97 (Winter 1968), 21–50.

203. Nichol, Davidson. 'Politics, Nationalism, and Universities in Africa,' *African Affairs* 62 (January 1963), 20–8.

204. Nichol, D. 'The Role of the Scholar Today in Developing Nations with Particular Reference to Africa,' *Présence Africaine* (No. 4, 1970), 3–15.

205. Ojiaku, Mazi Okoro. 'Two University Traditions in Africa: Contrast in Profile' in Ann Heiss *et al.*, *Participants and Patterns in Higher Education: Research and Reflections*. Berkeley, Calif.: Program in Higher Education, University of California, 1973, pp. 55–70.

206. Pedler, F. 'Universities and Polytechnics in Africa,' *Africa* 42 (October 1972), 264–74.

207. Richards, Audrey I. 'The Adaptation of Universities to the African Situation: Review Article,' *Minerva* 3 (Spring 1965), 336–42.

208. Rimmington, Gerald. 'The Development of Universities in Africa,' *Comparative Education* 1 (March 1965), 105–12.

209. Salifou, André. 'On Refusing the Balkanization of the African University,' *Prospects* 4 (Winter 1974), 471–9.

210. Sutton, F. X. 'African Universities and the Process of Change in Middle Africa' in S. Kertesz, ed., *The Task of Universities in a Changing World*. South Bend, Ind.: Notre Dame University Press, 1971, pp. 383–404.

Algeria

211. Ottaway, David B. 'Algeria' in D. Emmerson, ed., *Students and Politics in Developing Nations*. New York: Praeger, 1968, pp. 3–36.

Botswana

212. Ulin, Richard O. 'African Leadership: National Goals and the Values of Botswana University Students,' *Comparative Education* 12 (June 1976), 145–51.

Egypt

Books
213. Dodge, Bayard. *Al-Azhar; A Millennium of Muslim Learning*. Washington, D.C.: Middle East Institute, 1961.

Articles
214. Crecelius, Daniel. 'Al-Azhar in the Revolution,' *Middle East Journal* 20 (Winter 1965), 31–49.

215. Kerr, Malcolm. 'Egypt' in J. S. Coleman, ed., *Education and Political Development*. Princeton, N.J.: Princeton University Press, 1965, pp. 169–94.

216. Kraemer, J. 'Tradition and Reform at Al-Azhar University', *Middle Eastern Affairs* 7 (March 1956), 89–94.

216a. Najjar, F. M. 'State and University in Egypt during the Period of Socialist Transformation, 1961–1967,' *Review of Politics* 38 (January 1976), 57–87.

217. Sarour, A. H. 'The University of Cairo' in T. M. Yesufu, ed., *Creating the African University*. Ibadan: Oxford University Press, 1973, pp. 218–25.

218. Von Grunebaum, G. E. 'The Political Role of the University in the Near East as Illustrated by Egypt' in G. E. Von Grunebaum, ed., *Modern Islam*. Berkeley, Calif.: University of California Press, 1962, pp. 258–75.

Ethiopia

219. Gillett, Margaret. 'Western Academic Role Concepts in an Ethiopian University,' *Comparative Education Review* 7 (October 1963), 149–62.

Ghana

220. Austin, Dennis. 'Et in Arcadia Ego: Politics and Learning in Ghana,' *Minerva* 13 (Summer 1975), 236–69.

221. Curle, Adam. 'Nationalism and Higher Education in Ghana,' *Universities Quarterly* 16 (June 1962), 229–42.

222. Dickson, K. B. 'The University of Ghana: Aspects of the Idea of an African University' in T. M. Yesufu, ed., *Creating the African University*. Ibadan: Oxford University Press, 1973, pp. 102–15.

223. Finlay, David J. 'Students and Politics in Ghana,' *Daedalus* 97 (Winter 1968), 51–69.

224. Finlay, David J., Roberta E. Koplin and Charles A. Ballard, Jr. 'Ghana' in D. Emmerson, ed., *Students and Politics in Developing Nations*. New York: Praeger, 1968, pp. 64–102.

226. Williams, Peter. 'Lending for Learning: An Experiment in Ghana,' *Minerva* 12 (July 1974), 325–45.

Ivory Coast

227. Zolberg, Aristide. 'Political Generations in Conflict: The

Ivory Coast Case' in W. J. Hanna and J. L. Hanna, eds., *University Students and African Politics*. New York: Africana, 1975, pp. 103–34.

Kenya

228. Anderson, C. A. 'University Planning in an Underdeveloped Country: A Commentary on the University of East Africa Plan, 1967–70.' *Minerva* 7 (Autumn-Winter 1968–9), 36–51.
229. McKown, Roberta E. 'Kenya University Students and Politics' in W. J. Hanna and J. L. Hanna, eds., *University Students and African Politics*. New York: Africana, 1975, pp. 215–57.

Malawi

230. Michael, Ian and Felix Mnthali. 'Political Independence and Higher Education in Malawi' in B. Holmes and D. Scanlon, eds., *Higher Education in a Changing World*. New York: Harcourt Brace Jovanovich, 1971, pp. 348–56.

Nigeria

Books
233. Fafunwa, A. B. *The Growth and Development of Nigerian Universities*. Washington, D.C.: Overseas Liaison Committee, American Council on Education, 1974.
234. – – –. *A History of Nigerian Higher Education*. Lagos: Macmillan, 1971.
235. Hanson, John W. *Education, Nsukka: A Study in Institution Building among the Modern Ibo*. East Lansing, Mich.: Michigan State University, 1968.
236. Mellanby, Kenneth. *The Birth of Nigeria's University*. London: Methuen, 1958.
237. Nigeria, Federal Ministry of Education. *University Development in Nigeria: Report of National Universities Commission, 1963*. Apapa: Nigerian National Press, 1963.
238. Okafor, Nduka. *The Development of Universities in Nigeria*. London: Longman, 1971.
239. Olubrummo, Adegoke. *The Emergent University; with Special Reference to Nigeria*. London: Longman, 1960.

240. Van den Berghe, Pierre L. *Power and Privilege at an African University*. London: Routledge and Kegan Paul, 1973.

Articles

241. Agbowuro, Joseph. 'Nigerianization and the Nigerian Universities,' *Comparative Education* 12 (October 1976), 243–54.

242. Fafunwa, A. Babs. 'The University of Ife' in T. M. Yesufu, ed., *Creating the African University*. Ibadan: Oxford University Press, 1973, pp. 116–30.

243. – – –. 'The University of Nigeria' in *Commonwealth Universities Yearbook, 1973*. London: Association of Commonwealth Universities, 1973, pp. 1614–22.

244. Fafunwa, A. B. and J. Hanson. 'The Post-Independence Nigerian Universities' in P. G. Altbach, ed., *University Reform*. Cambridge, Mass.: Schenkman, 1974, pp. 95–115.

245. Hanson, J. W. 'Academic Freedom and Responsibility' in O. Ikejiani, ed., *Education in Nigeria*. New York: Praeger, 1965, pp. 209–22.

246. Ikejiani, O. and J. O. Anowi. 'Nigerian Universities' in O. Ikejiani, ed., *Nigerian Education*. Ikeja: Longman, 1964, pp. 128–82.

247. Koehl, Robert. 'The Uses of the University: Past and Present in Nigerian Educational Culture, Parts 1 and 2,' *Comparative Education Review* 15 (June and October 1971), 116–32 and 367–77.

248. Okafor, Nduka. 'The University of Nigeria, Nsukka' in T. M. Yesufu, ed., *Creating the African University*. Ibadan: Oxford University Press, 1973, pp. 185–95.

249. 'University Development in Nigeria: Report of the National Universities Commission,' *Minerva* 3 (Winter 1965), 210–28.

250. 'The University of Lagos Crisis, Nigeria,' *Minerva* 3 (Summer 1965), 592–609.

251. Yesufu, T. M. 'The University of Lagos: Profile of an African Urban University' in T. M. Yesufu, ed., *Creating the African University*. Ibadan: Oxford University Press, 1973, pp. 251–71.

Rhodesia (Zimbabwe)

252. 'Academic Freedom at University College, Rhodesia,' *Minerva* 5 (Autumn 1966), 123–47.

253. Cefkin, J. Leo. 'Rhodesian University Students in National Politics' in W. J. Hanna and J. L. Hanna, eds., *University Students and African Politics*. New York: Africana, 1975, pp. 135–66.

South Africa

254. 'Academic Freedom in South Africa: The Open Universities in South Africa and Academic Freedom, 1957–1974,' *Minerva* 13 (Autumn 1975), 428–65.

255. Legassick, Martin and John Shindler. 'South Africa' in D. Emmerson, ed., *Students and Politics in Developing Nations*. New York: Praeger, 1968, pp. 103–45.

Sudan

256. Sanyal, B. and J. Versluis. *Higher Education, Human Capital, and Labor Market Segmentation in the Sudan*. Paris: International Institute for Educational Planning, 1976.

257. Sanyal, Bikas C. and El Sammani A. Yacoub. *Higher Education and Employment in the Sudan*. Paris: International Institute for Educational Planning, 1975.

Tanzania

258. 'College Reform, Excerpts from Report and Recommendations of the Academic Board Committee' in I. Resnick, ed., *Tanzania: Revolution by Education*. Arusha: Longman, 1967, pp. 146–52.

259. Court, David. 'The Experience of Higher Education in East Africa: The University of Dar Es Salaam as a New Model?' *Comparative Education* 11 (October 1975), pp. 193–218.

260. 'Draft Recommendations of the Conference on the Role of the University College, Dar-es-Salaam, in a Socialist Tanzania,' *Minerva* 5 (Summer 1967), 558–70.

261. Nhenoli, A. M. 'The University of Dar-es-Salaam: Emerging Issues of the 1970's' in T. M. Yesufu, ed., *Creating the African University*. Ibadan: Oxford University Press, 1973, pp. 174–84.

262. Schutte, Donald G. W. 'The University of Dar-es-Salaam; A Socialist Enterprise' in W. R. Niblett and R. F. Butts, eds. *Universities Facing the Future*. San Francisco: Jossey-Bass, 1972, pp. 75–96.

Uganda

Books
263. Goldthorpe, J. E. *An African Elite: Makerere College Students 1922–1960*. Nairobi: Oxford University Press, 1966.

Articles

264. Atwoki, Kagenda. 'Makerere University: The Crisis of Identity' in T. M. Yesufu, ed., *Creating the African University*. Ibadan: Oxford University Press, 1973, pp. 91–101.

264a. Langlands, Bryan. 'Students and Politics in Uganda,' *African Affairs* 76 (January 1977), 3–20.

265. Larby, Norman. 'A Case Study in East African Higher Education: Makerere' in G. Bereday and J. Lauwerys, eds., *Yearbook of Education, 1959*. London: Evans, 1959, pp. 432–42.

266. Pratt, R. C. 'University and State in Independent Tropical Africa,' *Universities Quarterly* 21 (December 1966), 91–100.

267. Prewitt, Kenneth. 'University Students in Uganda: Political Consequences of Selection Patterns' in W. J. Hanna and J. L. Hanna, eds., *University Students and African Politics*. New York: Africana, 1975, pp. 167–86.

Zaire

Books

268. Rideout, William M., Jr. *The Reorganization of Higher Education in Zaire*. Washington, D.C.: Overseas Liaison Committee of the American Council on Education, 1974.

Articles

269. Ngobassu, Akwesi. 'The National University of Zaire (UNAZA)' in T. M. Yesufu, ed., *Creating the African University*. Ibadan: Oxford University Press, 1973, pp. 164–73.

270. Willame, Jean-Claude. 'The Congo' in D. Emmerson, ed., *Students and Politics in Developing Nations*. New York: Praeger, 1968, pp. 37–63.

Zambia

Books

271. Sanyal, Bikas *et al. Higher Education and the Labor Market in Zambia*. Paris: Unesco Press, 1976.

Articles

272. 'Report on the Development of a University in Northern Rhodesia,' *Minerva* 3 (Winter 1965), 245–60.

273. Tembo, Lyson P. 'The University of Zambia' in T. M. Yesufu, ed., *Creating the African University*. Ibadan: Oxford University Press, 1973, pp. 226–43.

ASIA

General

Books

274. Fischer, Joseph. *Universities in Southeast Asia.* Columbus, Ohio: Ohio State University Press, 1964.

275. Hayden, Howard, ed. *Higher Education and Development in Southeast Asia.* 4 vols. Paris: UNESCO, 1957.

276. International Association of Universities. *The Social Responsibility of Universities in Asian Countries.* Paris: I.A.U., 1973.

278. Muhammadi, ed. *Development Strategies and Manpower Needs: The Response of Southeast Asian Universities.* Singapore: Regional Institute for Higher Education and Development, 1976.

279. Noss, Richard. *Higher Education and Development in Southeast Asia: Language Policy.* Paris: UNESCO, 1967.

280. Silcock, T. H. *Southeast Asian University: A Comparative Account of Some Development Problems.* Durham, N.C.: Duke University Press, 1964.

281. Tapingkae, Amnuay. *The Growth of Southeast Asian Universities: Expansion versus Consolidation.* Singapore: Regional Institute for Higher Education and Development, 1974.

282. — — —, ed. *Higher Education and Economic Growth in Southeast Asia.* Singapore: Regional Institute for Higher Education and Development, 1976.

283. Yip, Y. H., ed., *Development of Higher Education in Southeast Asia: Problems and Issues.* Singapore: Regional Institute for Higher Education and Development, 1978.

284. — — —. *Development Planning in Southeast Asia: Role of the University.* Singapore: Regional Institute for Higher Education and Development, 1973.

285. — — —. *Role of Universities in National Development Planning in Southeast Asia.* Singapore: Regional Institute for Higher Education and Development, 1971.

Articles

286. Altbach, Philip G. 'Student Movements in Historical Perspective: The Asian Case,' *Youth and Society* 1 (March 1970), 333–57.

287. Fischer, Joseph. 'Universities and the Political Process in Southeast Asia,' *Pacific Affairs* 36 (Spring 1963), 3–15.

288. — — —. 'The University Student in South and South-East Asia,' *Minerva* 2 (Autumn 1963), 39–53.

289. Lyman, Princeton M. 'Students and Politics in Indonesia and Korea,' *Pacific Affairs* 38 (Fall-Winter 1965–6), 582–93.

290. Myint, Hla. 'The Universities of Southeast Asia and Economic Development,' *Pacific Affairs* 35 (Summer 1962), 116–27.

291. Pieris, Ralph. 'The Implantation of Sociology in Asia,' *International Social Science Journal* 21 (No. 3, 1969), 433–44.

292. Silcock, T. H. 'The Development of Universities in South-East Asia to 1960,' *Minerva* 2 (Winter 1964), 169–96.

293. Silverstein, Josef. 'Burmese and Malaysian Student Politics: A Preliminary Comparative Inquiry,' *Journal of Southeast Asian Studies* 1 (March 1970), 3–22.

293a. — — —. 'Students in Southeast Asian Politics,' *Pacific Affairs* 49 (Summer 1976), 189–212.

Bangladesh

294. Ritzen, Josef M. and Judith Balderston. *Methodology for Planning Technical Education: With a Case Study of Polytechnics in Bangladesh.* New York: Praeger Special Studies, 1975.

Burma

295. Silverstein, Josef and Julian Wohl. 'University Students and Politics in Burma,' *Pacific Affairs* 37 (Spring 1964), 50–65.

296. Wohl, Julian and Josef Silverstein. 'The Burmese University Student: An Approach to Personality and Subculture,' *Public Opinion Quarterly* 30 (Summer 1966), 237–48.

China

Books

297. Chen, Theodore. *The Maoist Educational Revolution.* New York: Praeger, 1974.

298. — — —. *The Popularization of Higher Education in Communist China.* Washington, D.C.: U.S. Office of Education, 1959.

299. Chow, Tse-Tung. *The May Fourth Movement.* Cambridge, Mass.: Harvard University Press, 1960.

300. Israel, John. *Student Nationalism in China: 1927–1937.* Stanford, Calif.: Stanford University Press, 1966.

301. Lutz, Jessie G. *China and the Christian Colleges, 1850–1950.* Ithaca, N.Y.: Cornell University Press, 1971.

303. West, Philip. *Yenching University and Sino-Western Relations, 1916–1952.* Cambridge, Mass.: Harvard University Press, 1976.

Articles

304. Bastid, Marianne. 'Economic Necessity and Political Ideals in Educational Reform during the Cultural Revolution,' *China Quarterly* No. 42 (April–June 1970), 16–45.

305. Boyer, Ernest. 'China: The People's Higher Education System' in M. Kaplan, ed., *The Monday Morning Imagination*. New York: Aspen Institute for Humanistic Studies, 1977, pp. 79–88.

306. Chambers, D. I. 'The 1975–1976 Debate over Higher Education in the People's Republic of China,' *Comparative Education* 13 (March 1977), 3–14.

307. 'The Cultural Revolution in China,' *Minerva* 5 (Autumn 1966), 112–16.

308. Goldman, René. 'Peking University Today,' *China Quarterly* No. 7 (July-September 1961), 101–11.

309. – – –. 'The Rectification Campaign at Peking University: May–June, 1957,' *China Quarterly* No. 12 (October–December 1962), 138–53.

310. Hsu, Immanuel. 'The Impact of Industrialization on Higher Education in Communist China' in F. Harbison and C. Myers, ed., *Manpower and Education*, New York: McGraw-Hill, 1965, pp. 202–31.

311. Hsu, Immanuel. 'The Reorganization of Higher Education in Communist China, 1949–1961,' *China Quarterly* No. 19 (July–September 1964), 128–60.

312. Hu, C. T. 'The Chinese Peoples' University: Bastion of Marxism-Leninism' in W. R. Niblett and R. F. Butts, eds., *Universities Facing the Future*. San Francisco: Jossey-Bass, 1972, pp. 63–74.

313. – – –. 'Higher Education in Mainland China,' *Comparative Education Review* 4 (February 1961), 159–68.

314. Hunt, R. C. 'Change in Higher Education in the People's Republic of China,' *Higher Education* 4 (February 1975), 45–60.

315. Israel, John. 'The Red Guards in Historical Perspective,' *China Quarterly* No. 30 (April–June 1967), 1–32.

316. – – –. 'Reflections on the Modern Chinese Student Movement,' *Daedalus* 97 (Winter 1968), 229–53.

317. Kun, Joseph C. 'Higher Education: Some Problems of Selection and Enrollment,' *China Quarterly* No. 8 (1961), 135–48.

318. Larkin, Bruce D. 'China' in D. Emmerson, ed., *Students and Politics in Developing Nations*. New York: Praeger, 1968, pp. 146–79.

319. Lubot, Eugene. 'Peking University Fifty-five Years Ago: Perspectives on Higher Education in China Today,' *Comparative Education Review* 17 (February 1973), 44–57.

320. Lutz, J. G. 'Chinese Student Movement of 1945–1949,'

Journal of Asian Studies 81 (November 1971), 89–110.

321. Munro, Julie W. 'A Major Turnaround in China,' *Chronicle of Higher Education* 15 (7 November 1977), 1, 10.

322. Nee, Victor. 'The Cultural Revolution at Peking University,' *Monthly Review* 21 (July–August 1969), 11–91.

323. Seybolt, Peter. 'Higher Education in China,' *Higher Education* 3 (August 1974), 265–84.

324. Wang, Chun. 'Current Trends in the Reform of Higher Education in Communist China,' *Chinese Education* 2 (Winter 1969–70), 27–52.

325. Young, L. C. 'Mass Sociology: The Chinese Style,' *American Sociologist* 9 (August 1974), 117–24.

Hong Kong

326. 'Report of the Fulton Commission, 1963: Commission to Advise on the Creation of a Federal-type Chinese University in Hong Kong,' *Minerva* 1 (Summer 1963), 493–507.

India

Books
327. Altbach, Philip G. *Student Politics in Bombay.* Bombay and New York: Asia Publishing House, 1968.

328. Altbach, Philip G., ed. *Turmoil and Transition: Higher Education and Student Politics in India.* New York: Basic Books, 1970.

329. Altbach, Philip G. *The University in Transition: An Indian Case Study.* Cambridge, Mass.: Schenkman, 1972.

330. Azad, J. L. *Financing of Higher Education in India.* New Delhi: Sterling, 1975.

331. Basu, Aparna. *The Growth of Education and Political Development in India, 1898–1920.* New Delhi: Oxford University Press, 1974.

332. Blaug, M., P. R. G. Layard and M. Woodhall. *The Causes of Graduate Unemployment in India.* London: Oxford University Press, 1969.

333. Di Bona, Joseph. *Change and Conflict in the Indian University.* Bombay: Lalvani, 1972.

334. Dongerkery, S. R. *University Autonomy in India.* Bombay: Lalvani, 1967.

336. Gaudino, Robert L. *The Indian University.* Bombay: Popular Prakashan, 1965.

337. Kaul, J. N. *Higher Education in India: Two Decades of Planned Drift.* Simla: Indian Institute of Advanced Study, 1974.

338. -— —, ed. *Higher Education, Social Change and National Development.* Simla: Indian Institute of Advanced Study, 1975.

339. Malik, S. C., ed. *Management and Organization of Indian Universities.* Simla: Indian Institute of Advanced Study, 1971.

340. McCully, Bruce T. *English Education and the Origins of Indian Nationalism.* New York: Columbia University Press, 1940.

342. Ministry of Education, Government of India. *Report of the Education Commission, 1964–66: Education and National Development.* New Delhi: Ministry of Education, 1966.

343. Ross, Aileen. *Student Unrest in India.* Montreal: Queens-McGill University Press, 1970.

344. Rudolph, Susanne and Lloyd Rudolph, eds. *Education and Politics in India: Studies in Organization, Society, Policy.* Cambridge, Mass.: Harvard University Press, 1972.

345. Sharma, G. D. *Enrollment in Higher Education: A Trend Analysis.* New Delhi: Association of Indian Universities, 1977.

346. Singh, Amrik and Philip G. Altbach, eds. *The Higher Learning in India.* Delhi: Vikas, 1974.

Articles

347. Ahmad, Karuna. 'Women's Higher Education: Recruitment and Relevance' in A. Singh and P. G. Altbach, eds., *The Higher Learning in India.* Delhi: Vikas, 1974, pp. 180–201.

348. Altbach, Philip G. 'Bibliography on Higher Education in India,' *New Frontiers in Education* 4 (October 1974), 85–106 and 5 (January 1975), 75–101.

349. — — —. 'Bombay Colleges,' *Minerva* 8 (October 1970), 520–41.

350. — — —. 'Higher Education in India' in B. Burn *et al., Higher Education in Nine Countries.* New York: McGraw-Hill, 1971, pp. 317–44.

351. — — —. 'Problems of University Reform in India,' *Comparative Education Review* 16 (June 1972), 251–66.

352. — — —. 'In Search of Saraswati: The Ambivalence of the Indian Academic,' *Higher Education* 6 (May 1977), 255–75.

353. Azad, J. L. 'Financing Institutions of Higher Education in India,' *Higher Education* 5 (February 1975), 1–8.

354. Chitnis, Suma. 'Teachers in Higher Education' in A. Singh and P. G. Altbach, eds., *The Higher Learning in India.* Delhi: Vikas, 1974, pp. 237–50.

355. Eisemon, Thomas. 'Institutional Correlates of Faculty

Outlooks and Professional Behaviours: A Study of Indian Engineering Faculty,' *Higher Education* 3 (November 1974), 419–38.

356. Elliott, Carolyn. 'The Problem of Autonomy: The Osmania University Case' in S. Rudolph and L. Rudolph, eds., *Education and Politics in India.* Cambridge, Mass.: Harvard University Press, 1972, pp. 273–312.

357. 'The English-Hindu Controversy,' *Minerva* 3 (Summer 1965), 560–91.

358. 'English, Hindi, and the Medium of Instruction,' *Minerva* 6 (Autumn 1967), 123–30.

359. 'English, Hindi, and the Medium of Instruction, II,' *Minerva* 6 (Winter 1968), 287–305.

360. 'Further Steps towards the Displacement of English,' *Minerva* 7 (Autumn-Winter 1968–9), 178–234.

361. Gilbert, Irene. 'The Indian Academic Profession: The Origins of a Tradition of Subordination,' *Minerva* 10 (July 1972), 384–411.

362. Goel, B. S. 'Changing Functional Character of the Indian University, 1905–1929,' *Paedagogica Historica* 14 (No. 1, 1974), 34–63.

363. Gore, M. S., I. P. Desai and Suma Chitnis. 'College Teachers' in M. S. Gore, I. P. Desai and Suma Chitnis, *Field Studies in the Sociology of Education.* New Delhi: National Council of Educational Research and Training, 1970, pp. 272–436.

364. ———. 'Students' in M. S. Gore, I. P. Desai and Suma Chitnis, *Field Studies in the Sociology of Education.* New Delhi: National Council of Educational Research and Training, 1970, pp. 56–178.

365. Ilchman, Warren and T. N. Dhar. 'Student Discontent and Educated Unemployment,' *Economic and Political Weekly* 5 (July 1970), 1259–66.

366. 'Indian University Reform,' *Minerva* 5 (Autumn 1966), 47–81.

367. 'Indian University Reform, II,' *Minerva* 5 (Winter 1967), 242–64.

368. 'Indian University Reform, III,' *Minerva* 5 (Spring 1967), 391–412.

369. Jayaraman, T. R. 'Higher Education and State Government' in A. Singh and P. G. Altbach, eds., *The Higher Learning In India.* Delhi: Vikas, 1974, pp. 38–47.

370. Jones, Dawn and Rodney Jones. 'The Scholars' Rebellion: Educational Interests and Agitational Politics in Gujarat,' *Journal of Asian Studies* 36 (May 1977), 457–76.

371. Kahane, Reuven. 'Education towards Mediatory Roles: An Interpretation of the Higher Education Policy in India in the 20th Century,' *Development and Change* 7 (July 1977), 291–309.

372. Karve, D. D. 'The Universities and the Public in India,' *Minerva* 1 (Spring 1963), 263–84.

373. Mathai, Samuel. 'The University Grants Commission' in A. Singh and P. G. Altbach, eds., *The Higher Learning in India*. Delhi: Vikas, 1974, pp. 25–37.

374. 'A Miscellany of Tribulations in India,' *Minerva* 7 (Autumn-Winter 1968–9), 256–7.

375. 'Perpetual Commotion in India,' *Minerva* 7 (Spring 1969), 545–60.

376. Rahman, A. 'Universities and Scientific Research' in A. Singh and P. G. Altbach, eds., *The Higher Learning in India*. Delhi: Vikas, 1974, pp. 355–72.

377. 'Rampant Disorder Continues,' *Minerva* 6 (Autumn 1967), 131–40.

378. 'Rampant Disorder in Indian Universities,' *Minerva* 5 (Winter 1967), 284–300.

379. Reddy, A. K. N. 'The Brain Drain' in A. Singh and P. G. Altbach, eds., *The Higher Learning in India*. Delhi: Vikas, 1974, pp. 373–94.

380. Ross, Aileen. 'The Silent Sufferers: The Lecturer's Role in Student Unrest in India,' in H. S. Becker *et al.*, *Institutions and the Person*. Chicago: Aldine, 1968, pp. 89–100.

381. Rudolph, S. and L. Rudolph. 'Parochialism and Cosmopolitanism in University Government: The Environment of Baroda University' in S. Rudolph and L. Rudolph, eds., *Education and Politics in India*. Cambridge, Mass.: Harvard University Press, 1972, pp. 207–72.

382. Rudolph, Lloyd and Susanne Rudolph. '"Standards" in Democratized Higher Education: An Analysis of the Indian Experience,' *Economic and Political Weekly* 5 (January 1970), 209–18.

383. Shils, Edward. 'The Academic Profession in India,' *Minerva* 7 (Spring 1969), 345–72.

384. Singh, Amar Kumar, 'The Impact of Foreign Study: The Indian Experience,' *Minerva* 1 (Autumn 1962), 43–53.

385. Singh, Amrik. 'The Education Commission and After,' *Asian Survey* 9 (October 1969), 734–41.

386. — — —. 'Restructuring Our Universities,' *Economic and Political Weekly* 10 (29 November 1975), 1847–53.

387. — — —. 'Universities and the Government' in A. B. Shah, ed., *Higher Education in India*. Bombay: Lalvani, 1968, pp. 66–75.

388. Verma, Manindra K. 'English in Indian Education' in A. Singh and P. G. Altbach, eds., *The Higher Learning in India*. Delhi: Vikas, 1974, pp. 251–77.

389. Wood, Glynn. 'National Planning and Public Demand in Indian Higher Education: The Case of Mysore,' *Minerva* 10 (January 1972), 83–106.

390. — — —. 'Planning University Reform: An Indian Case Study,' *Comparative Education Review* 16 (June 1972), 267–80.

391. — — —. 'The University of Mysore: A Case Study in Decentralization,' *Economic and Political Weekly* 6 (12 June 1971), 1177–82.

Indonesia

Books
392. Douglas, Stephan A. *Political Socialization and Student Activism in Indonesia.* Urbana, Ill.: University of Illinois Press, 1970.

393. Thomas, R. Murray. *A Chronicle of Indonesian Higher Education.* Singapore: Chopmen Enterprises, 1973.

Articles
394. Bachtiar, Harsja W. 'Indonesia' in D. Emmerson, ed., *Students and Politics in Developing Nations.* New York: Praeger, 1968, pp. 180–214.

395. 'Continuing Student Agitation in Indonesia,' *Minerva* 5 (Autumn 1966), 116–22.

396. Geertz, Clifford. 'Social Science Policy in a New State: A Programme for the Stimulation of the Social Sciences in Indonesia,' *Minerva* 12 (July 1974), 365–81.

397. 'The Indonesian University Situation,' *Minerva* 4 (Spring 1966), 433–41.

399. Smith, Theodore M. and Harold F. Carpenter. 'Indonesian University Students and Their Career Aspirations,' *Asian Survey* 14 (September 1974), 807–26.

Iran

Books
400. Atanassian, L. S. *The Reform of Higher Education, Iran.* Paris: UNESCO, 1969.

Articles
401. Moghaddas, Ali Pour. 'Higher Education and Development in Iran,' *Higher Education* 4 (April 1975), 369–77.

Iraq

402. Al-Qazzaz, Ayad. 'Sociology in Underdeveloped Countries: A Case Study of Iraq,' *Sociological Review* 20 (February 1972), 93–103.

Israel

403. 'Israel Students' Strike,' *Minerva* 5 (Spring 1967), 439–45.
404. Rabinowitz, Dorothy. 'Israeli Universities in a Time of Siege,' *Change* 4 (February 1972), 42–7.
405. Shapira, Rina and Yeal Enoch. 'Ivory Tower or Social Involvement: University Professors in Israel,' *Universities Quarterly* 28 (Autumn 1974), 437–49.

Japan

Books
406. Blewett, John, ed. *Higher Education in Postwar Japan.* Tokyo: Sophia University, 1965.
407. Dowsey, Stewart, ed. *Zengakuren: Japan's Revolutionary Students.* Berkeley, Calif.: Ishii Press, 1970.
408. Kokusai Bunka Shinkokai. *Higher Education and the Student Problem in Japan.* Tokyo: Kokusai Bunka Shinkokai, 1972.
409. Krauss, Ellis S. *Japanese Radicals Revisited: Student Protest in Postwar Japan.* Berkeley, Calif.: University of California Press, 1974.
410. Massey, Joseph. *Youth and Politics in Japan.* Lexington, Mass.: Heath-Lexington, 1976.
411. Nagai, Michio. *Higher Education in Japan: Its Take-off and Crash.* Tokyo: University of Tokyo Press, 1971.
412. Passin, Herbert. *Society and Education in Japan.* New York: Bureau of Publications, Teachers College, 1965.
413. Teichler, Ulrich. *Das Dilemma der Modern Bildungsgesellschaft: Japans Hochschulen unter den Zwangen der Statuszuteilung.* Stuttgart: Ernst Klett, 1975.
414. − − −. *Geschichte und Struktur des Japanischen Hochschulwesens.* Stuttgart: Ernst Klett, 1975.
415. Teichler, Ulrich and Friedrich Voss. *Bibliography on Japanese Education.* Munich: Verlag Dokumentation, 1974.

Articles
416. Altbach, Philip G. 'Japanese Students and Japanese Politics,' *Comparative Education Review* 7 (October 1963), 181–8.
417. Burn, Barbara. *Higher Education in Nine Countries.* New York: McGraw-Hill, 1971, pp. 227–76.
418. Cummings, William K. 'The Conservatives Reform Higher Education,' *Japan Interpreter* 8 (Winter 1974), 421–31.
419. − − −. 'The Japanese Private University,' *Minerva* 11 (July 1973), 348–71.

420. Cummings, William K. 'Understanding Behavior in Japan's Academic Marketplace,' *Journal of Asian Studies* 34 (February 1975), 313–40.

421. Cummings, William K. and Ikuo Amano. 'The Changing Role of the Japanese Professor,' *Higher Education* 6 (May 1977), 209–34.

422. — — —. 'Japanese Higher Education' in P. G. Altbach, ed., *Comparative Higher Education Abroad: Bibliography and Analysis.* New York: Praeger, 1976, pp. 222–62.

423. Eto, Jun. 'The University: Myths and Possibilities,' *Journal of Social and Political Ideas in Japan* 5 (December 1967), 179–94.

424. Fuse, Toyomasa. 'Student Radicalism in Japan: A Cultural Revolution?' *Comparative Education Review* 13 (October 1969), 325–42.

425. Halliday, Jon. 'Education and the Student Movement' in J. Halliday, *A Political History of Japanese Capitalism.* New York: Pantheon, 1975, pp. 41–58.

426. Kida, Hiroshi. 'Higher Education in Japan,' *Higher Education* 4 (No. 3, 1975), 261–72.

427. Kitamura, K. and W. K. Cummings. 'The "Big Bang" Theory and Japanese University Reform,' *Comparative Education Review* 16 (June 1972), 303–24.

428. Kobayashi, Tetsuya. 'Changing Policies in Higher Education: The Japanese Case' in B. Holmes and D. Scanlon, eds., *Higher Education in a Changing World.* New York: Harcourt Brace Jovanovich, 1971, pp. 368–75.

429. Nakayama, Shigeru. 'The Role Played by Universities in Scientific and Technological Development in Japan,' *Journal of World History* 9 (No. 2, 1965), 340–62.

430. Orihara, H. 'Test Hell and Alienation: A Study of Tokyo University Freshmen,' *Journal of Social and Political Ideas in Japan* 5 (No. 2–3, 1967), 225–50.

431. Pempel, T. J. 'The Politics of Enrollment Expansion in Japanese Universities,' *Journal of Asian Studies* 33 (November 1973), 67–86.

432. 'The Reform of Japanese Higher Education: Report of the Central Council for Education in Japan,' *Minerva* 1 (July 1963), 387–414.

433. Shimbori, Michiya. 'The Academic Marketplace in Japan,' *The Developing Economies* 7 (December 1969), 617–39.

434. — — —. 'Comparative Study of Career Patterns of College Professors,' *International Review of Education* 10 (No. 3, 1964), 284–96.

435. — — —. 'Comparison between Pre- and Post-War Student

Movements in Japan,' *Sociology of Education* 37 (Fall 1963), 59–70.

436. Shimbori, Michiya. 'Nepotism versus Meritocracy: The Institutional Framework for Inbreeding in the Academic Marketplace in Japan,' *Indian Sociological Bulletin* 3 (January 1966), 122–35.

437. — — —. 'Sociology of a Student Movement — A Japanese Case Study,' *Daedalus* 97 (Winter 1968), 204–28.

438. — — —. 'Zengakuren: A Japanese Case Study of a Student Political Movement,' *Sociology of Education* 37 (Spring 1964), 229–53.

439. Tsurumi, Kazuko. 'The Japanese Student Movement: Group Portraits,' *Japan Quarterly* 16 (January–March 1969), 25–44.

440. — — —. 'Some Comments on the Japanese Student Movement in the 1960s,' *Journal of Contemporary History* 5 (No. 1, 1970), 104–12.

441. 'University Reform in Japan,' *Minerva* 8 (October 1970), 581–93.

442. 'University and Society,' *Journal of Social and Political Ideas in Japan* 5 (December 1967), 117–345.

Korea

Books
443. Adams, Don. *Higher Education Reforms in the Republic of Korea*. Washington, D.C.: U.S. Department of Health, Education and Welfare, Office of Education, 1965.

Articles
444. Douglas, William A. 'Korean Students and Politics,' *Asian Survey* 3 (December 1963), 584–95.

Lebanon

Books
445. Barakat, Halim. *Lebanon in Strife: Student Preludes to the Civil War*. Austin, Tex.: University of Texas Press, 1977.

Articles
446. Bashshur, M. A. 'Higher Education and Political Development in Syria and Lebanon,' *Comparative Education Review* 10 (October 1966), 451–61.

Malaysia

447. Johnson, Harry G. 'The Role of the University in Development

Planning in Malaysia,' *Minerva* 12 (January 1974), 32–8.

448. Lim, David. 'The Role of the University in Development Planning in Malaysia,' *Minerva* 12 (January 1974), 18–31.

Middle East

Books

449. Qubain, Fahim I. *Education and Science in the Arab World.* Baltimore, Md.: Johns Hopkins University Press, 1966.

450. Waardenburg, J. J. *Les universités dans le monde arabe actuel.* 2 vols. Paris: Mouton, 1966.

Articles

450a. Akrawi, Matta. 'Arab World' in A. Knowles, ed., *International Encyclopedia of Higher Education,* San Francisco: Jossey-Bass, 1977, pp. 361–79.

451. Gottschalk, Hans Ludwig. 'Idee und Aufgabe der Universitäten in den arabischen Ländern' in Richard Schwarz, ed., *Universität und moderne Welt.* Berlin: De Gruyter, 1962, pp. 457–83.

452. Waardenburg, J. D. J. 'Some Institutional Aspects of Muslim Higher Education and Their Relation to Islam,' *Numen* 12 (April 1964), 96–138.

453. Zahlen, A. B. 'Science in the Arab Middle East,' *Minerva* 8 (January 1970), 8–35.

Pakistan

454. 'Major Student Victory in Pakistan,' *Minerva* 7 (Spring 1969), 569–78.

455. Maniruzzaman, T. 'Political Activism of University Students in Pakistan,' *Journal of Commonwealth Political Studies* (November 1971), 234–45.

456. 'Pakistan,' *Minerva* 3 (Winter 1965), 272–76.

457. 'Pakistan: A Brief Triumph for Student Power,' *Minerva* 7 (Summer 1969), 783–812.

Philippines

458. Case, Harry and Robert Bunnell. *The University of the Philippines: External Assistance and Development.* East Lansing, Mich.: Michigan State University, 1970.

Singapore

459. Puccetti, Roland. 'Authoritarian Government and Academic Subservience: The University of Singapore,' *Minerva* 10 (April 1972), 223-41.

460. Pye, Lucian and Arthur L. Singer. 'Higher Education and Politics in Singapore,' *Minerva* 3 (Spring 1965), 321-35.

461. Spector, S. 'Students and Politics in Singapore,' *Far East Survey* 25 (May 1956), 65-73.

462. Ten, C. L. 'Politics in the Academe' in A. Montefiore, ed., *Neutrality and Impartiality*. Cambridge: Cambridge University Press, 1975, pp. 149-64.

Sri Lanka

463. 'The Higher Education Act, Ceylon,' *Minerva* 5 (Autumn 1966), 102-11.

464. Pieris, Ralph. 'Universities, Politics, and Public Opinion in Ceylon,' *Minerva* 2 (Summer 1964), 435-54.

465. 'Report of the Ceylon Universities Commission,' *Minerva* 2 (Summer 1964), 492-518.

466. 'University Autonomy in Ceylon,' *Minerva* 4 (Summer 1966), 568-78.

Thailand

Books

467. Prizzia, Ross and Narong Sinsawasdi. *Thailand: Student Activism and Political Change*. Bangkok: D. K. Book House, 1974.

468. Sanguanruang, Saeng. *Development Planning in Thailand: The Role of the University*. Singapore: Regional Institute for Higher Education and Development, 1973.

469. Wyatt, David. *The Politics of Reform in Thailand: Education under Chulalongkorn*. New Haven, Conn.: Yale University Press, 1969.

Articles

470. Darling, Frank. 'Student Protest and Political Change in Thailand,' *Pacific Affairs* 47 (Spring 1974), 5-19.

471. Guskin, Alan. 'Tradition and Change in a Thai University' in T. B. Textor, ed., *Cultural Frontiers of the Peace Corps*. Cambridge, Mass.: M.I.T. Press, 1966, pp. 87-106.

472. Heinze, Ruth-Inge. 'Ten Days in October—Students vs. the Military: An Account of the Student Uprising in Thailand,' *Asian Survey* 14 (June 1974), 491–508.

473. Nimmanheminda, Nai Sukich. 'Higher Education in Thailand' in Stephen D. Kertesz, ed., *The Task of Universities in a Changing World.* South Bend, Ind.: Notre Dame University Press, 1971, pp. 445–54.

474. Zimmerman, Robert F. 'Student "Revolution" in Thailand: The End of the Thai Bureaucratic Policy?' *Asian Survey* 14 (June 1974), 509–29.

Turkey

Books

475. Szyliowicz, Joseph S. *A Political Analysis of Student Activism: The Turkish Case.* Beverly Hills, Calif.: Sage Publications, 1972.

Articles

476. Krueger, Anne. 'Rates of Return to Turkish Higher Education,' *Journal of Human Resources* 7 (Fall 1972), 482–99.

477. Okyar, Osman. 'Universities in Turkey,' *Minerva* 6 (Winter 1968), 213–43.

478. Reed, Howard A. 'Haceteppe and Middle East Technical University: New Universities in Turkey,' *Minerva* 13 (Summer 1975), 200–35.

479. Roos, Leslie L., Jr. and Noralou Roos. 'Student and Politics in Turkey,' *Daedalus* 97 (Winter 1968), 184–203.

480. Szyliowicz, Joseph S. 'Students and Politics in Turkey,' *Middle Eastern Studies* 6 (May 1970), 150–62.

481. Tinto, Vincent. 'University Organization and Scientific Productivity in Turkey' in P. G. Altbach, ed., *University Reform.* Cambridge, Mass.: Schenkman, 1974, pp. 28–41.

482. — — —. 'University Productivity and the Organization of Higher Education in Turkey,' *Higher Education* 3 (August 1974), 285–302.

483. Weiker, W. F. 'Academic Freedom and Problems of Higher Education in Turkey,' *Middle East Journal* 16 (Summer 1962), 279–94.

EUROPE

General

Books

484. *Access to Higher Education in Europe: Comparative Background.* Paris: UNESCO, 1969.

485. Agoston, G. *et al. Case Study on the Development of Higher Education in Some East European Countries.* Paris: UNESCO, 1974.

486. Baldwin, John W. and Richard A. Goldthwaite, eds., *Universities in Politics: Case Studies from the Late Middle Ages and Early Modern Period.* Baltimore, Md.: Johns Hopkins University Press, 1972.

487. Berstecher, Dieter *et al. A University of the Future.* The Hague: Martinus Nijhoff, 1974.

488. Bockstael, Eric and Otto Feinstein. *Higher Education in the European Community: Reform and Economics.* Lexington, Mass.: Heath-Lexington, 1970.

489. Cobban, A. B. *The Medieval Universities: Their Development and Organization.* London: Methuen, 1975.

490. Cockburn, Alexander and Robin Blackburn, eds. *Student Power: Problems, Diagnosis, Action.* Baltimore, Md.: Penguin Books, 1969.

491. Council for Cultural Cooperation, Council of Europe. *Mobility of University Staff.* Strasbourg: Council of Europe, 1973.

492. –––. *Reform and Expansion of Higher Education in Europe: National Reports.* Strasbourg: Council of Europe, 1967.

493. –––. *Structure of University Staff.* Strasbourg: Council of Europe, 1966.

494. Ehrenreich, John and Barbara. *Long March, Short Spring.* New York: Monthly Review Press, 1969.

495. Embling, Jack. *A Fresh Look at Education: European Implications of the Carnegie Commission Reports.* Amsterdam: Elsevier, 1974.

496. Entwistle, Noel, ed. *Strategies for Research and Development in Higher Education.* Amsterdam: Swets and Zeitlinger, 1976.

497. Haskins, Charles H. *The Rise of Universities.* Ithaca, N.Y.: Cornell University Press, 1965.

498. Kibre, Pearl. *The Nations in Medieval Universities.* Cambridge, Mass.: Mediaeval Academy of America, 1948.

499. Lesguillons, H. *Mobility of University Staff.* Strasbourg: Council of Europe, 1973.

500. Lomas, Donald E., ed. *European Perspectives in Teacher Education.* New York: Wiley, 1976.

501. King, Edmund *et al. Post Compulsory Education: A New Analysis in Western Europe.* Beverly Hills, Calif.: Sage Publications, 1974.

502. *L'Université Européenne.* Brussels: Institut de Sociologie de l'Université Libre de Bruxelles, 1973.

503. McGuigan, Gerald F., ed. *Student Protest.* Toronto: Methuen, 1969.

504. Nagel, Julian, ed. *Student Power*. London: Merlin Press, 1969.

505. Neave, Guy. *Patterns of Equality: The Influence of New Structures in European High Education upon the Equality of Educational Opportunity*. Windsor, England: N.F.E.R. Publishing, 1977.

506. Organization for Economic Cooperation and Development. *Development of Higher Education, 1950–1967: Analytical Report*. Paris: O.E.C.D., 1971.

507. — — —. *Development of Higher Education, 1950–1967: Statistical Survey*. Paris: O.E.C.D., 1970.

508. — — —. *The Development of Higher Education 1950–1967: Quantitative Trends*. Paris: O.E.C.D., 1969.

509. — — —. *Economic Aspects of Higher Education*. Paris: O.E.C.D., 1964.

510. — — —. *Policies for Higher Education (General Report)*. Paris: O.E.C.D., 1974.

511. — — —. *Quantitative Trends in Teaching Staff in Higher Education*. Paris: O.E.C.D., 1971.

512. — — —. *Short-Cycle Higher Education: A Search for Identity*. Paris: O.E.C.D., 1973.

513. — — —. *Structures of Studies and Place of Research in Mass Higher Education*. Paris: O.E.C.D., 1974.

514. — — —. *Towards Mass Higher Education: Issues and Dilemmas*. Paris: O.E.C.D., 1974.

515. — — —. *Towards New Structures of Post-Secondary Education: A Preliminary Statement of Issues*. Paris: O.E.C.D., 1971.

516. Rait, Robert S. *Life in the Medieval University*. Cambridge: Cambridge University Press, 1912.

517. Rashdall, Hastings. *The Universities of Europe in the Middle Ages*. Oxford: Clarendon Press, 1936.

518. Schachner, Nathan. *The Mediaeval Universities*. New York: A. S. Barnes, 1962.

519. Shryock, Richard H., ed. *The Status of University Teachers*. Ghent: International Association of University Professors, 1961.

520. Spender, Stephen. *The Year of the Young Rebels*. New York: Vintage Books, 1969.

521. Standing Conference of Rectors and Vice-Chancellors of the European Universities. *The European Universities, 1975–1985*. Oxford: Pergamon Press, 1975.

522. Statera, Gianni. *Death of a Utopia: The Development and Decline of Student Movements in Europe*. New York: Oxford University Press, 1975.

523. Stone, Lawrence, ed. *The University in Society. Vol. 2. Europe, Scotland, and the United States from the 16th to the 20th*

Century. Princeton, N.J.: Princeton University Press, 1974.

524. Szczepanski, Jan. *Higher Education in Eastern Europe*. New York: I.C.E.D., 1974.

525. UNESCO. *Higher Education in Europe: Problems and Prospects: Statistical Study*. Paris: UNESCO, 1973.

526. — — —. *Reform and Development of Higher Education in Europe: France, the Netherlands, and Poland*. Paris: UNESCO, 1964.

527. Verger, J. *Les Universités au Moyen Age*. Paris: Presses Universitaires de France, 1973.

528. Wieruszowski, Helene. *The Medieval University*. Princeton, N.J.: Van Nostrand, 1966.

Articles

529. Altbach, Edith H. 'Vanguard of Revolt: Students and Politics in Central Europe, 1815–1848' in S. M. Lipset and P. G. Altbach, eds., *Students in Revolt*. Boston, Mass.: Houghton Mifflin, 1969, pp. 451–74.

530. Ben-David, Joseph. 'Scientific Productivity and Academic Organization in Nineteenth Century Medicine,' *Sociological Review* 25 (1960), 828–43.

531. — — —. 'The Scientific Role: The Conditions of Its Establishment in Europe,' *Minerva* 4 (Autumn 1965), 15–54.

532. Boudon, Raymond *et al.* 'Short Cycle Higher Education and the Pitfalls of Collective Action,' *Minerva* 14 (Spring 1976), 33–60.

533. Buschbeck, M. 'Politicization of the University,' *Western European Education* 3 (Winter 1971–2), 329–48.

534. Campos, C. 'Mobility of University Staff of Europe,' *Universities Quarterly* 25 (Winter 1970), 28–48.

535. Cerych, Ladislav. 'Academic Reforms of Higher Education in Europe: Overview of Major Trends and Innovations' in Carnegie Commission on Higher Education, *Reform on Campus*, New York: McGraw-Hill, 1972, pp. 105–19.

536. Cerych, Ladislav and D. Furth. 'On the Threshold of Mass Higher Education' in W. R. Niblett and R. F. Butts, eds., *Universities Facing the Future*. San Francisco: Jossey-Bass, 1972, pp. 14–28.

537. Clerk, J. P. and C. Debbasch. 'Student Participation in University Governance,' *Western European Education* 3 (Winter 1971–2), 349–54.

538. Cobban, A. B. 'The Academic Community' in A. B. Cobban, *The Medieval Universities*. London: Methuen, 1975, pp. 196–217.

539. Cornell, Richard. 'Students and Politics in the Communist Countries of Eastern Europe,' *Daedalus* 97 (Winter 1968), 166–83.

540. Cornwall, Malcolm. 'Authority versus Experience in Higher Education: Project-Orientation in Some Continental Universities,'

Comparative Higher Education

Universities Quarterly 29 (Summer 1975), 272–98.

540a. De Moor, R. A. 'Western Europe and the United Kingdom' in A. Knowles, ed., *International Encyclopedia of Higher Education*, San Francisco: Jossey-Bass, 1977, pp. 4365–75.

541. 'Diversifying Post-Secondary Education in Europe,' *Paedagogica Europaea* 7 (1972), 7–129.

542. Draheim, Hans. 'The Gesamthochschule: A Model of Mobility,' *Prospects* 3 (Winter 1973), 504–14.

543. Eith, Wolfgang. 'The State of European University Cooperation,' *Western European Education* 5 (Winter 1973–4), 56–70.

544. 'European Universities a Century Ago,' *Minerva* 6 (Summer 1968), 561–76.

545. Farmer, Paul. 'Nineteenth Century Ideas of the University: Continental Europe' in M. Clapp, ed., *The Modern University*. Ithaca, N.Y.: Cornell University Press, 1950, pp. 3–26.

546. Ford, Boris. 'Changing Relations between Universities and Colleges of Education: West Germany, Sweden, and Denmark,' *Universities Quarterly* 28 (Autumn 1974), 404–36.

547. Goldschmidt, Dietrich. 'Participating Democracy in Schools and Higher Education: Emerging Problems in the Federal Republic of Germany and Sweden,' *Higher Education* 4 (May 1976), 113–34.

548. Janne, Henri. 'The European University in Society,' *Prospects* 3 (Winter 1973), 482–92.

549. Legrand, Louis. 'European Research Policies: Analysis of 16 Country Reports,' *Western European Education* 6 (Fall 1974), 63–90.

550. 'Mass Higher Education and the Elitist Tradition,' *Western European Education* 8 (Spring-Summer 1976).

551. 'Mass Higher Education,' *Higher Education* 2 (May 1973), 133–270.

551a. 'New Trends in European Post-Secondary Education (Case Studies),' *Paedagogica Europaea* 12 (No. 1, 1977), 7–101.

552. Pinner, Frank A. 'Student Trade Unionism in France, Belgium, and Holland,' *Sociology of Education* 37 (Spring 1964), 1–23.

553. — — —. 'Transition and Transgression: Some Characteristics of Student Movements in Western Europe,' *Daedalus* 97 (Winter 1968), 137–55.

554. Reeves, Marjorie. 'The European University from Medieval Times' in W. R. Niblett, ed., *Higher Education: Demand and Response*. San Francisco: Jossey Bass, 1970, pp. 61–84.

555. Robbins, Lord. 'Reflections on Eight Years of Expansion in Higher Education,' *Higher Education* 1 (May 1972), 229–34.

556. Robinson, Eric. 'A Comprehensive Reform of Higher Education,' *Western European Education* 3 (Winter 1971–2).

557. 'University Reforms: 1' (special issue), *Western European Education* 2 (Winter 1970–1), 275–365.

558. Von Gizycki, Rainald. 'Center and Periphery in the International Scientific Community; Germany, France and Great Britain in the 19th Century,' *Minerva* 11 (October 1973), 474–94.

559. Weissman, Ann B. 'Widening the Base for Higher Education: A Study of Scandinavian Institutions,' *Western European Education* 6 (Summer 1974), 5–86.

Austria

Books

560. *Educational Policy and Planning: Higher Education and Research in Austria.* Paris: O.E.C.D., 1975.

561. Organization for Economic Cooperation and Development. *Reviews of National Policy for Education: Austria: Higher Education and Research.* Paris: O.E.C.D., 1976.

Articles

561a. 'Austria' in A. Knowles, ed., *International Encyclopedia of Higher Education.* San Francisco: Jossey-Bass, 1977, pp. 561–72.

562. McGrath, William. 'Student Radicalism in Vienna,' *Journal of Contemporary History* 2 (July 1967), 183–202.

563. Posch, Peter. 'The Klagenfurt Institute: A New Model of University Education,' *Western European Education* 2 (Winter 1970–71), 314–29.

564. Torrance, John. 'The Emergence of Sociology in Austria,' *European Journal of Sociology* 17 (No. 2, 1976), 185–219.

Belgium

Books

565. Dejean, Christian and C. L. Binnemans. *L'Université Belge: De Pari au Défi.* Brussels: Editions de l'Institut de Sociologie, Université Libre de Bruxelles, 1971.

Articles

566. Boxus, L. *et al.* 'A University Information System: A Case Study Carried Out at the Catholic University of Louvain, Belgium' in V. Onushkin, ed., *Planning the Development of Universities,* Vol. 4. Paris: Unesco Press, 1975, pp. 317–410.

567. Philippart, André. 'The University in Belgian Politics since

the Contestation of 1968,' *Government and Opposition* 7 (Autumn 1972), 450–63.

567a. Van de Vijvere, J., 'L'Enseignement Post-Secondaire en Belgique: Entre l'Evolution et la Mutation,' *Paedagogica Europaea* 12 (No. 1, 1977), 41–62.

Britain

Books

568. Arblaster, Anthony. *Academic Freedom.* Harmondsworth, England: Penguin Books, 1974.

569. Armytage, W. H. G. *Civic Universities.* New York: Arno Press, 1977.

570. Ashby, Eric. *Masters and Scholars: Reflections on the Rights and Responsibilities of Students.* London: Oxford University Press, 1970.

571. Ashby, Eric and Mary Anderson. *The Rise of the Student Estate in Britain.* Cambridge, Mass.: Harvard University Press, 1970.

572. Bell, R. E. and A. J. Youngson, eds. *Present and Future in Higher Education.* London: Tavistock, 1973.

573. Beloff, Michael. *The Plateglass Universities.* London: Secker and Warburg, 1968.

574. Berdahl, Robert O. *British Universities and the State.* Berkeley, Calif.: University of California Press, 1959.

575. Bottomley, J. A. *et al. Costs and Potential Economics.* Paris: O.E.C.D., 1972.

576. Butcher, H. J. and E. Rudd, eds. *Contemporary Problems in Higher Education: An Account of Research.* London: McGraw-Hill, 1972.

577. Caine, Sydney. *British Universities: Purpose and Prospects.* London: Bodley Head, 1969.

578. Committee on Higher Education (Robbins Committee). *Higher Education: Report of the Committee.* London: H.M.S.O., 1963.

579. Crooks, S. B. *The Open University in the United Kingdom.* Paris: International Institute for Educational Planning, 1976.

581. Daiches, David, ed. *The Idea of a New University: An Experiment at Sussex.* Cambridge, Mass.: M.I.T. Press, 1964.

582. Davie, George E. *The Democratic Intellect: Scotland and Her Universities in the Nineteenth Century.* Edinburgh: Edinburgh University Press, 1961.

583. Donaldson, Lex. *Policy and Polytechnics: Pluralistic Drift in Higher Education.* Westmead, England: Saxon House, 1975.

584. Entwistle, Noel and Dai Hounsell, eds. *How Students Learn*. Lancaster, England: Institute for Research and Development in Post-Compulsory Education, University of Lancaster, 1975.

585. Falk, Barbara and Kwong Lee Dow. *The Assessment of University Teaching*. London: Society for Research into Higher Education, 1971.

586. Ferguson, John. *The Open University from Within*. London: Hodder and Stoughton, 1975.

587. Green, V. H. *The Universities*. Harmondsworth, England: Penguin Books, 1969.

588. Group for Research and Innovation in Higher Education. *The Drift of Change*. London: Nuffield Foundation, 1975.

589. Halsey, A. H. and Martin Trow. *The British Academics*. Cambridge, Mass.: Harvard University Press, 1971.

592. Kearney, Hugh. *Scholars and Gentlemen: Universities and Society in Pre-Industrial Britain, 1500–1700*. Ithaca, N.Y.: Cornell University Press, 1970.

593. Lawlor, John, ed. *Higher Education: Patterns of Changes in the 1970's*. London: Routledge and Kegan Paul, 1972.

594. — — —. *The New University*. London: Routledge and Kegan Paul, 1968.

595. Layard, Richard, John King and Claus Moser. *The Impact of Robbins*. Harmondsworth, England: Penguin Books, 1969.

596. Livingstone, Hugh. *The University: An Organizational Analysis*. Glasgow: Blackie, 1974.

599. McIntosh, Naomi E. *A Degree of Difference: The Open University of the United Kingdom*. New York: Praeger, 1977.

600. Moodie, Graeme and Rowland Eustace. *Power and Authority in British Universities*. Montreal: McGill-Queens University Press, 1974.

601. Mountford, James. *British Universities*. London: Oxford University Press, 1966.

602. Page, Colin Flood and Mary Yates, eds., *Power and Authority in Higher Education*. Guildford, England: Society for Research into Higher Education, 1976.

604. Perkin, Harold. *Innovations in Higher Education: New Universities in the United Kingdom*. Paris: O.E.C.D., 1969.

605. — — —. *Key Profession: The History of the Association of University Teachers*. London: Routledge and Kegan Paul, 1969.

606. Pickford, Michael. *University Expansion and Finance*. Brighton, England: Sussex University Press, 1975.

607. Pratt, John and Tyrrell Burgess. *Polytechnics: A Report*. London: Pitman, 1975.

608. Rothblatt, Sheldon. *The Revolution of the Dons: Cambridge*

and Society in Victorian England. London: Faber, 1968.

609. Rudd, Ernest and Renate Simpson. *The Highest Education: A Study of Graduate Education in Britain.* London: Routledge and Kegan Paul, 1975.

610. Sanderson, Michael. *The Universities and British Industry 1850–1970.* London: Routledge and Kegan Paul, 1972.

611. — — —, ed. *The Universities in the Nineteenth Century.* London: Routledge and Kegan Paul, 1975.

613. Silver, Harold and S. J. Teague. *The History of British Universities, 1800–1969: A Bibliography.* London: Society for Research into Higher Education, 1970.

614. Simpson, M. G. *et al. Planning University Development.* Paris: O.E.C.D., 1972.

616. Stone, Lawrence, ed. *The University in Society.* Vol. 1. *Oxford and Cambridge from the 14th to the Early 19th Century.* Princeton, N. J.: Princeton University Press, 1974.

617. Truscot, Bruce. *Red Brick University.* Harmondsworth, England: Penguin Books, 1951.

618. Tunstall, Jeremy, ed. *The Open University Opens.* Amherst, Mass.: University of Massachusetts Press, 1974.

619. Verry, Donald and Bleddyn David. *University Costs and Outputs.* Amsterdam: Elsevier, 1976.

620. Williams, Gareth, Tessa Blackstone and David Metcalf. *The Academic Labour Market: Economic and Social Aspects of a Profession.* Amsterdam: Elsevier, 1974.

Articles

621. Andrewski, S. 'Observations of How Book Worms are Changing into Red Tape Worms,' *European Journal of Sociology* 18 (No. 1, 1977), 160–75.

622. Ashby, Eric. 'Government, the University Grants Committee and the Universities: Hands Off the Universities?" *Minerva* 6 (Winter 1968), 244–56.

624. Beloff, Max. 'British Universities and the Public Purse,' *Minerva* 5 (Summer 1967), 520–32.

625. Betsky, S. 'Concepts of Excellence: Universities in an Industrial Culture,' *Universities Quarterly* 24 (Winter 1969), 7–28.

626. Beyer, Janice and Thomas Lodahl. 'A Comparative Study of Patterns of Influence in United States and English Universities,' *Administrative Science Quarterly* 21 (March 1976), 104–29.

627. Blackstone, Tessa and Oliver Fulton. 'Men and Women Academics: An Anglo-American Comparison of Subject Choices and Research Activity,' *Higher Education* 3 (April 1974), 119–40.

628. Blackstone, T. and R. Hadley. 'Student Protest in a British

University: Some Comparisons with American Research,' *Comparative Education Review* 15 (February 1971), 1–19.

629. Bottomley, J. A. and John Dunworth. 'Rates of Return on University Education With Economies of Scale,' *Higher Education* 3 (February 1974), 91–102.

630. Bowden, Lord. 'English Universities — Problems and Prospects' in S. Kertesz, ed., *The Task of Universities in a Changing World*. South Bend, Ind.: Notre Dame University Press, 1971, 235–58.

631. – – –. 'The Universities, the Government and the Public Accounts Committee,' *Minerva* 6 (Autumn 1967), 28–42.

632. Boyle, Edward. 'Parliament and University Policy,' *Minerva* 5 (Autumn 1966), 3–19.

633. Boyle, Edward *et al*. 'Report on James,' *Universities Quarterly* 26 (Spring 1972), 127–63.

634. Briggs, Asa. 'Development of Higher Education in the United Kingdom' in W. R. Niblett, ed., *Higher Education: Demand and Response*. San Francisco, Jossey-Bass, 1970, pp. 95–116.

635. Caine, Sydney. 'Universities and the State,' *Political Quarterly* 37 (July–September 1966), 237–54.

636. Campbell-Balfour, W. 'The Academic Working Week,' *Universities Quarterly* 24 (Autumn 1970), 353–9.

637. Carter, Charles. 'The Efficiency of Universities,' *Higher Education* 1 (February 1972), 77–92.

638. Chester, Robert. 'Role Conflict and the Junior Academic' in David Martin, ed., *Anarchy and Culture*. London: Routledge and Kegan Paul, 1969, pp. 77–84.

639. Christopherson, Derman G. 'Current Trends in the United Kingdom,' *Higher Education* 4 (April 1975), 133–48.

641. 'The Comprehensive Principle at Work' in W. R. Niblett and R. F. Butts, eds., *Universities Facing the Future*. San Francisco: Jossey-Bass, 1972, 311–96.

642. Driver, Christopher. 'Higher Education in Britain: The Cow Ruminant,' *Comparative Education Review* 16 (June 1972), 325–39.

643. Dunworth, John and Rupert Cook. 'Budgetary Devolution as an Aid to University Efficiency,' *Higher Education* 5, (May 1976), 153–68.

644. Eggleston, S. J. 'Innovations in Teacher Education in England and Wales,' *Paedagogica Europaea* 10 (No. 1, 1975), 43–71.

645. Engel, Arthur. 'The Emerging Concept of the Academic Profession at Oxford, 1800–1854' in L. Stone, ed. *The University in Society*, Vol. 1. Princeton, N.J.: Princeton University Press, 1974, pp. 305–51.

646. 'Experiment and Innovation in Methods of Teaching' in H. J. Butcher and E. Rudd, eds., *Contemporary Problems in Higher*

Education. London: McGraw-Hill, 1972, pp. 103–59.

647. Fowler, G. 'The Binary Policy in England and Wales' in W. R. Niblett and R. F. Butts, eds., *Universities Facing the Future*. San Francisco: Jossey-Bass, 1972, pp. 268–80.

648. Gabarino, J. W. 'Academic Unionism in Great Britain' in J. W. Gabarino, *Faculty Bargaining*. New York: McGraw-Hill, 1975, pp. 213–50.

649. Gould, Julius. 'Politics and the Academy,' *Government and Opposition* 3 (Winter 1968), 23–47.

650. Halsey, A. H. 'British Universities,' *Archives of European Sociology* 3 (1962), 85–101.

651. — — —. 'British Universities and Intellectual Life,' *Universities Quarterly* 12 (February 1958), 141–52.

652. — — —. 'Universities and the State,' *Universities Quarterly* 23 (Spring 1969), 123–48.

653. Halsey, A. H. and Stephen Marks. 'British Student Politics' in S. M. Lipset and P. G. Altbach, eds., *Students in Revolt*. Boston, Mass.: Houghton Mifflin, 1969, pp. 35–59.

654. Halsey, A. H. and Thomas Pakenham. 'The Study of the University Teacher,' *Universities Quarterly* 17 (March 1963), 165–76.

656. Harrison, M. J. and Keith Weightman. 'Academic Freedom and Higher Education in England,' *British Journal of Sociology* 25 (March 1974), 32–46.

657. Hornsby-Smith, M. P. 'The Working Life of the University Lecturer,' *Universities Quarterly* 28 (Spring 1974), 149–63.

658. Hutchinson, Eric. 'The Origins of the University Grants Committee,' *Minerva* 13 (Winter 1975), 583–620.

659. 'The James Report: Radical Reforms Proposed for Teacher Education,' *Times Higher Education Supplement* (28 January 1972), 1–12.

660. Laidlaw, Bruce and Richard Layard. 'Traditional versus Open University Teaching Methods: A Cost Comparison,' *Higher Education* 3 (November 1974), 439–67.

661. McConnell, T. R. 'Beyond the Universities: The Movement towards Mass Higher Education in Britain,' *Higher Education* 2 (May 1973), 160–71.

662. McConnell, T. R. and Robert O. Berdahl. 'Planning Mechanisms for British Transition to Mass Higher Education,' *Higher Education Review* 3 (Autumn 1971), 3–22.

663. McMahon, Walter. 'Policy Issues in the Economics of Higher Education and Related Research Opportunities in Britain and the United States,' *Higher Education* 3 (April 1974), 165–86.

664. Mellanby, Kenneth. 'The Disorganization of Scientific Research,' *Minerva* 12 (January 1974), 67–82.

665. 'Militants and Moderates in British Universities.' *Minerva* 7 (Autumn–Winter 1968–9), 282–309.

666. O'Connor, R. E. 'Political Activism and Moral Reasoning: Political and Apolitical Students in Great Britain and France' *British Journal of Political Science* 4 (January 1974), 53–78.

667. Percy, K. A. and F. W. Salter, 'Student and Staff Perceptions and the "Pursuit of Excellence" in British Higher Education,' *Higher Education* 5 (November 1975), 457–74.

668. Perkin, Harold. 'Adaptation to Change by British Universities,' *Universities Quarterly* 28 (Autumn 1974), 389–403.

669. – – –. 'A British University Designed for the Future: Lancaster' in W. R. Niblett and R. F. Butts, eds., *Universities Facing the Future*. San Francisco: Jossey-Bass, 1972, pp. 183–94.

670. – – –. 'Mass Higher Education and the Elitist Tradition: The English Experience,' *Western European Education* 8 (No. 1–2, 1976), 11–35.

671. – – –. 'The New Universities in Britain,' *Western European Education* 2 (Winter 1970–1), 290–313.

672. – – –. 'University Planning in Britain in the 1960's,' *Higher Education* 1 (February 1972), 111–20.

673. Phillipson, Nicholas. 'Culture and Society in the 18th Century Province: The Case of Edinburgh and the Scottish Englightenment' in L. Stone, ed., *The University in Society,* Vol. 2. Princeton, N.J.: Princeton University Press, 1974, pp. 407–48.

674. Riesman, David. 'Notes on New Universities: British and American,' *Universities Quarterly* 20 (March 1966), 128–46.

675. Rothblatt, Sheldon. 'The Past and Future Freedom of the British University,' *Minerva* 14 (Summer 1976), 251–62.

676. Rudd, Ernest. 'The Research Orientation of British Universities,' *Higher Education* 2 (August 1973), 301–24.

677. Stretch, K. L. 'Academic Ecology: On the Location of Institutions of Higher Education', *Minerva* 2 (Spring 1964) 320–35.

678. Taylor, William. 'The University Teacher of Education in England,' *Comparative Education* 1 (June 1965), 193–202.

679. Trow, Martin. 'The Idea of a New University,' *Universities Quarterly* 19 (March 1965), 162–72.

680. – – –. 'A Question of Size and Shape: The Robbins Report on British Higher Education,' *Universities Quarterly* 18 (March 1964), 136–52.

681. Wagner, Lesley. 'The Economics of the Open University,' *Higher Education* 1 (May 1972), 159–84.

682. – – –. 'The Economics of the Open University Revisited,' *Higher Education* 6 (August 1977), 359–82.

683. Williams, Bruce. 'University Values and University

Organization,' *Minerva* 10 (April 1972), 259–79.

684. Williams, Gareth. 'The Events of 1973–4 in a Long Term Planning Perspective,' *Higher Education Bulletin* 3 (Autumn 1974), 17–44.

Czechoslovakia

685. Golan, Galia. 'Youth and Politics in Czechoslovakia,' *Journal of Contemporary History* 5 (No. 1, 1970), 3–22.

686. Kaminsky, Howard. 'The University of Prague in the Hussite Revolution: The Role of the Masters' in J. Baldwin and R. Goldthwaite, eds., *Universities in Politics*. Baltimore, Md.: Johns Hopkins University Press, 1972, pp. 79–106.

687. Kubickova, Miluse. 'The Student Movement in Czechoslovakia' in P. G. Altbach, ed., *Student Revolution: A Global Analysis*. Bombay: Lalvani, 1970, pp. 267–85.

Denmark

Books
688. Jensen, Arne *et al. Decision, Planning and Budgeting*. Paris: O.E.C.D., 1972.

Articles
689. Cane, Alan. 'Something Modern in the State of Denmark,' *Times Higher Education Supplement* No. 150 (August 30 1974), 6–7.

France

Books
690. Antoine, Gerald and Jean-Claude Passeron. *La Réforme de l'Université*. Paris: Calmann-Levy, 1966.

691. Bayan, Maurice. *Histoire des Universités*. Paris: Presses Universitaires de France, 1973.

692. Bourdieu, Pierre and Jean-Claude Passeron. *Les Etudiants et Leurs Etudes*. Paris: Mouton, 1964.

693. — — —. *Les Héritiers, les Etudiants, et la Culture*. Paris: Editions de Minuit, 1965.

694. Bourricaud, François. *Universités à la Dérive*. Paris: Stock, 1971.

695. Clark, Terry N. *Prophets and Patrons: The French University*

and the Emergence of the Social Sciences. Cambridge, Mass.: Harvard University Press, 1973.

696. Debeauvais, Michel. *L'Université Ouverte; Les Dossiers de Vincennes.* Grenoble: Presses Universitaires de Grenoble, 1976.

697. Escarpit, Robert. *Les I.U.T.: Du Temps Gagné.* Lorrez le Bogage: E.L.P. Editions, 1974.

698. Faure, Edgar. *Philosophie d'une Réforme.* Paris: Plon, 1969.

699. Gabriel, A. L. *Student Life in Ave Maria College: Medieval Paris.* South Bend, Ind.: University of Notre Dame Press, 1955.

700. Gerbod, Paul. *La Condition Universitaire en France au XIXe Siècle.* Paris: Presses Universitaires de France, 1965.

701. Grignon, C. and J.-C. Passeron. *Innovation in Higher Education: French Experience before 1968.* Paris: O.E.C.D., 1970.

702. Keylor, William R. *Academy and Community: The Foundation of the French Historical Profession.* Cambridge, Mass.: Harvard University Press, 1975.

703. Lefebvre, Henri. *The Explosion: Marxism and the French Upheaval.* New York: Monthly Review Press, 1969.

704. McLaughlin, Mary M. *Intellectual Freedom and Its Limitations in the University of Paris in the Thirteenth and Fourteenth Centuries.* New York: Arno Press, 1977.

705. Priaulx, Allen and Sanford Ungar. *The Almost Revolution: France, 1968.* New York: Dell, 1969.

706. Quattrocchi, Angelo and Tom Nairn. *The Beginning of the End: France, May 1968.* London: Panther Books, 1968.

707. *Quelle Université? Quelle Société?* Paris: Le Seuil, 1968.

708. Schnapp, Alain and Pierre Vidal-Nacquet. *The French Student Uprising, November, 1967–June, 1968: An Analytical Documentary.* Boston: Beacon, 1971.

709. Touraine, Alain. *The May Movement: Reform and Revolt.* New York: Random House, 1971.

Articles

710. Antoine, Gerald. 'An Innovative University in France: Orléans-La Source — A Stocktaking' in W. R. Niblett and R. F. Butts, eds. *Universities Facing the Future.* San Francisco: Jossey-Bass, 1972, pp. 195–206.

711. Aron, Raymond. 'Some Aspects of the Crisis in the French Universities,' *Minerva* 2 (Spring 1964), 279–85.

711a. Boudon, Raymond. 'La Crise Universitaire Française: Essai de Diagnostic,' *Annales* 24 (May–June 1969), 738–64.

711b. — — —. 'The French University since 1968,' *Comparative Politics* 10 (October 1977), 89–119.

712. Bourdieu, Pierre, C. Grignon and J.-C. Passeron. 'L'Evolution

des Chances d'Accès à L'Enseignement Supérieur en France, 1962–66,' *Higher Education* 2 (November 1973), 407–22.

713. 'Examinations, Reforms, and Irreconcilables in France,' *Minerva* 7 (Spring 1969), 507–26.

714. 'Faire l'Université,' *Esprit* 32 (May–June 1964), 705–1214.

715. Fomerand, Jacques. 'The French University: What Happened after the Revolution?' *Higher Education* 6 (February 1977), 93–116.

716. Gagnon, Paul. 'The French Lesson: The Right to Culture,' *Change* 7 (December–January 1975–6), 36–41.

717. Gaussen, F. 'The Human Cost of French University Expansion, Academics without Careers,' *Minerva* 11 (July 1973), 372–86.

718. Griset, Antoine and Marc Kravets. 'De l'Algérie à la Réforme Fouchet: Critique du Syndicalisme Etudiant: I,' *Temps Modernes* No. 227 (April 1965), 1880–1902.

719. – – –. 'De l'Algérie à la Réforme Fouchet: Critique du Syndicalisme Etudiant: II,' *Temps Modernes* No. 228 (May 1965), 2066–2089.

720. Hahn, Roger. 'Scientific Research as an Occupation in Eighteenth Century Paris,' *Minerva* 13 (Winter 1975), 501–13.

721. Kravets, Marc. 'Naissance d'un Syndicalisme Etudiant,' *Temps Modernes* No. 213 (February, 1964), 1447–75.

722. 'Law No. 68–978 of November 12, 1968, Orientation Law on Higher Education: France,' *Western European Education* 6 (Spring 1974), 82–102.

722*a*. Levy-Garboua, Louis. 'Les Demandes de l'Etudiant ou les Contradictions de l'Université de Masse,' *Revue Française de Sociologie* 17 (January–March 1976), 53–80.

723. Lowenthal, M. 'Unsanctioned Projects for French University Reform,' *Universities Quarterly* 22 (September 1968), 371–84.

724. 'Mai, 1968,' *Esprit* 36 (June–July 1968), 961–1080.

725. Nye, Mary Jo. 'The Scientific Periphery in France: The Faculty of Science at the University of Toulouse, 1880–1930,' *Minerva* 13 (Autumn 1975), 374–403.

726. Patterson, Michelle. 'French University Reform: Renaissance or Restoration,' *Comparative Education Review* 16 (June 1972), 281–302.

727. – – –. 'Governmental Policy and Equality in Higher Education: The Junior Collegization of the French University,' *Social Problems* 24 (December 1976), 173–83.

728. 'A Phantasm of Revolution and the Possibility of Reform in French Universities,' *Minerva* 6 (Summer 1968), 630–89.

729. 'Prelude to Disorder: Late Opening and Overcrowding in French Universities,' *Minerva* 6 (Spring 1968), 441–7.

730. 'Réforme de l'Enseignement Supérieur en France,' *Esprit* (May–June, 1964), 705–1214.

731. 'University Reform in France,' *Minerva* 7 (Summer 1969), 706–27.

732. Van de Graaff, John. 'The Politics of Innovation in French Higher Education: The University Institute of Technology,' *Higher Education* 5 (May 1976), 189–210.

733. Walters, Stuart. 'University Reform: A Case Study from France,' *Universities Quarterly* 18 (March 1964), 169–79.

734. Williamson, Ann. 'Innovation in Higher Education: French Experience before 1968' in B. Holmes and D. Scanlon, eds., *Higher Education in a Changing World*. New York: Harcourt Brace Jovanovich, 1971, pp. 251–64.

735. Zeldin, Theodore. 'Higher Education in France, 1848–1940,' *Journal of Contemporary History* 2 (No. 3, 1967), 53–80.

Germany, Democratic Republic

Books
736. Richert, Ernst. *Sozialistische Universität: die Hochschul-Politik der S.E.D.* Berlin: Colloquium, 1967.

Articles
737. Lehmann, H. *et al.* 'Planning the Teaching Work at Humboldt University, Berlin,' in V. Onushkin, ed. *Planning the Development of Universities—IV* Paris: Unesco Press, 1975, pp. 59–102.

738. Nast, Manfred. 'The Planning of Higher Education in the German Democratic Republic,' *Higher Education* 3 (April 1974), 201–12.

739. Wirzberger, Karl-Heinz. 'The Third Reform of Higher Education in the German Democratic Republic,' *Prospects* 3 (Winter 1973), 497–503.

Germany, Federal Republic

Books
740. Anger, Hans *et al. Probleme der Deutschen Universität.* Tübingen: Mohr, 1960.

741. Arnold, Matthew. *Higher Schools and Universities in Germany.* New York: Macmillan, 1892.

742. Asche, Holger. *Hochschulautonomie-Wissenschaftsfreiheit im Abseits.* Darmstadt: Luchterhand, 1975.

743. Bergmann, Uwe, R. Deutschke, W. Lefevre and B. Rabehl. *Rebellion der Studenten oder die Neue Opposition.* Reinbeck: Rowohlt, 1968.

744. Berndt, E. B. *et al. Erziehung der Erzieher: Das Bremer Reformmodell—Ein Lehrstück zur Bildungspolitik.* Reinbeck: Rowohlt, 1972.

745. Bleuel, Hans Peter. *Deutschlands Bekenner, Professoren zwischen Kaiserreich und Diktatur.* Munich: Scherz, 1968.

746. Boning, E. and K. Roeloffs. *Innovation in Higher Education: Three German Universities: Aachen, Bochum, Konstanz.* Paris: O.E.C.D., 1970.

747. Broch, Hermann, ed. *Zur Universitätsreform.* Frankfurt am Main: Suhrkamp, 1969.

748. Busch, Alexander. *Die Geschichte des Privatdozenten.* New York: Arno Press, 1977.

749. Carnegie Foundation for the Advancement of Teaching. *The Financial Status of the Professor in America and Germany.* New York: Arno Press, 1977.

750. Habermas, Jurgen. *Protestbewegung und Hochschulreform.* Frankfurt am Main: Suhrkamp, 1969.

752. Helms, E. *Die Hochschulreform in den U.S.A. und ihre Bedeutung für die B.R.D.* Hanover: Hermann Schroedel, 1971.

754. International Association of Universities. *Problems of Integrated Higher Education: An International Case Study of the Gesamtschule.* Paris: I.A.U. 1972.

755. International Council on the Future of the University. *Report on German Universities.* New York: International Council on the Future of the University, 1977.

756. Kluge, Alexander. *Die Universitäts-Selbstverwaltung.* New York: Arno Press, 1977.

757. Leibfried, Stephan. *Die Angepasste Universität zur Situation der Hochschulen in der Bundesrepublik und den U.S.A.* Frankfurt am Main: Suhrkamp, 1968.

758. — — —, ed. *Wider die Undertanenfabrik: Handbuch zur Demokratisierung der Hochschule.* Cologne: Rugenstein, 1967.

759. Lilge, Frederick. *The Abuse of Learning: The Failure of the German University.* New York: Macmillan, 1948.

760. Nitsch, Wolfgang *et al Hochschule in der Demokratie.* Berlin: Luchterhand, 1965.

761. Nitsch, Wolfgang. *Hochschule: soziologische Materialien.* Heidelberg: Quelle and Meyer, 1967.

762. — — —. *Die Soziale Dynamik Akademischer Institutionen.* Weinheim: Beltz, 1973.

763. Plessner, Helmuth, ed. *Untersuchunger zur Lage der*

Deutschen Hochschullehrer. 3 vols. Göttingen: Vandenhoeck and Ruprecht, 1956.

764. Ringer, Fritz. *The Decline of the German Mandarins: The German Academic Community, 1890-1933.* Cambridge, Mass.: Harvard University Press, 1969.

765. Schelsky, Helmut. *Einsamkeit und Freiheit: zur Idee und Gestalt der Deutschen Universität und ihrer Reformen.* Reinbeck: Rowohlt, 1963.

766. Schwan, Alexander and Kurt Sontheimer, eds. *Reform als Alternative: Hochschullehrer Antworten auf die Herausforderung der Studenten.* Cologne: Westdeutscher Verlag, 1969.

767. Shils, Edward, ed. *Max Weber on Universities: The Power of the State and the Dignity of the Academic Calling in Imperial Germany.* Chicago: University of Chicago Press, 1973.

768. Steinberg, M. S. *Sabers and Brown Shirts: The German Students' Path to National Socialism.* Chicago: University of Chicago Press, 1977.

769. Von Friedeburg, Ludwig *et al. Freie Universität und Politisches Potential der Studenten.* Berlin: Luchterhand, 1968.

Articles

770. 'The Academic Consequences of Disorder in the German Universities.' *Minerva* 12 (October 1974), 510-14.

771. Ben-David, Joseph. 'The Universities and the Growth of Science in Germany and the United States,' *Minerva* 7 (Autumn-Winter 1968-9), 1-35.

773. Busch, Alexander. 'The Vicissitudes of the Privatdozent: Breakdown and Adaptation in the Recruitment of the German University Teacher,' *Minerva* 1 (Spring 1963), 319-41.

774. Dahrendorf, Ralf. 'Starre und Offenheit der Deutschen Universität: die Chancen der Reform,' *European Journal of Sociology* 3 (1962), 263-93.

775. Domes, Jurgen and A. P. Frank. 'The Tribulations of the Free University of Berlin,' *Minerva* 13 (Summer 1975), 183-99.

776. Doring, Herbert. 'Deutsche Professoren zwischen Kaiserreich und Drittem Reich,' *Neue politische Literatur* No. 3 (July-September 1974), 340-52.

777. Fischer, A. 'American University Planning and Its Relevance to West German Educational Policy,' *International Review of Education* 20 (No. 2, 1974), 138-54.

778. Forman, Paul. 'The Financial Support and Political Alignment of Physicists in Weimar Germany,' *Minerva* 12 (January 1974), 39-66.

779. Goldschmidt, Dietrich. 'Autonomy and Accountability of

Higher Education in the Federal Republic of Germany' in P. G. Altbach, ed., *The University's Response to Societal Demands.* New York: I.C.E.D., 1975, pp. 151–72.

780. Goldschmidt, Dietrich. 'Teachers in Institutions of Higher Learning in Germany' in A. H. Halsey, J. Floud, and C. A. Anderson, eds., *Education, Economy and Society.* New York: Free Press, 1962, pp. 577–88.

781. — — —. 'West Germany' in M. S. Archer, ed., *Students, University, and Society.* London: Heinemann Educational Books, 1972, pp. 154–66.

784. Hahn, Walter. 'Higher Education in West Germany: Reform Movements and Trends,' *Comparative Education Review* 7 (June 1963), 51–60.

785. 'Halting Movements towards University Reform in West Germany,' *Minerva* 7 (Spring 1969), 527–32.

786. Hamm-Bruecher, Hildegard. 'Towards the Comprehensive University in Germany' in W. R. Niblett and R. F. Butts, eds., *Universities Facing the Future.* San Francisco: Jossey-Bass, 1972, pp. 325–35.

787. Heald, David. 'The Transformation of the German Universities,' *Universities Quarterly* 23 (Autumn 1969), 408–19.

788. Herz, Otto. 'Plans for Comprehensive Higher Institutions,' *Western European Education* 2 (Winter 1970–1), 351–65.

789. 'Irreconcilables and Fumbling Reformers in West Germany,' *Minerva* 7 (Autumn–Winter 1968–9), 153–77.

790. Jarausch, Konrad. 'The Sources of German Student Unrest, 1815–1848' in L. Stone, ed., *The University in Society,* Vol. 2. Princeton, N.J.: Princeton University Press, 1974, pp. 533–70.

792. Kloss, G. 'The Growth of Federal Power in the West German University System,' *Minerva* 9 (October 1971), 510–27.

793. — — —. 'University Reform in West Germany: The Burden of Tradition,' *Minerva* 6 (Spring 1968), 323–53.

794. 'The Krippendorff Case and the Free University of West Berlin,' *Minerva* 6 (Winter 1968), 274–86.

795. Krueger, M. and B. Wallisch-Prinz. 'University Reform in West Germany,' *Comparative Education Review* 16 (June 1972), 340–51.

797. McClelland, Charles E. 'The Aristocracy and University Reform in Eighteenth Century Germany' in L. Stone, ed., *Schooling and Society.* Baltimore, Md.: Johns Hopkins University Press, 1976, pp. 146–76.

798. Mason, H. L. 'Reflections on the Politicized University: The Academic Crisis in the Federal Republic of Germany,' *AAUP Bulletin* 60 (September 1974), 299–312.

799. Merritt, Richard. 'The Student Protest Movement in West Berlin,' *Comparative Politics* 1 (July 1969), 516–32.

800. Nitsch, Wolfgang. 'Zur Struktur der Bremer "Reformsuniversität",' *Zeitschrift der Technischen Universität Berlin* No. 1 (1972), 1–36.

801. Pfetsch, Frank. 'Scientific Organization and Science Policy in Imperial Germany, 1872–1914: The Foundation of the Imperial Institute of Physics and Technology,' *Minerva* 8 (October 1970), 557–80.

802. 'Recommendations of the Science Council on the Reorganization of University Teaching Staffs in Western Germany,' *Minerva* 4 (Winter 1966), 246–53.

803. 'Relentless Revolutionaries, Reluctant Reformers in West Germany,' *Minerva* 6 (Summer 1968), 690–739.

804. Ringer, Fritz. 'Higher Education in Germany in the Nineteenth Century,' *Journal of Contemporary History* 2 (July 1967), 123–38.

805. Ruegg, Walter. 'The Intellectual Situation in German Higher Education,' *Minerva* 13 (Spring 1975), 103–20.

806. Schelsky, Helmut. 'The Wider Setting of Disorder in the German Universities,' *Minerva* 10 (October 1972), 614–26.

807. Shils, Edward. 'The Freedom of Teaching and Research,' *Minerva* 11 (October 1973), 433–41.

808. — — —. 'Stanford and Berlin: The Spheres of Politics and Intellect,' *Minerva* 10 (July 1972), 351–61.

809. Sommerkorn, I. N. 'The Free University of Berlin: Case Study of an Experimental Seminar' in W. R. Niblett and R. F. Butts, eds., *Universities Facing the Future*. San Francisco: Jossey-Bass, 1972, pp. 336–46.

810. Sontheimer, Kurt. 'Student Opposition in Western Germany,' *Government and Opposition* 3 (Winter 1968), 49–87.

811. 'A Steady State of Disorder: The S.D.S. at Work,' *Minerva* 7 (Spring 1969), 533–44.

812. 'Students as an Anti-Parliamentary Opposition in West Germany,' *Minerva* 6 (Spring 1968), 448–56.

814. Teichler, Ulrich. 'Problems of West German Universities on the Way to Mass Higher Education,' *Western European Education* 8 (No. 1–2, 1976), 81–120.

815. — — —. 'University Reform and Skeleton Legislation on Higher Education in the Federal Republic of Germany,' *Western European Education* 5 (Winter 1973–4), 34–55.

816. Turner, R. Steven. 'The Growth of Professorial Research in Prussia, 1818–1848—Causes and Context,' *Historical Studies in the Physical Sciences* 3 (1971), 137–82.

817. — — —. 'University Reformers and Professional Scholarship in

Germany, 1760–1806' in L. Stone, ed., *The University in Society*, Vol. 2. Princeton, N.J.: Princeton University Press, 1974, pp. 495–532.

818. 'University Reform in Germany,' *Minerva* 8 (April 1970), 242–67.

819. Von Friedeburg, Ludwig. 'Youth and Politics in the Federal Republic of Germany,' *Youth and Society* 1 (September 1969), 91–109.

820. Wildenmann, Rudolph. 'Higher Education in Transition: The Case of the Universities in the Federal Republic of Germany' in S. Kertesz, ed., *The Task of Universities in a Changing World*. South Bend, Ind.: Notre Dame University Press, 1971, pp. 336–52.

821. Zorn, Wolfgang. 'Student Politics in the Weimar Republic,' *Journal of Contemporary History* 5 (No. 1, 1970), 128–43.

Greece

822. Haniotis, George. 'The Situation of the Universities in Greece,' *Minerva* 6 (Winter 1968), 163–84.

823. Roberts, Steven V. 'Greek Universities Try Balancing Act,' *Change* 7 (March 1975), 19–21.

Hungary

824. Kopeczi, B. 'Hungarian University Reform,' *New Hungarian Quarterly* No. 35 (1969), 11–21.

Italy

Books
825. Burn, Barbara B., ed. *The Emerging System of Higher Education in Italy: Report of a Seminar*. New York: I.C.E.D., 1973.

826. Clark, Burton R. *Academic Power in Italy: Bureaucracy and Oligarchy in a National University System*. Chicago: University of Chicago Press, 1977.

827. Martinotti, Guido. *Studenti universitari: profilo sociologico*. Padova: Marsilio, 1968.

Articles
828. Codignola, Trislano. 'The University Reform,' *Western European Education* 3 (Winter 1971–2), 316–28.

829. Coppola Pignatelli, Paola. 'Currents and Crises in Italian Higher Education' in P. G. Altbach, ed., *The University's Response to*

Societal Demands. New York: I.C.E.D., 1975, pp. 59–74.

830. Hyde, J. K. 'Commune, University, and Society in Early Medieval Bologna' in J. Baldwin and R. Goldthwaite, eds., *Universities in Politics.* Baltimore, Md.: Johns Hopkins University Press, 1972, pp. 17–46.

831. Karp, Angela. 'Student Unrest, Italian Style,' *Change* 9 (June 1977), 15–17.

832. Mancini, Fredrico. 'The Italian Student Movement,' *AAUP Bulletin* 54 (December 1968), 427–44.

833. Martinotti, Guido. 'The Positive Marginality: Notes on Italian Students in Periods of Political Mobilization' in S. M. Lipset and P. G. Altbach, eds., *Students in Revolt.* Boston, Mass.: Houghton Mifflin, 1969, pp. 167–201.

834. Martinotti, Guido and Alberto Giasanti. 'The Robed Baron: The Academic Profession in the Italian University,' *Higher Education* 6 (May 1977), 189–208.

835. 'Rebels and Factions in Italian Universities,' *Minerva* 6 (Summer 1968), 740–56.

835a. Ryan, Desmond, 'The University of Calabria in its Regional Context,' *Paedagogica Europaea* 12 (No. 1, 1977), 63–92.

836. Wurliger, Robert. 'Italian Universities and the Social Crisis,' *AAUP Bulletin* 61 (October 1975), 233–7.

Netherlands

837. Daalder, Hans. 'The Dutch Universities Between the "New Democracy" and the "New Management",' *Minerva* 12 (April 1974), 221–57.

838. Gaff, J. G., H. F. M. Crombagm and T. M. Chang. 'Environments for Learning in a Dutch University,' *Higher Education* 5 (August 1976), 285–300.

839. Lammers, C. J. 'Localism, Cosmopolitanism and Faculty Response: Case Study of Leyden University,' *Sociology of Education* 48 (Winter 1974), 129–58.

840. Mason, Henry L. 'Reflections on the Politicized University: II. Triparity and Tripolarity in the Netherlands,' *AAUP Bulletin* 60 (December 1974), 383–400.

Poland

841. 'The Aftermath of *Dziady* in Poland,' *Minerva* 6 (Summer 1968), 759–70.

842. Gella, Aleksander. 'Student Youth in Poland: Four Generations, 1945–70,' *Youth and Society* 6 (March 1975), 309–43.

843. Kupisiewicz, Czeslaw and Franciszek Januskiewick. 'The Development of Teaching and Learning in Polish Higher Education,' *Higher Education* 3 (April 1974), 141–8.

844. Matejko, A. 'Planning and Tradition in Polish Higher Education,' *Minerva* 7 (Summer 1969), 621–48.

845. Narkiewicz, Olga. 'Polish or Socialist?' *Universities Quarterly* 19 (September 1965), 345–60.

846. Simon, B. 'Higher Education in Poland,' *Universities Quarterly* 7 (February 1953), 176–83.

Spain

Books
847. Kagan, Richard L. *Students and Society in Early Modern Spain*. Baltimore, Md.: Johns Hopkins University Press, 1974.

Articles
848. Bela, Ramon. 'Spanish Educational Reform — Three Views' in S. Kertesz, ed., *The Task of Universities in a Changing World*. South Bend, Ind.: Notre Dame University Press, 1971, pp. 353–69.

849. 'Free Student Unions in Spain: Adamant Demands, Adamant Refusals,' *Minerva* 6 (Spring 1968), 463–73.

850. 'Free Students' Unions in Spain,' *Minerva* 4 (Summer 1966), 597–604.

851. 'A Further Digging in of Heels in Spain,' *Minerva* 6 (Summer 1968), 772–87.

852. 'Higher Education in Spain — II,' *Minerva* 8 (July 1970), 428–49.

853. Horowitz, Morris H. 'The University System in Spain: An Analysis of Structure,' *Higher Education* 3 (August 1974), 341–52.

854. Galvin, Enrique Tierno. 'Student Opposition in Spain,' *Government and Opposition* 1 (May–August 1966), 467–86.

855. Kagan, Richard L. 'Universities in Castile, 1500–1810' in L. Stone, ed., *The University in Society*, Vol. 2. Princeton, N.J.: Princeton University Press, 1974, pp. 355–406.

856. Moncada, Alberto. 'Directions of Development in Higher Education in Spain' in W. R. Niblett and R. F. Butts, eds., *Universities Facing the Future*. San Francisco: Jossey-Bass, 1972, pp. 207–19.

857. 'Spain,' *Minerva* 3 (Spring 1965), 421–8.

858. 'The Struggle Broadens in Spain,' *Minerva* 5 (Spring 1967), 447–54.

Sweden

Books

859. Boalt, G. and L. Herman. *Universities and Research: Observations on the United States and Sweden.* Stockholm: Almqvist and Wiksell, 1970.

860. Duster, Troy. *Aims and Control of the Universities: A Comparative Study of Academic Governance in Sweden and the United States.* Berkeley, Calif.: Center for Research and Development in Higher Education, 1972.

861. *Higher Education: Proposals by the Swedish 1968 Educational Commission.* Stockholm: Allmanna, 1973.

Articles

862. Anderson, C. Arnold. 'Sweden Re-examines Higher Education: A Critique of the U68 Report,' *Comparative Education* 10 (October 1974), 167–580.

863. Bergendal, Gunnar. 'U68 — A Reform Proposal for Swedish Higher Education,' *Higher Education* 3 (August 1974), 353–64.

864. Burn, Barbara. 'Higher Education in Sweden' in B. Burn *et al.*, *Higher Education in Nine Countries.* New York: McGraw-Hill, 1971, pp. 197–226.

865. Foyer, Lars. 'The 1955 Commission on the Swedish Universities,' *Minerva* 3 (Autumn 1964), 83–90.

866. Husen, Torsten. 'Swedish University Research at the Crossroads,' *Minerva* 14 (Winter 1976–7), 419–46.

867. 'The Reorganization of Higher Education in Sweden,' *Minerva* 12 (January 1974), 83–114.

868. 'Swedish University Policy,' *Minerva* 3 (Autumn 1964), 83–98.

869. Tomasson, Richard. 'Some Observations on Higher Education in Sweden,' *Journal of Higher Education* 37 (December 1966), 493–501.

Switzerland

870. Papke, David. 'Restricted Admissions in Switzerland,' *Change* 6 (November 1974), 14–17.

U.S.S.R.

Books

871. DeWitt, Nicholas. *Education and Professional Employment in the U.S.S.R.* Washington, D.C.: National Science Foundation, 1961.

872. Korol, Alexander G. *Soviet Education for Science and Technology.* New York: Wiley, 1957.

Articles

873. Belyaev, S. T. and T. Golenpolsky. 'The State University of Novosibirsk: Experience and Problems' in W. R. Niblett and R. F. Butts, eds., *Universities Facing the Future.* San Francisco: Jossey-Bass, 1972, pp. 255–66.

874. Burg, David. 'Observations on Soviet University Students,' *Daedalus* 89 (Summer 1960), 520–40.

875. Burn, Barbara. 'Higher Education in the Soviet Union' in B. Burn *et al., Higher Education in Nine Countries.* New York: McGraw-Hill, 1971, pp. 277–316.

876. Dobson, Richard. 'Social Status and Inequality of Access to Higher Education in the U.S.S.R.' in J. Karabel and A. H. Halsey, eds., *Power and Ideology in Education.* New York: Oxford University Press, 1977, pp. 254–74.

877. 'The Economics of Higher Education,' *Soviet Education* 18 (November 1975), 3–113.

878. Harasymiw, B. 'Post-Secondary Education in the U.S.S.R.' in T. H. McLeod, ed., *Post-Secondary Education in a Technological Society.* Montreal: McGill-Queens University Press, 1973, pp. 129–44.

879. Jacoby, Susan. 'Toward an Educated Elite: The Soviet Universities,' *Change* 3 (November 1971), 33–9.

880. Mathes, William L. 'University Courts in Imperial Russia,' *Slavonic and East European Review* 52 (July 1974), 366–81.

881. Rabkin, Yakov. '"Naukovedenie": The Study of Scientific Research in the Soviet Union,' *Minerva* 14 (Spring 1976), 61–78.

882. Stolyetov, V. 'Methodology of Planning of the University System in the U.S.S.R.' in V. Onushkin, ed., *Planning the Development of Universities—IV.* Paris: Unesco Press, 1975, pp. 9–58.

Yugoslavia

Books

883. Filipovic, Marijan. *Higher Education in Yugoslavia.* Belgrade: Yugoslav Institute for Educational Research, 1971.

884. Institute for Social Research, University of Zagreb. *Innovation in Higher Education: Reforms in Yugoslavia*. Paris: O.E.C.D., 1970.

Articles

885. Pribicevic, Branko and Jovan Gligorijevic. 'Self-Management in Yugoslav Universities,' *Prospects* 3 (Winter 1973), 515–21.

886. 'Student Demands in Yugoslavia: Pop Concert Tickets and Socialist Ideals,' *Minerva* 7 (Autumn–Winter 1968–9), 336–41.

887. Trahan, Richard. 'The Dilemma of Decentralization and Reform: Yugoslav Universities in Transition' in P. G. Altbach, ed., *University Reform*. Cambridge, Mass.: Schenkman, 1974, pp. 199–211.

LATIN AMERICA

General

Books

888. Albornoz, Orlando. *Ideologia y politica en la universidad latinoamericana*. Carácas: Instituto Societas, 1972.

889. Atcon, Rudolph. *The Latin American University*. Bogotá: ECO, 1972.

890. – – –. *La universidad latinoamericana*. Bogotá: Libreria Buchholz, 1966.

891. Benjamin, Harold R. W. *Higher Education in the American Republics*. New York: McGraw-Hill, 1965.

892. Cardozo, Manuel, ed. *Higher Education in Latin America*. Washington, D.C.: Catholic University of America Press, 1961.

893. Lanning, John Tate. *Academic Culture in the Spanish Colonies*. New York: Oxford University Press, 1940.

894. Liebman, Arthur, Kenneth Walker and Myron Glazer. *Latin American University Students: A Six-Nation Study*. Cambridge, Mass.: Harvard University Press, 1972.

895. Mazo, Gabriel del. *La reforma universitaria*. 6 vols. Buenos Aires: Publicaciones del Circulo Medico Argentino, 1927.

896. – – –. *Reforma universitaria y cultura nacional*. Buenos Aires: Editorial Raigal, 1955.

897. Ocampo Londono, Alfonso. *Higher Education in Latin America: Current and Future*. New York: I.C.E.D., 1973.

898. Schiefelbein, Ernesto and Noel McGinn. *Universidad contemporanea: un intento de analysis empírico*. Santiago. Chile: Ediciones C.P.U., 1974.

899. Smith, David H. *Latin American Student Activism.* Lexington, Mass.: Heath-Lexington, 1973.

900. Steger, Hans-Albert. *Las universidades en el desarrollo social de la America Latina.* Mexico City: Fondo de Cultura Economica, 1974.

901. Sunkel, Osvaldo. *Reforma universitaria: sub desarrollo y dependencia.* Mexico City: Editorial Universitaria, 1969.

Articles

902. Albornoz, Orlando. 'Academic Freedom and Higher Education in Latin America,' *Comparative Education Review* 10 (June 1966), 250–6.

903. — — —. 'Excellence of Equality at the University: The Latin American Case,' *Latin American Research Review* 11 (No. 1, 1976), 125–36.

904. — — —. 'Student Opposition in Latin America,' *Government and Opposition* 2 (October 1966–January 1967), 105–18.

905. Allard Neumann, R. 'Bases fundamentales de la reforma universitaria,' *Universidades* 13 (April–June 1973), 9–31.

906. Arnove, Robert F. 'A Survey of Literature and Research on Latin American Universities,' *Latin American Research Review* 3 (Fall 1967), 45–62.

907. Atcon, Rudolph. 'The Latin American University,' *Deutsche Universitätszeitung* 17 (February 1962), 9–49.

908. — — —. 'La reforma universitaria,' *ECO* 20 (December 1969), 10–39.

909. Einaudi, Luigi. 'University Autonomy and Academic Freedom in Latin America,' *Law and Contemporary Problems* 28 (Summer 1963), 636–46.

910. Germani, Gino. 'O profesor e a catedra,' *America Latina* 13 (January–March 1970), 83–101.

911. Goodman, Margaret. 'The Political Role of the University in Latin America,' *Comparative Politics* 5 (January 1973), 279–92.

912. Harrison, John P. 'Confrontation with the Political University,' *American Academy of Political and Social Science Annals* 334 (March 1961), 74–83.

913. — — —. 'The Latin American University—Present Problems Viewed through the Recent Past' in S. Kertesz, ed., *The Task of Universities in a Changing World.* South Bend, Ind.: Notre Dame University Press, 1971, pp. 414–32.

914. — — —. 'Learning and Politics in Latin American Universities,' *Proceedings of the Academy of Political Science* 27 (May 1964), 331–42.

915. Havighurst, Robert. 'Latin American and North American

Higher Education,' *Comparative Education Review* 4 (February 1961), 174–82.

916. Hennessy, Alastair. 'University Students in National Politics' in C. Veliz, ed., *The Politics of Conformity in Latin America*. New York: Oxford University Press, 1967, pp. 119–57.

917. Pelczar, Richard. 'The Latin American Professoriate: Progress and Prospects,' *Higher Education* 6 (May 1977), 235–54.

918. Peterson, John. 'Recent Research on Latin American Students,' *Latin American Research Review* 5 (Spring 1969), 37–58.

919. Renner, Richard. 'The Expansion of Educredit in Latin American Higher Education: Promise or Peril?' *Higher Education* 3 (February 1974), 81–90.

920. Riberio, Darcy. 'Rethinking the University in Latin America,' *Prospects* 4 (Autumn 1974), 315–30.

921. – – –. 'Universities and Social Development' in S. M. Lipset and A. Solari, eds., *Elites in Latin America*. New York: Oxford University Press, 1967, pp. 343–81.

922. Scherz-Garcia, Luis. 'Some Disfunctional Aspects of Inter-National Assistance and the Role of the University in Social Change,' *International Social Science Journal* 19 (No. 3, 1967), 387–403.

923. Sherlock, Philip. 'The Caribbean' in J. Perkins, ed., *Higher Education: From Autonomy to Systems*. New York: I.C.E.D., 1972, pp. 159–74.

924. Silvert, Kalman. 'The University Student' in John Johnson, ed., *Continuity and Change in Latin America*. Stanford. Calif.: Stanford University Press, 1964, pp. 206–26.

925. Soares, Glaudio A. D. 'The Active Few: Student Ideology and Participation in Developing Countries' in S. M. Lipset, ed., *Student Politics*. New York: Basic Books, 1967, pp. 124–47.

926. Suchlicki, Jaime. 'Sources of Student Violence in Latin America: An Analysis of the Literature,' *Latin American Research Review* (Fall 1972), 31–46.

927. Thomas, Dani and R. B. Craig. 'Student Dissent in Latin America: A Comparative Analysis,' *Latin American Research Review* 8 (Spring 1973), 71–96.

928. Tierney, James F. 'Higher Education in Latin America in an Era of Change' in W. R. Niblett and R. F. Butts, eds., *Universities Facing the Future*. San Francisco: Jossey-Bass, 1972, pp. 97–114.

929. Waggoner, Barbara and George, and G. Wolfe. 'Higher Education in Contemporary Central America,' *Journal of Inter-American Studies* 6 (1964), 445–61.

930. Waggoner, G. R. 'Problems in the Professionalization of the University Teaching Career in Central America,' *Journal of Inter-American Studies* 8 (April 1966), 193–211.

931. Wagley, Charles W. 'Latin America' in J. Perkins, ed., *Higher Education: From Autonomy to Systems.* New York: I.C.E.D., pp. 229–42.

932. Walker, K. N. 'A Comparison of the University Reform Movements in Argentina and Colombia,' *Comparative Education Review* 10 (June 1966), 257–72.

933. Wedge, B. 'A Case Study of Student Political Violence: Brazil, 1964 and Dominican Republic, 1965,' *World Politics* 21 (January 1969), 183–206.

Argentina

Books
934. Walter, Richard J. *Student Politics in Argentina: The University Reform and Its Effects, 1918–1964.* New York: Basic Books, 1968.

Articles
935. 'The Anniversary of the Cordoba Declaration and its Ramifications in the Argentine,' *Minerva* 7 (Autumn–Winter 1968-9), 95–112.

936. Mantonani, Juan. 'Freedom in the Argentine Universities before and after the Peron Regime' in G. Bereday and J. Lauserys, eds., *Yearbook of Education—1959.* London: Evans, 1959, pp. 405–15.

937. Munger, William L. 'Academic Freedom under Peron,' *Antioch Review* 7 (June 1947), 275–90.

938. Nasatir, David. 'Education and Social Change: The Argentina Case,' *Sociology of Education* 39 (Spring 1966), 167–82.

939. — — — . 'Higher Education and the Perception of Power, The Case of Argentina,' *Social Science Quarterly* 49 (September 1968).

940. — — — . 'University Experience and Political Unrest of Students in Buenos Aires' in S. M. Lipset, ed., *Student Politics.* New York: Basic Books, 1967, pp. 318–31.

941. Newton, Ronald C. 'Students and the Political System of the University of Buenos Aires,' *Journal of Inter-American Studies* 8 (October 1966), 633–56.

942. Romero Brest, G. de. 'Ten Years of Change at the University of Buenos Aires, 1956–66: Innovations and the Recovery of Autonomy' in W. R. Niblett and R. F. Butts, eds., *Universities Facing the Future.* San Francisco: Jossey-Bass, 1972, pp. 124–36.

943. Socolow, Daniel. 'Argentine Professoriate: Occupational

Insecurity and Political Interference,' *Comparative Education Review* 17 (October 1973), 375–88.

944. Socolow, Daniel. 'El profesorado de tiempo completo en Argentina,' *Revista del Centro de Estudios Educativos* 2 (No. 3, 1972), 37–52.

945. 'Student Power in Latin America: The Cordoba Manifesto,' *Minerva* 7 (Autumn–Winter 1968–9), 82–7.

946. 'Suspension of University Autonomy in the Argentine,' *Minerva* 5 (Autumn 1968), 93–9.

947. Tulchin, J. S. 'Origins of Student Reform in Latin America: Cordoba, 1918,' *Yale Review* 61 (June 1972), 575–90.

948. Van Aken, M. J. 'University Reform Before Cordoba,' *Hispanic–American Historical Review* 51 (August 1971), 447–62.

949. Walker, Kenneth. 'A Comparison of University Reform Movements in Argentina and Colombia' in S. M. Lipset, ed., *Student Politics*. New York: Basic Books, 1967, pp. 293–317.

950. Walter, R. J. 'Intellectual Background of the 1918 University Reform in Argentina' *Hispanic–American Historical Review* 49 (May 1969), 233–53.

Bolivia

951. Cohen, S. 'Problems in Bolivian Higher Education: Their Origin and Proposals for their Solution,' *Journal of Higher Education* 36 (February 1965), 80–7.

Brazil

Books
952. Haar, Jerry. *Higher Education and Politics in Brazil.* New York: Praeger, 1977.

Articles
953. Abu-Merhy, N. F. 'Emerging National Policies for Higher Education in Brazil' in B. Holmes and D. Scanlon, eds., *Higher Education in a Changing World*. New York: Harcourt Brace Jovanovich, 1971. pp. 334–47.

954. Carneiro, David, Jnr. 'The University in Brazil: Expansion and the Problem of Modernization' in W. R. Niblett and W. F. Butts, eds., *Universities Facing the Future*. San Francisco: Jossey-Bass, 1972, pp. 11–23.

955. Myhr, Robert O. 'Brazil' in D. Emmerson, ed., *Students and Politics in Developing Nations*. New York: Praeger, 1968, pp. 249–85.

956. Myhr, Robert O. 'Nationalism in the Brazilian University Student Movement,' *Inter-American Economic Affairs* 22 (Spring 1969), 81–94.

957. O'Neil, Charles. 'Problems of Innovation in Higher Education: The University of Brasilia, 1961–64,' *Journal of Inter-American Studies* 15 (November 1973), 415–31.

Chile

Books

958. Bonilla, Frank and Myron Glazer. *Student Politics in Chile.* New York: Basic Books, 1970.

959. Fagen, Patricia W. *Chilean Universities: Problems of Autonomy and Dependency.* Beverly Hills, Calif.: Sage Publications, 1973.

960. Huneeus Madge, Carlos. *La reform en la Universidad de Chile.* Santiago: Corporación de Promoción Universitaria, 1973.

Articles

961. Avaos, Beatrice. 'University Reforms and Changes in Teaching in Chile,' *Higher Education* 8 (Autumn 1975), 59–70.

962. Bonilla, Frank. 'The Student Federation of Chile: 50 Years of Political Action,' *Journal of Inter-American Studies* 2 (July 1960), 311–34.

963. Glazer, Myron. 'Chile' in D. Emmerson, ed., *Students and Politics in Developing Nations.* New York: Praeger, 1968, pp. 286–314.

964. — — —. 'The Professional and Political Attitudes of Chilean University Students' in S. M. Lipset, ed., *Student Politics.* New York: Basic Books, 1957, pp. 332–54.

965. Glazer, M. and P. Glazer. 'Chile: estudiantes y profesores en la reforma universitaria,' *Aportes* No. 22 (January 1972), 101–17.

Colombia

966. Pelczar, Richard. 'University Reform in Latin America: The Case of Colombia,' *Comparative Education Review* 16 (June 1972), 230–50.

Cuba

Books
967. Suchlicki, Jaime. *University Students and Revolution in Cuba, 1920–68*. Coral Gables: University of Miami Press, 1969.

Articles
968. Hochschild, A. 'Student Power in Action,' *Trans-Action* 6 (April 1969), 16–21.
969. Suchlicki, Jaime. 'Cuba' in D. Emmerson, ed., *Students and Politics in Developing Nations*. New York: Praeger, 1968, pp. 315–49.

Guatemala

970. Lanning, John T. *The Eighteenth Century Enlightenment in the University of San Carlos de Guatemala*. Ithaca, N.Y.: Cornell University Press, 1956.
971. — — —. *The University in the Kingdom of Guatemala*. Ithaca, N.Y.: Cornell University Press, 1955.

Mexico

Books
972. King, Richard G. *The Provincial Universities of Mexico: An Analysis of Growth and Development*. New York: Praeger, 1971.
972a. Osborn, T. W. *Higher Education in Mexico*. El Paso, Tex.: Texas Western Press, 1976.
973. Scott, Robert. *Universities and Political Change in Latin America: Case Studies in Mexico and Peru*. Washington, D.C.: Brookings Institution, 1968.

Articles
974. 'Bus Fares and Student Demonstrations in Mexico,' *Minerva* 5 (Winter 1967), 301–7.
975. 'A Conflagration of Obscure Origin in Mexico City,' *Minerva* 7 (Autumn–Winter 1968–9), 256–67.
976. Liebman, A. 'Student Activism in Mexico,' *Annals of the American Academy of Political and Social Science* 395 (May 1971), 159–70.
977. 'The Movement Finds a Cause in Mexico,' *Minerva* 7 (Spring 1969), 563–8.
978. 'The University Crisis in Mexico City,' *Minerva* 4 (Summer 1966), 588–94.

Peru

979. Scott, Robert. *Universities and Political Change in Latin America: Case Studies in Mexico and Peru.* Washington: Brookings Institution, 1968.

Venezuela

Books
980. Arnove, Robert. *Student Alienation: A Venezuelan Study.* New York: Praeger, 1971.

Articles
981. Washington, S. Walter. 'Student Politics in Latin America: The Venezuelan Example,' *Foreign Affairs* 37 (April 1959), 463–73.

AUSTRALIA

Books
982. Harman, Grant and C. Selby Smith, eds. *Australian Higher Education: Problems of a Developing System.* Sydney: Angus and Robertson, 1972.
983. Macmillan, David S. *Australian Universities.* Sydney: Sydney University Press, 1968.
984. *Report of the Committee on Australian Universities.* Canberra, 1957.

Articles
985. Anderson, D. S. 'Post-Secondary Education and Manpower Planning in Australia' in T. H. McLeod, ed., *Post-Secondary Education in a Technological Society.* Montreal: McGills—Queen's University Press, 1973, pp. 73–88.
986. Burn, Barbara. 'Higher Education in Australia' in B. Burn *et al.*, *Higher Education in Nine Countries.* New York: McGraw-Hill, 1971, pp. 125–64.
987. Davies, Denis J. 'Some Effects of Ph.D. Training on the Academic Labor Markets of Australian and British Universities,' *Higher Education* 5 (February 1976), 67–78.
988. Harman, Grant. 'Academic Staff and Academic Drift in Australian Colleges of Advanced Education,' *Higher Education* 6 (August 1977), 313–36.

989. Harman, G. S. and C. S. Smith. 'Some Current Trends and Issues in the Governance of Australian Colleges of Advanced Education,' *Australian Journal of Education* 20 (June 1976), 129–48.

990. 'Higher Education in Australia,' *Minerva* 4 (Summer 1966), 505–41.

991. 'The Knopfelmacher Case,' *Minerva* 3 (Summer 1965), 538–55.

992. Partridge, P. H. 'Universities in Australia,' *Comparative Education* 2 (November 1965), 19–30.

993. Peters, H. W. 'System of Indicators for Planning and Management at the Western Australian Institute of Technology' in V. Onushkin, ed., *Planning the Development of Universities—IV*. Paris: Unesco Press, 1975, pp. 213–316.

994. Saha, L. J. 'How Deviant are Left Wing Academics?: An Australian Test,' *Sociology of Education* 49 (January 1976), 80–9.

995. — — —. 'Recruitment Trends and Academic Inbreeding in an Australian University,' *Australian Journal of Higher Education* 5 (December 1973), 3–14.

996. Smith, C. S. 'Faculty Costs in Australian Universities,' *The Australian University* 11 (September 1973), 87–108.

997. 'Tertiary Education in Australia: Report of the Committee on the Future of Tertiary Education in Australia to the Australian Universities Commission,' *Minerva* 4 (Summer 1966), 505–41.

CANADA

Books

998. Dadson, D. F., ed., *On Higher Education*. Toronto: University of Toronto Press, 1966.

999. Duff, James and Robert Berdahl. *University Government in Canada*. Toronto: University of Toronto Press, 1966.

1000. Economic Council of Canada. *Canadian Higher Education in the Seventies*. Ottawa: Information Canada, 1972.

1001. Harris, Robin S. *A History of Higher Education in Canada, 1663–1960*. Toronto: University of Toronto Press, 1976.

1002. Harris, R. S. and A. B. Tremblay. *A Bibliography of Higher Education in Canada*. Toronto: University of Toronto Press, 1960.

1003. Harvey E. B. and J. L. Lennards. *Key Issues in Higher Education*. Toronto: Ontario Institute for Studies in Education, 1973.

1004. Hettich, Walter. *Expenditures, Output, and Productivity in Canadian University Education*. Ottawa: Information Canada, 1971.

1005. Hurtubise, René, ed. *L'université québecoise du proche avenir*. Montreal: Hurtubise H.M.H., 1973.

1006. Hurtubise, René and Donald Rowat. *The University, Society and Government*. Ottawa: University of Ottawa Press, 1970.

1007. *The Learning Society: Report of the Commission on Post-Secondary Education in Ontario*. Toronto: Ministry of Government Services, 1972.

1008. McLeod, T. H., ed. *Post-Secondary Education in a Technological Society*. Montreal: McGill-Queen's University Press, 1973.

1009. Sheffield, Edward, ed. *Teaching in the Universities: No One Way*. Montreal: Queens-McGill University Press, 1975.

1010. Symons, T. H. B. *To Know Ourselves: The Report of the Commission on Canadian Studies*. Vols. 1 and 2. Ottawa: Association of Universities and Colleges of Canada, 1975.

1011. Trotter, Bernard and A. W. R. Carrothers. *Planning for Planning: Relationships between Universities and Governments*. Ottawa: Association of Universities and Colleges of Canada, 1974.

1012. Watson, Cicely. *New College Systems in Canada*. Paris: O.E.C.D., 1973.

Articles

1013. Barkans, John and Norene Pupo. 'The Boards of Governors and the Power Elite: A Case Study of Eight Canadian Universities,' *Sociological Focus* 7 (Summer 1974), 81–98.

1014. Berdahl, Robert O. 'The Reform of University Government in Canada,' *Educational Record* 47 (Spring 1966), 203–17.

1015. Bissell, Claude. 'Institutions of Higher Education in Canada' in W. R. Niblett, ed., *Higher Education: Demand and Response.* San Francisco: Jossey-Bass, 1970, pp. 139–51.

1016. Burn, Barbara. 'Higher Education in Canada' in B. Burn *et al., Higher Education in Nine Countries*. New York: McGraw-Hill, 1971, pp. 91–124.

1017. Halliday, Terence C. 'The Politics of "Universial Participatory Democracy": A Canadian Case Study,' *Minerva* 13 (Autumn 1975), 404–27.

1018. Handa, M. L. and M. L. Skolnik. 'Unemployment, Expected Returns, and the Demand for University Education in Ontario: Some Empirical Results,' *Higher Education* 4 (February 1975), 27–44.

1019. Harvey, Edward B. 'Canadian Higher Education and the Seventies,' *Interchange* 5 (No. 2, 1974), 42–52.

1020. Munroe, D. C. 'Post-Secondary Education in Canada' in T. H. McLeod, ed., *Post-Secondary Education in a Technological Society*. Montreal: McGill-Queens University Press, 1973, pp. 31–50.

1021. Porter, John. 'The Democratization of the Canadian Universities and the Need for a National System,' *Minerva* 8 (July 1970), 325–56.

1022. Ross, Murray. 'The Dilution of Academic Power in Canada: The University of Toronto Act,' *Minerva* 10 (April 1972), 242–58.

1023. Ryan, Doris. 'Organizational Adaptation to Professional Differentiation in the University,' *Interchange* 5 (No. 3, 1974), 55–66.

1024. Scarfe, Janet and Edward Sheffield. 'Notes on the Canadian Professoriate,' *Higher Education* 6 (August 1977), 337–58.

1025. Sheffield, Edward. 'Innovation in Higher Education in Canada' in R. A. Brecher *et al.*, *Innovation in Higher Education*. London: Society for Research into Higher Education, 1972, 61–76.

1026. Wright, Douglas. 'Recent Developments in Higher Education in Ontario' in W. R. Niblett and R. F. Butts, eds., *Universities Facing the Future*. San Francisco: Jossey-Bass, 1972, pp. 297–310.

NEW ZEALAND

1027. McLaren, Ian. 'Developments in Tertiary Education' in I. McLaren, *Education in a Small Democracy: New Zealand*. London: Routledge and Kegan Paul, 1974, pp. 134–52.

U.S.A.

Books

1028. Altbach, Philip G. and David Kelly. *American Students: A Select Bibliography on Student Activism and Related Topics*. Lexington, Mass.: Lexington Books, 1973.

1029. Anderson, Charles and John Murray, eds. *The Professors*. Cambridge, Mass.: Schenkman, 1971.

1030. Ashby, Eric. *Any Person, Any Study: An Essay on Higher Education in the United States*. New York: McGraw-Hill, 1971.

1031. Bakke, E. Wight and Mary S. *Campus Challenge: Student Activism in Perspective*. Hamden, Conn.: Archon Books, 1971.

1032. Baldridge, J. V. *Power and Conflict in the University*. New York: Wiley, 1971.

1034. Ben-David, Joseph. *American Higher Education*. New York: McGraw-Hill, 1972.

1035. Blau, Peter. *The Organization of Academic Work*. New York: Wiley, 1973.

1036. Bowman, Mary Jean and C. Arnold Anderson. *Mass Higher*

188 — Comparative Higher Education

Education: Some Perspectives from Experience in the United States. Paris: O.E.C.D., 1974.

1037. Brubacher, John S. and Willis Rudy. *Higher Education in Transition.* New York: Harper and Row, 1976.

1037a. Carnegie Commission on Higher Education. *A Digest of Reports of the Carnegie Commission on Higher Education.* New York: McGraw-Hill, 1974.

1038. — — —. *Less Time, More Options: Education beyond the High School.* New York: McGraw-Hill, 1971.

1039. — — —. *New Students and New Places: Policies for the Future Growth and Development of American Higher Education.* New York: McGraw-Hill, 1971.

1040. — — —. *Priorities for Action: Final Report of the Carnegie Commission on Higher Education.* New York: McGraw-Hill, 1973.

1041. — — —. *The Purposes and the Performance of Higher Education in the United States: Approaching the Year 2000.* New York: McGraw-Hill, 1973.

1042. — — —. *Reform on Campus.* New York: McGraw-Hill, 1972.

1043. — — —. *Sponsored Research on the Carnegie Commission on Higher Education.* New York: McGraw-Hill, 1975.

1044. Clark, Burton and Ted I. K. Youn. *Academic Power in the United States.* Washington, D.C.: American Association for Higher Education, 1976.

1045. Corson, John J. *The Governance of Colleges and Universities.* New York: McGraw-Hill, 1975.

1046. Curti, Merle and Vernon Carstensen. *The University of Wisconsin: A History, 1848–1925.* Madison, Wis.: University of Wisconsin Press, 1949.

1047. Dressel, Paul and Lewis Mayhew. *Higher Education as a Field of Study.* San Francisco: Jossey-Bass, 1974.

1048. Dugger, Ronnie. *Our Invaded Universities.* New York: Norton, 1974.

1049. Epstein, Leon. *Governing the University.* San Francisco: Jossey-Bass, 1974.

1050. Feldman, Kenneth and Theodore Newcomb. *The Impact of College on Students.* San Francisco: Jossey-Bass, 1969.

1051. Flacks, Richard. *Youth and Social Change.* Chicago: Markham, 1971.

1052. Gilman, Daniel Coit. *University Problems in the United States.* New York: Century, 1898.

1052a. Hartnett, Rodney. *The British Open University in the United States: Adaptation and Use at Three Universities.* Princeton, N.J.: Educational Testing Service, 1974.

1053. Heiss, Ann. *An Inventory of Academic Innovations and Re-*

form. New York: McGraw-Hill, 1973.

1054. Henry, David D. *Challenges Past, Challenges Present: An Analysis of American Higher Education since 1930.* San Francisco: Jossey-Bass, 1975.

1055. Hofstadter, Richard and Wilson Smith, eds. *American Higher Education: A Documentary History.* 2 vols. Chicago: University of Chicago Press, 1961.

1056. Hook, Sidney. *Academic Freedom and Academic Anarchy.* New York: Cowles, 1969.

1057. Hutchins, Robert M. *The Higher Learning in America.* New Haven, Conn.: Yale University Press, 1936.

1058. ― ― ―. *The University of Utopia.* Chicago: University of Chicago Press, 1953.

1059. Jencks, Christopher and David Riesman. *The Academic Revolution.* Chicago: University of Chicago Press, 1977.

1060. Keniston, Kenneth. *Youth and Dissent.* New York: Harcourt Brace Jovanovich, 1971.

1061. Kerr, Clark. *The Uses of the University.* New York: Harper Torchbooks, 1966.

1062. Ladd, E. C. and S. M. Lipset. *The Divided Academy: Professors and Politics.* New York: McGraw-Hill, 1975.

1063. Leslie, Larry L. and Howard F. Miller, Jr. *Higher Education and the Steady State.* Washington, D.C.: American Association for Higher Education, 1974.

1063a. Lewis, Lionel. *Scaling the Ivory Tower: Merit and Its Limits in Academic Careers.* Baltimore, Md.: Johns Hopkins University Press, 1975.

1064. Lipset, S. M. *Rebellion in the University.* Chicago: University of Chicago Press, 1977.

1066. Mayhew, Lewis B. *The Carnegie Commission on Higher Education.* San Francisco: Jossey-Bass, 1973.

1067. McHenry, Dean E. *et al. Academic Departments: Problems, Variations and Alternatives.* San Francisco: Jossey-Bass, 1977.

1068. Metzger, Walter, ed. *Reader on the Sociology of the Academic Profession.* New York: Arno Press, 1977.

1069. Miles, Michael. *The Radical Probe: The Logic of Student Rebellion.* New York: Atheneum, 1971.

1070. Mortimer, Kenneth P. *Accountability in Higher Education.* Washington, D.C.: American Association for Higher Education, 1972.

1071. Nagai, Michio. *An Owl before Dusk.* New York: McGraw-Hill, 1975.

1072. National Commission on the Financing of Post-secondary Education. *Financing Post-secondary Education in the United States.* Washington, D.C.: U.S. Government Printing Office, 1973.

1073. Nisbet, Robert. *The Degradation of the Academic Dogma.* New York: Basic Books, 1971.

1074. Novak, Steven J. *The Rights of Youth: American Colleges and Student Revolt, 1798–1815.* Cambridge, Mass.: Harvard University Press, 1977.

1075. Parsons, Talcott and Gerald Platt. *The American University.* Cambridge, Mass.: Harvard University Press, 1973.

1076. Perkins, James, ed. *The University as an Organization.* New York: McGraw-Hill, 1973.

1077. *Report of the President's Commission on Campus Unrest.* New York: Arno Press, 1970.

1078. Ridgeway, James. *The Closed Corporation: American Universities in Crisis.* New York: Ballantine, 1968.

1079. Riesman, David. *Constraint and Variety in American Education.* Garden City, N.Y.: Doubleday, 1958.

1080. Riley, Gary and J. V. Baldridge, eds. *Governing Academic Organizations.* Berkeley, Calif.: McCutcheon, 1977.

1081. Rudolph, Frederick. *The American College and University: A History.* New York: Vintage, 1965.

1082. Sale, Kirkpatrick. *SDS.* New York: Random House, 1973.

1083. Sampson, Edward E. and Harold A. Korn, eds. *Student Activism and Protest.* San Francisco: Jossey-Bass, 1970.

1084. Schwab, Joseph. *College Curriculum and Student Protest.* Chicago: University of Chicago Press, 1969.

1085. *The Second Newman Report: National Policy and Higher Education.* Cambridge, Mass.: M.I.T. Press, 1974.

1086. Shulman, Carol Herrnstadt. *Enrollment Trends in Higher Education.* Washington, D.C.: American Association for Higher Education, 1976.

1087. Smith, Bruce L. R. and Joseph J. Karlesky. *The State of Academic Science: The Universities in the Nation's Research Effort.* New York: Change Magazine Press, 1977.

1088. Smith, David N. *Who Rules the Universities? An Essay in Class Analysis.* New York: Monthly Review Press, 1974.

1089. Storr, Richard J. *The Beginning of the Future: A Historical Approach to Graduate Education in the Arts and Sciences.* New York: McGraw-Hill, 1973.

1090. Touraine, Alain. *The Academic System in American Society.* New York: McGraw-Hill, 1974.

1091. Trivett, David A. *Goals for Higher Education: Definitions and Directions.* Washington, D.C.: American Association for Higher Education, 1973.

1092. Trow, Martin. *Aspects of American Higher Education, 1969–1975.* Berkeley, Calif.: Carnegie Council on Policy Studies in

Higher Education, 1977.

1093. Trow, Martin, ed. *Teachers and Students*. New York: McGraw-Hill, 1975.

1094. Veblen, Thorstein. *The Higher Learning in America*. New York: Hill and Wang, 1965.

1095. Veysey, Laurence. *The Emergence of the American University*. Chicago: University of Chicago Press, 1965.

1096. Wallerstein, Immanuel and Paul Starr, eds. *The University Crisis Reader*. Vols. 1 and 2. New York: Random House, 1971.

1097. Wolff, Robert Paul. *The Ideal of the University*. Boston, Mass.: Beacon, 1969.

1098. Wood, James L. *The Sources of American Student Activism*. Lexington, Mass.: Lexington Books, 1974.

Articles

1099. 'American Higher Education: Toward an Uncertain Future, Volumes 1 and 2,' *Daedalus* 133 (Fall 1974) and 104 (Winter 1975), 1–345 and 1–346.

1100. Bickel, Alexander. 'The Aims of Education and the Proper Standards of the University,' *Minerva* 12 (April 1974), 199–206.

1101. Darknell, Frank. 'The Carnegie Council for Policy Studies in Higher Education: A New Policy Group for the Ruling Class,' *Insurgent Sociologist* 5 (Spring 1975), 106–14.

1102. Finn, Chester E., Jr. 'Federal Patronage of Universities in the United States: A Rose by Many Other Names,' *Minerva* 14 (Winter 1976–7), 496–529.

1103. Fogarty, Robert S. 'A Nice Piece of Change,' *Antioch Review* 29 (Fall 1969), 305–28.

1103a. Folger, John, ed. 'Increasing the Public Accountability of Higher Education,' *New Directions for Institutional Research* No. 16 (1977), 1–97.

1104. McDonald, Donald. 'A Six Million Dollar Misunderstanding: The Carnegie Commission on Higher Education,' *Center Magazine* 6 (September–October 1973), 32–50.

1105. Moynihan, Daniel P. 'On Universal Higher Education,' *Minerva* 9 (April 1971), 256–71.

1106. Parsons, Talcott and Gerald M. Platt. 'Considerations on the American Academic System,' *Minerva* 6 (Summer 1968), 497–523.

1107. Pierson, G. W. 'American Universities in the Nineteenth Century: The Formative Period' in M. Clapp, ed., *The Modern University*. Ithaca, N.Y.: Cornell University Press, 1950, pp. 59–96.

1108. Razik, T. A. 'Planning the Development of Universities: State University of New York at Buffalo' in V. Onushkin, ed.,

Planning the Development of Universities—IV. Paris: Unesco Press, 1975, pp. 103–212.

1109. Riesman, David. 'The Future of Diversity in a Time of Retrenchment,' *Higher Education* 4 (November 1975), 461–82.

1110. Shils, Edward. 'The American Private University,' *Minerva* 11 (January 1973), 6–29.

1111. — — —, 'The Confidentiality and Anonymity of Assessment,' *Minerva* 13 (Summer 1975), 135–51.

1112. Smith, Virginia B. 'More for Less: Higher Education's New Priority' in *Universal Higher Education Costs and Benefits*. Washington, D.C.: American Council on Education, 1971, pp. 123–42.

1113. Trow, Martin. 'The Democratization of Higher Education in America,' *European Journal of Sociology* 3 (1962), 231–62.

1114. — — —. 'Elite Higher Education: An Endangered Species,' *Minerva* 14 (Autumn 1976), 355–76.

1115. — — —. 'Notes on American Higher Education: "Planning" for University Access in the Context of Uncertainty,' *Higher Education* 4 (February 1975), 1–12.

1116. Weinberg, Ian and Kenneth Walker. 'Student Politics and Political Systems: Toward a Typology,' *American Journal of Sociology* 75 (July 1969), 77–96.

Topic Cross-Reference Index

References are to item numbers.

1. Academic profession 3, 26, 32, 45, 56, 90, 91, 125, 204, 219, 352, 354, 355, 361, 363, 380, 383, 405, 420, 421, 433, 434, 436, 491, 493, 499, 511, 519, 534, 538, 589, 605, 620, 627, 636, 638, 645, 648, 654, 657, 678, 717, 740, 745, 748, 749, 763, 764, 773, 776, 780, 817, 834, 839, 910, 917, 930, 943, 987, 988, 994, 995, 996, 1024, 1029, 1035, 1062, 1068, 1111

2. Accountability, autonomy and academic freedom 40, 64, 132, 137, 147, 186, 191, 245, 252, 254, 334, 356, 466, 483, 537, 568, 656, 742, 756, 779, 794, 807, 902, 909, 936, 937, 942, 946, 991, 1056, 1070.

3. Administration, institutional management and governance 37, 47, 68, 104, 108, 127, 255, 339, 362, 373, 381, 391, 482, 547, 596, 621, 626, 683, 837, 853, 860, 885, 989, 999, 1013, 1014, 1017, 1021, 1022, 1023, 1032, 1044, 1045, 1049, 1067, 1076, 1080

4. Comparative studies 1, 10, 12, 13, 13a, 14, 15, 16, 17, 19, 20, 21, 22, 25, 27, 30, 31, 35, 39, 43, 46, 51, 58, 59, 60, 69, 70, 71, 72, 73, 74, 75, 77, 79, 80, 81, 83, 87, 94, 95, 97, 99, 100, 101, 103, 105, 111, 112, 117, 120, 121, 134, 140, 141, 144, 157, 159, 160, 161, 162, 505, 521, 543, 549, 550, 551, 757

5. Curriculum and teaching 116, 291, 584, 585, 646, 660, 838, 843, 1009, 1084

6. Economics of higher education 33, 36, 67, 86, 88, 102, 128, 149, 150, 156, 165, 169, 178, 194, 226, 256, 257, 272, 330, 332, 353, 379, 476, 488, 509, 606, 619, 629, 637, 643, 663, 681, 682, 877, 880, 1004, 1018, 1072, 1112

7. Historical studies 9, 23, 92, 93, 115, 126, 131, 153, 176, 184, 205, 236, 247, 299, 301, 319, 331, 340, 345, 486, 489, 497, 498, 516, 518, 523, 527, 528, 530, 544, 545, 554, 558, 564, 582, 592, 608, 610, 611, 613, 616, 673, 686, 691, 695, 699, 700, 702, 704, 720, 725, 735, 741, 759, 767, 768, 771, 778, 797, 801, 804, 816, 830, 847, 855, 893, 948, 950, 1001, 1037, 1046, 1052, 1054, 1055, 1081, 1089, 1095, 1107

8. Philosophy of higher education 42, 57, 63, 698, 1057, 1058, 1097, 1100

Country and Region Index

References are to page numbers.

Author Index

References are to item numbers.